I0134740

# SIXTEEN

Joseph Giuffrida Jr.

This book or parts thereof may not be reproduced in any form, stored in a retrieval system, or transmitted in any form  by any mean – electronic, mechanical, photocopy, recording, or otherwise – without prior written permission of the author, except as provided by United States of America copyright law.

◆◆◆◆◆◆◆◆◆◆◆◆◆◆

**SIXTEEN**

◆◆◆◆◆◆◆◆◆◆◆◆◆◆

Cover Illustration and Design by Jeanine Giuffrida

Unless otherwise noted, all Scripture quotations are from the King James Bible.

Available @ Amazon U.S., Amazon Europe, Kindle, and hardcopy.

© 2013 by Joseph Giuffrida Jr.

All rights reserved

ISBN-13: 978-0615886848
ISBN-10: 0615886841

Contact Joseph Giuffrida Jr. at: newcovrealities@gmail.com

Several years ago I was introduced to a young man and what I saw was passion, integrity and a heart to see people's lives changed and touched by the presence and power of God. Today, I am honored to call him a friend and brother. He has travelled and preached with our ministry and his knowledge of the word of God is fine-tuned and sharp. This book will not only shake you to the core but bring great revelation to your life. The content of his writing reveals his passion for people. I know you will be greatly blessed, inspired and encouraged as you dive deep into this writing that will ultimately change the perspective you have on life!

– Prophet John Natale

Founder & Overseer, Northeast Revival Centre

Author, Journey of Destiny

Joseph does a tremendous job at unpacking the lives of these men and women of faith mentioned in Hebrews. The insight he shares spurs growth in our personal journey with Jesus. As we look at their examples they offer encouragement to press on and fight the good fight of faith. Through his writing he so beautifully portrays this thread of faith throughout the Old and New Testament. As you take the time to dive into the lives of these heroes of the faith I pray you will go to new depths in your relationship with the Father!

– Pastor Michelle Skorski

Co-Founder, Whole Hearted Youth Outreach

Overseer, The Front Ministries

I highly recommend reading Joseph's book, as casual reading or for the biblical scholar – especially if you are looking for something to bolster your faith. It is the best treatise that I have read on the biblical personalities we call 'men and women of faith'.

– Dr. Jeff Victor

President & Founder, Summit Bible College

# Acknowledgements

♦♦♦♦♦♦♦♦♦♦♦♦♦♦♦

I would like to acknowledge my father who has been my chief editor for this book. He brought great clarity to ideas and words that were not as clear nor developed as they should have been. I am deeply indebted to him for his expertise in the English language, along with the thousands of hours of biblical discussions we have had, sharpening each other's theological foundations. I would also like to acknowledge my sister Jessica for revising this work, and for her skill in language as well as her appreciation for the Gospel. Lastly, I would like to thank my sister Jeanine for her stellar work designing the graphics for the front and back of this book. She is a professional artist with a real passion to see the Gospel preached to the nations.

# Dedication

For My Mother,

A woman who epitomized the life of faith. Faithful to the Lord.
Faithful to her husband. Faithful to her children. Faithful to her work.
Faithful to the Church.

# Dedication

# TABLE OF CONTENTS

# WHAT IS FAITH?

From cover to cover, the Bible is a book about faith. From the children of Adam to the final generations mentioned in the Book of Revelation, we see faith personified throughout. Faith recognizes what has always existed in the realm of timeless eternity. Faith transcends time and space, allowing us to access the past, present, and future of God's eternal nature. Hebrews 11:4 says that, "Through faith we understand the worlds were framed by the word of God." It is only through faith that we can truly grasp our existence, as well as the existence of the created universe. The Bible declares that faith is the very substance and evidence of God's word. It is *substance* in that by faith, we possess the timeless reality of what God has said, even before it manifests. The reality of God's word spoken to us provides a supreme knowing that we already possess what has been spoken. It is *evidence*, because by faith we are made aware supernaturally of God's competence in accomplishing His word.

We may understand faith as the eternal eyesight of God. It is that part of God's nature that sees a work accomplished even before that work ever begins. Since God is able to see the end from the beginning, He has confidence that what He desires to do will actually manifest. God never sets out to do anything without first seeing that thing accomplished. If God wants to create a galaxy, He sees that galaxy created even before He forms it. Since God is eternal, His sight is not limited by time and space. Faith is divine sight, which pierces through time, space, and matter, seeing the finished work before that work even commences.

Although faith is not a physical entity, it can be likened to a pair of eyes. Eyes are on the body simply for one purpose: to recognize reality as it is made visible. The faith of God recognizes what He is about to do, the creation which He is about to create. Now faith, though spiritual and intangible in the physical world, has a "weight" and "matter" in the spiritual world. That weight and matter is not experienced physically until the word of God has created a physical entity. For example, a tree is a physical reality that has physical substance to it. If God says "Let there be a tree" a physical tree must manifest, for that is the way God designed creation to come into existence. The word is spiritual, the creation is physical. Nothing can be created physically, without a spiritual word from God. This is why 2 Corinthians 4:18 declares that "the things which are seen" were created by the even greater spiritual reality of the "things which are not seen." We know that God is a spirit being, and though He is not physically walking the earth right now, He is still made up of real, spiritual substance. In fact, the Bible says that Christ – who is God – "fills all things" implying that His spiritual substance is everywhere. Although God is a spiritual entity, He always manifests Himself physically. Faith is the acute recognition of spiritual reality, translating what is of God into the physical creation.

# Faith Needs the Word

Faith recognizes spiritual realities, however it cannot recognize what is in the spiritual realm without being intimately joined to the word of God. Now, as we have likened faith to a pair of eyes, we know that without light, a pair of eyes cannot function properly. Similarly, faith needs the word of God like a pair of eyes needs light. Since the purpose of the eye is to see, the necessity of sight is light. *The Bible describes the word of God as light.* The psalmist says "Your word is a lamp unto my feet, a light unto my path." The apostle John says "In Him (the Word) was light, and that light was the light of men." From these verses, it is clear that the word of God contains divine light, which illuminates the understanding of man to see what God's purpose is. Faith is therefore dependent upon the word of God to see God's preordained purpose, before that purpose manifests into creation. When God created the earth, there needed to be light in order for that creation to exist. And so, when God said "Let there be light," light came into physical existence, illuminating all of the earth. Here we see a picture of faith and the word together. When God speaks His word to a man, immediately his vision becomes illuminated, and the word begins to create something in his life. The geography of that word is seen, the time of that word is understood, and the instructions needed to fulfill that word are revealed. This is why *light* is always connected with *the word of God*. Psalm 36:10 declares "In thy light, we shall see light." Faith is therefore the sight that recognizes what the word of God has illuminated about our future.

4

# Walk By Faith

Although faith is often taught in the context of the works that it produces, biblical faith should not be understood merely by the works we perform, but as the very *life that we live*. The outworking of faith does manifest in works, however faith does not merely involve doing something, but *being* someone. Faith affects our perceptions – what we believe to be true – therefore it is affects how we live. Since our subconscious and conscious realities are based upon what we believe to be true, the capacity of belief becomes the rudder that steers the course of our lives. In 2 Corinthians 5:7, the apostle Paul declares "For we walk by faith, not by sight." Now, there is a clear line of delineation here between faith and sight. Faith is speaking of spiritual vision, and sight speaks of natural vision. The first is the vision we are instructed to walk by, the second we are told to abandon. The word "walk" here is the Hebrew word *peripateo* which means "to regulate one's life, to conduct one's life, to pass one's life," literally to "live."[1] When the apostle Paul tells us that we "walk by faith," he is not merely instructing us to operate in faith, but that faith would literally operate us! The life we are to live is rooted in the very ground of faith. When we are instructed to "walk by faith" we are being invited to live a life energized by the supernatural life of God. The life of God *is* the life of faith. We see this great truth in Paul's epistle to the Galatians. He says, "I am crucified with Christ: nevertheless I live; yet not I, but Christ liveth in me: and the life which I now live in the flesh I live by the faith of the Son of God, who loved me, and gave himself for me." Notice that this verse says, "I live by the faith *of* the Son of God." The

5

faith that we have belongs to Jesus Christ; the lives that we live are therefore enabled by the faith of Jesus Christ. Notice how the apostle doesn't say that we "do works" by the faith of Jesus. He said that we *live* by Jesus' faith. In other words, our very existence is to be energized by the same spiritual power that possessed the Lord Jesus in His earthly ministry.    Romans 14:23 says "For whatever is not of faith is sin." The Greek word for "sin" is *hamartia* which means "to miss the mark."[2] In other words, the essence of sin is imperfection. Only God's life is perfect, and therefore the only way to live without sin is to possess His life. When we "walk by faith" we are walking in the reality of God's life, therefore we are walking perfectly. God's faith creates within our conscience a continual testimony that we are perfect. Not only that, but when God speaks to us, that divine word infuses His faith into our consciousness until we see ourselves vitally one with the word we have received. Our belief in God's word is what causes that word to manifest in our lives.

# Not Much Has Changed

When we look at the last six thousand years of church and biblical history, we see faith coming to mankind the same way – nothing has changed. Civilizations have changed, however the life of faith has not changed. Biblical history includes a plethora of different time periods, from the pre-diluvium Age of Adam and Eve and the Governmental Age of the Judges, to the age of Rome's great ascent to the top of the world's kingdoms. Throughout these various ages, cultures have changed, languages have developed, technology has evolved and become super sophisticated, but faith has never changed, neither in the way it is given nor the way it is received. Faith has always come by the word of God, and has always been received by the heart of the hearer. It is important to understand that the history of faith is not traced back to the Church, nor in the physical life of Jesus when He walked the earth – faith was in God even before He created the world. Before He created anything, God's faith was mixed with His word. Creation came as a result of Him speaking that word forth. Even though He created the world *ex nihilo* – out of nothing – He still saw the substance of the world created before He spoke His word. The *seeing* and the *speaking* of God both happened by faith. This reveals to us an important fact that can help us understand the lives of those who came before Christ's advent and the Church's beginning. Faith has always been God's gift to man, so that man would please God in all that he did. The Old Testament was not instituted to give man yet another way he might be pleasing to the Creator. It wasn't as though God deemed His original plan as a failure, and so instead of humanity's simple trust in Him, He decided to impose a strenuous, unattainable system of regulations that had to be adhered to in order to please Him. He instituted the Law of the Old Testament, not to show man how to live, but to expose fallen man's failed attempts at pleasing Him through human effort. The will of the Father was always that His sons and daughters would approach Him by faith, believing that they were made bone of His bone, and they could do nothing to add anything to their already given perfection.

In the following chapters, there are three major themes which emerge throughout each person's life: the *word* of God, the *faith* of

God, and the *destiny* of God. These three divine elements are essential to every person's calling. First, we know that the word of God is the means by which all things are created. According to the first chapter of John, not only is the word of God creative, but it is described as the very Person of God. When God speaks His word, that word is infused with the personality, energy, and substance of God Himself. Since all of creation was created *by* the word, we know that creation has come *out of* the very person of God. Everything created finds its existence necessarily joined to the Lord. By this truth we understand that when God's word goes forth there is a certainty of its fulfillment, even as the Lord spoke through the prophet Isaiah, saying "So shall my word be that goeth forth out of my mouth: it shall not return unto me void, but it shall accomplish that which I please, and it shall prosper in the thing whereto I sent it" (Isaiah 55:11). The certainty of God's word exists because God Himself is the omnipotent force within what is spoken, insuring the success of what He has said. What we will see in each biblical figure is the power of God's word demonstrated through their lives.

After the word of the Lord is released into the heart of a man or woman, the faith of God is simultaneously released as well. That faith can be likened to a map. When going out on an exploration, we may use a map to guide us toward a particular location. The map outlines the terrain of our journey, whether it is the roadways or the mountains, including the potential dangers as well as the beauty we might expect. Spiritually speaking, we may call this map *faith*. Faith enables us to see the "terrain" of our future. Just as God's word began to form the heavens and the earth after he spoke them into existence, the word we

8

receive begins to form the landscape of our destiny *within our minds* – a kind of vision. The *seeing* of that vision is the seeing of faith. God speaks a word to us and instantly we begin to see something in the future – a specific mission, a particular people group, or a physical location. Furthermore, faith infuses us with a plethora of holy emotions. These emotions fill the waiting period between the time the word is spoken and the destiny fulfilled. God has designed this time of waiting to be saturated with feeling, because it is in those feelings that we are empowered to continue believing in the word we have received. It is commonly believed that faith and feeling are mutually exclusive, but true biblical faith has always been connected to intense human emotion. We will likewise see the power of emotion in the lives of those presented within this book.

It is after we have received the word of God and the faith of God that the final piece is revealed: the God-ordained destiny for each person. Now, since God and His word are one, and a *destiny* is the physical manifestation of that word, we may conclude that a person's destiny reveals the very person of God. For example, if a man is destined to become a deliverer to some oppressed nation, the manifestation of deliverance to that nation is a *manifestation* of God. Therefore the people whom God reveals His word to are called to be a mirror reflection of the God who called them. Although the destiny of each individual may be different, all share the same common purpose, which is to reveal the Lord to those whom they are sent. We are about to recall the life of faith in sixteen individuals. Although each one's personal history reveals a great deal of cultural, religious, and social diversity, they all reached their destiny, because they encountered the word of God and by it, lived the life of faith.

# CHAPTER ONE

# ABEL

*"By faith Abel offered unto God a more excellent sacrifice than Cain,
by which he obtained witness that he was righteous, God testifying of
his gifts: and by it he being dead yet speaketh."*

*- Hebrews 11:4*

Out of the hundreds of individuals named in scripture, there were only sixteen specifically noted in the eleventh chapter of Hebrews. At the very beginning of this historic list, we are introduced to the second-born of Adam and Eve. The significance of his life is simplified to only a handful of verses, yet in what is revealed we discover a fascinating truth: Abel is the first person in biblical history who is called righteous. Furthermore, it is Abel who is noted as performing the first act of faith. It was this act of faith that revealed in him the characteristic of righteousness, which would become the testimony of his life.

Before we explore Abel's life, it is worth mentioning that the Bible is not a mere storybook, nor are the people contained within its pages simply characters, filling up the fantastical tales of great storytellers. From cover to cover, the Bible is a divine revelation that

12

tells of the Creator, His creation, and the eternal purpose of all that has been created. Furthermore, given the theological complexity of the Scripture, it is important to return to the book of beginnings – Genesis, to discover the seed thoughts and ideas that are continually developed throughout God's word. Therefore, it is fitting that the writer of Hebrews begins with Abel. Whereas in the chronology of the Bible, he is not the first person to be called "righteous," we know that genealogically he was the first figure to be described as "righteous." According to the writer of Hebrews, he is also genealogically the first person to have done an "act of faith." Since Abel is the earliest person to have been regarded as having both of these characteristics, we understand that both righteousness and faith are inextricably linked throughout the entirety of scripture.

Now, Abel's father had walked with the Lord in the Garden. He saw the Creator's image and likeness, he heard His voice audibly, and it was upon his head that this awesome Creator placed a crown of glory. Abel's mother had the same breathtaking experience without the veil of sin-made separation darkening the splendor. After the fall, the tragic consequences of sin caused the defiling of mankind's conscience. It was in the conscience of man that the guilt of sin was found. This guilty conscience created an invisible curtain, veiling man's ability to fellowship with the Divine. The aftereffect of this was immediate spiritual death, resulting in eventual physical death. Humanity's father and mother were thus sent out from the Garden under the banner of this curse. The consequences of sin were not limited to Adam and Eve, however, as Eve's first-born child became the first to inherit the corrupt nature of sin. The erosion of life brought about by sin was manifested in Eve's first child who eventually murdered his younger brother. The name "Eve" means "spring of life"[1] which is the essence of God's original intent for her. However, sin caused her to reproduce the seed of corruption in her children, and thus she became a "spring of death." Not only were her children doomed to die physically, but they inherited spiritual death as well. They too had corrupted consciences which interrupted their ability to commune with their Creator the way He had originally intended. Therefore the infinitely wise God revealed a gift to His creation which would become the golden thread throughout all the ages – that gift was faith. It was by faith that mankind would be allowed to not only communicate with his Creator, but please Him as well. In fact, it would be impossible to communicate or to please Him any other way. Faith was and is the bridge that crosses the invisible divide between man and his Creator.

In order to understand some fundamental differences between Cain and Abel and the significance of Abel's faith, we must first take another look at their father. Before the Fall, Adam was commanded to "dress" the Garden (Genesis 2:15). After the fall, Adam was again told by God to "till the ground from whence he was taken" (3:23). The word in Hebrew for "dress" and "till" is "abad" which means "to labor or to work."[2] This reveals to us that Adam's function before the Fall and after the Fall was the same. The difference was that, after the Fall, Adam and his progeny would sweat, bleed, and eventually break down physically due to the strenuous conditions upon their mortal bodies. Now, Adam's eldest son Cain was right by his side in this work, as Cain was also a "tiller of the ground" (4:2). Furthermore, Cain's name

14

means "possessor."[3] As we see throughout scripture, the firstborn always occupied a position of preeminence amongst the lineage of a family. Cain's name sets this precedent as he was likely to possess a greater inheritance than his younger brothers.

*"And in process of time it came to pass, that Cain brought of the fruit of the ground and offering unto the lord. And Abel, he also brought of the firstlings of his flock and of the fat thereof. And the Lord had respect unto Abel and his offering: But unto Cain and his offering He had not respect." - Genesis 4:3-5*

Now these verses give us great insight into the nature of these two offerings. Contrary to the thought of some, the acceptance of Abel's offering over Cain's is *not* a matter of the *content* of the offering. God had given Cain one area of creation to steward over, and Abel another. As a tiller of the field, Cain worked through fields and forests, vines and thickets. Abel, on the other hand, was a shepherd who cared for animals. In a momentous act of worship, both of the brothers offered up a portion of their labor to the Creator. Both were to give of the substance in their particular sphere of dominion. If God preferred one offering over the other based upon content, He would have been unjust in respecting one offering over the other. Remember, there was no law that placed specific requirements upon offerings at this time. But notice the wording in verses four and five: "And the Lord had respect unto Abel *and* his offering: But unto Cain *and* his offering He had not respect" (emphasis mine). The Lord was looking

15

not merely at the offering, but the person giving it! God first looked at the man bringing the offering, and then at the content of the offering. The fact is, God had "respect" unto Abel's offering because God respected Abel. The Hebrew word for "respect" here is *sha'ah,* which translates as, "to look at or to, regard, gaze at or about."[4] God was actually looking at, gazing at, and regarding Abel before He had even looked at the offering! *Abel amazed God. His life was something that God gazed at in amazement.* Now, the Lord was not merely amazed with what Abel had done, but with the mirror reflection that Abel had become, reflecting the very person of the Lord. A physical offering could not have impressed God; however the man behind that offering made the act impressive because the man performing it *was* impressive. What was so impressive about Abel? The writer of Hebrews tells us that it was the *faith of Abel* that caused his sacrifice to become "excellent." The Greek word for "excellent" means "greater in quality, superior."[5] It is a fact that an act of faith is the only action that God considers excellent and therefore impressive. Both Cain and Abel were doing the same thing – offering their livelihood to the Lord. However, God reveals to us that our religious works are sinful if they do not come from a life of faith.

*"But unto Cain and to his offering he had not respect. And Cain was very wroth, and his countenance fell. And the LORD said unto Cain, Why art thou wroth? and why is thy countenance fallen? If thou doest well, shalt thou not be accepted? and if thou doest not well, sin lieth at the door. And unto thee [shall be] his desire, and thou shalt rule over him." – Genesis 4:5-7*

16

There are two apparent revelatory truths in the above verses. The first truth is that Cain's reaction to the Lord reveals the sinful condition of his heart. Much like the elder brother in Jesus' parable of the Prodigal Son, Cain worked the land of his father tilling the field. And just as the elder brother was envious of his younger brother's acceptance, so Cain was envious of God's acceptance of Abel. Similarly, the relationship between the Pharisees and Jesus also mirrored Cain's relationship with Abel. Matthew 27:18 declares that it was *envy* which caused the Pharisees to crucify the Son of God. Envy is akin to *jealousy*, which is described as the "rage of man" according to Proverbs 6:24. The Hebrew word for "rage" denotes heat, venom, poison, and anger.[6] We are told that Cain "was very wroth." The word "wroth" literally means "to be hot, furious, burn, become angry, be kindled."[7] Cain's anger was a result of the jealousy he had toward his brother, and anger toward the Lord for accepting Abel's offering and Abel's lifestyle of faith. We may gather that the life which pleases God will attract the anger of jealous souls who have allowed Satan to influence them.

The second truth is that Cain's offering was the result of *self-righteousness*. The Lord says, "If thou doest well, shalt thou not be accepted?" Literally, God was revealing His requirement for Cain's acceptance, "Don't you realize that I will accept you if you do what is right?" The problem is that no man could possibly be acceptable by his works, especially in the fallen state which began in the Garden. And this was the point of the divine command. Cain was trying to be pleasing to God with his offering, rather than with a life of faith. The life of faith is not based upon the works of a man, but upon the already

17

given work of God in making man acceptable. Cain's work was the essence of a self-righteous action. Self-righteousness is the mindset of those trying to please God by their own abilities. The Lord was giving Cain a preview of the Law which would be enacted some thousand years later. That divine Law would expose man's utter sinfulness in trying to become righteous by his works. This statement by the Lord reveals that Cain was not living under the original life of grace, but of the works of self-effort; not of God's righteousness but of his own. Thus, the Lord was using language that addressed a person trying to be justified by their works. Jesus used this same approach with the rich young man, who desired to have eternal life (see Matthew 19). When the young man approached Jesus, he came under the guise of having done all the works of the Law. In response, Jesus found the one thing that this young man could not do – sell everything he had and give it to the poor. The Bible says that the young man went away from the Lord "sorrowful," for his self-righteousness had an inevitable limit which could not translate him into the eternal life he was seeking. After having received the divine exhortation from the Lord, Cain went out into the field and killed his brother. This act reveals the utter weakness of Cain's flesh in trying to keep God's requirements, even though God had personally explained this requirement as we saw in verse 7.

*"And Cain talked with Abel his brother: and it came to pass, when they were in the field, that Cain rose up against Abel his brother, and slew him." Genesis 4:8*

This hatred that Cain manifested toward his brother typifies the same hatred that Jesus' brothers had toward Him. In the same way that Abel was killed by his brother, so Christ was crucified by his brothers. It is fascinating that, according to Hebrews 11:4 and 12:24, the blood that Cain shed gave off a sound that can still be heard! These verses declare that his blood is still "speaking." This "speaking" indicates that Abel's life represents something much larger than his short lifespan on earth. Abel's blood represents all of humanity under the curse of sin and death. Abel's blood cries out "judgment!" on humanity's cursed state. It wasn't until four thousand years later when Jesus was crucified that the cry of Abel's blood was answered! On the Cross of Calvary, Jesus' blood spoke of "better things." Jesus's blood was shed for all humanity, representing all of humanity, so that not only did it judge the sin of humanity, but completely removed the penalty of that sin from all of mankind. Abel could not have known the depth of significance placed upon his life; however because of faith, he lived and died righteously, foreshadowing the very life and death of the Messiah.

Abel's name in Hebrew is *hebel* which literally means "breath" or "vapor."[8] When considering the fact that his life was cut short by the hand of his brother, and the relatively small amount of content written about him, it is apparent that Abel's existence was like a vapor of smoke which was only visible for a moment. All throughout King Solomon's writings, he continually used the word "vanity" to describe the natural life of man. The word "vanity" used by Solomon is also *hebel*.[9] The apostle James asks the rhetorical question, "What is your life? It is even a *vapour*, that appeareth for a little time, and then vanisheth away" (James 4:14, emphasis mine). Compared with eternity, James is saying that this temporal life is like a breath that comes and goes. And yet, the breath of Abel's life impacted future generations simply because his life was lived in faith. That faith translated his life and death into a representative voice, echoing throughout every century of man. The sound that was given off would resound in each generation until Christ's death occurred, being met with an infinitely greater sound. It is apparent that, having done only a handful of works, Abel did not need the praise of men to make his life meaningful. Through the offering of his work and the offering of his blood, this man will be remembered eternally as he bares the testimony of God – that he was a righteous man, having lived the life of faith.

# CHAPTER TWO

---

# ENOCH

*"By faith Enoch was translated that he should not see death; and was not found, because God had translated him: for before his translation he had this testimony, that he pleased God."*

*- Hebrews 11:5*

Enoch is a mystical figure who lived in the first centuries of Creation. By faith, he would become the central figure in one of the most supernatural events recorded in scripture. Like the account of Abel, there is little detail given about Enoch's life; his journey is shrouded in mystery. Yet, moments of clarity do appear throughout, creating the silhouette of faith behind each detail recorded. We know that his communion with God was extraordinary, and his journey would take him to his heavenward destination; however the most magnificent fact recorded about this man is that "he pleased God." This is the account of his life which manifested the faith of God.

*"And Enoch walked with God." – Genesis 5:4*

He was the 7<sup>th</sup> generation of man from Adam, the son of Jared. His occupation is unknown, however we know that he "walked with God." The Hebrew word for "walk" here is *halak*. Strong's Greek Lexicon translates "halak" in this verse as "to live."[1] Scripture is declaring that Enoch actually *lived* with God! This truth opens a door of revelation for us to understand more about Enoch's faith and his prophetic utterances. As we have discovered, God was no longer fellowshipping with man the way he had intended to in Garden. Sinfulness had veiled man's ability to live conscious of God's abiding presence. Man did not possess the inherent spiritual eyes that he once had, to see the spiritual life of God the way Adam had prior to the Fall. And yet, man had been given a divine lifeline called faith, which flipped open the shutters of man's soul to experience the invisible God and the light of His invisible realm. By faith, man was able to access the realm of God, which made two-way communication possible. A relationship was established so that he could live in a place of fellowship with God, even though that communion was frequently interrupted by the static of sin. Enoch had accessed the realm of God to the point that he was *living* in a place of divine ecstasy.

Now, the name "Enoch" means "dedicated."[2] It is apparent that he was dedicated to the spiritual reality that had been revealed to him by God. The enabling force behind such dedication was faith, as it is by faith that a man is able to "walk" or "live" with God. We must realize that sin, while a deterrent to the consistent consciousness of God's presence, has never been able to trump God's ability to reveal that presence to man. Just as a dark room cannot withstand the beams of light that come through the cracks of the doorway, so the life of God cannot ultimately be shut out of the heart of man, even though that man may be living in the darkness of unbelief. Faith is the key that opens the door, so that man can fully experience the divine light. In Romans 5:2, the apostle Paul says of the Lord Jesus Christ, "By whom also we have *access by faith* into this grace wherein we stand, and rejoice in hope of the glory of God" (emphasis mine). The access point into the grace of God is faith. Even though Jesus Christ had not yet been revealed, Enoch was accessing the divine grace of God by the faith which he had received. Any person who accesses that divine realm will begin to see and hear the eternal counsel of God. It is in this place that man learns to prophesy. The word "prophesy" in Hebrew is *naba*, which means "to cause to bubble up."[3] The image most of us receive when we think of "bubbling" is that of water when it is heated. As the temperature increases, the water molecules begin to move violently, faster and faster, which produce bubbles. Similarly, when a person walks by faith, the Spirit of the Lord will begin to stir up words within their heart, until the violence of that stirring causes an explosion of divinely inspired words to bubble out of their mouth. This outflow of words will immediately begin affecting the course of the natural, physical world around us. Enoch had a word bubble up out of him, which is recorded by Jude:

*"And Enoch also, the seventh from Adam, prophesied of these, saying,*
*Behold, the Lord cometh with ten thousands of his saints, to execute*
*judgment upon all, and to convince all that are ungodly among them of*
*all their ungodly deeds which they have ungodly committed, and of all*

24

*their hard [speeches] which ungodly sinners have spoken against*
*him." – Jude 1:14-15*

Enoch lived almost 6 thousand years ago, and he prophesied of an event that has yet to take place! It is in the realm of the Spirit that time and space no longer determines what we see and hear. A man or woman may gain insight into events, thousands of years into the future; and yet, when these events are perceived they can seem as near to us as the air we are breathing. Although the Bible does not speak of him as a prophet, we know that he was a man acquainted with the prophetic oracles of God. According to the apostle Paul, it takes faith to prophesy. Since prophecy involves speaking forth divinely inspired revelation, it takes God's word combined with God's faith to not only hear the word but to speak it out as well. Scripture declares that "faith cometh by hearing, and hearing by the word of God." Therefore, it becomes clear that Enoch's prophesying came by faith, and that his faith was received through personal communion with God. Now, many people have wrongly taught that man was physically and spiritually separated from God as a result of sin. If this was the case, then how could Enoch have prophesied God's word, much less "walk with God"? The truth is that man's sin separated him within his own consciousness – man was made an enemy of God *in his mind* (see Colossians 2). Sin darkened the consciousness of man to the point that man perceived God as being his enemy, and therefore in the distance. And yet, it has always been the desire of God to commune with mankind, even through the age of Law which would be ushered in centuries later. The Lord has *always* been intervening into the affairs of

His Creation. Much more, God upholds all things by His word; therefore all things are still being upheld by the word of God, by His very presence. By faith, man has always been able to continue in unbroken fellowship with the Lord. Enoch shows us that, even in his fallen condition, he was able to commune with his Creator, receive the divine word, and walk toward his destiny.

*"Enoch lived sixty-five years, and begot Methuselah..."* - Genesis 5:21

The name that Enoch chose for his first born gives us yet another insight into his prophetic life of faith. *Methuselah* has two possible meanings. The first is "man of the dart" which is derived from two Hebrew words; "metu" which translates as "man," and the word "shelach" which means "a weapon or missile" (or the English variation of "dart"). However, The second meaning reveals that the root word "metu" is derived from the word "mot" which means "death," and the "u" meaning "their"; when put together, you have "their death." Combined with "shelach" which is more literally translated as "to send something" (hence "missile" or "dart") you could say that *metu shelach* means "their death sends" or "his death sends." It is fascinating to note that the very year Methuselah died, God sent the flood to destroy the inhabitants of the earth, saving only Noah and his family. It was as though Enoch was prophesying through his son's name, that the death of his son would usher in the flood that would be sent to destroy the entire earth! Once again, we see that a life of faith

26

will inspire a person to say and do things that may very well confirm future events.[4]

Perhaps one of the most mystical details of Enoch's journey was what occurred at the end of his time on earth. We read:

*"And Enoch walked with God; and he was not, for God took him." -*
*Genesis 5:24*

The English word "took" is the Hebrew word laqach which means "to receive" or "to take away."[5] Hebrews 11 tells us that Enoch was "translated," which is the Greek word *metatithēmi* meaning "to transfer."[6] Enoch was literally transferred from one realm to another, received from the physical, natural world, into the spiritual, supernatural dimension of the Lord. The writer of Hebrews says it this way, "By faith Enoch was translated that he should not see death" (11:5). Notice the words of the writer "...that he should not see death." Faith is the substance of things hoped for and the evidence of things not seen. By faith Enoch did not experience death because he did not see death! The future did not hold death for this man, because he did not see death in his future. Rather, he saw the supernatural realm of God as his reality. At the Fall of mankind, the human race was blinded to the truth of their inclusion into God's nature. Sickness, poverty and death all were incurred as a result of that blindness. Man could not see himself as perfect anymore, therefore all that was imperfect became part of man's existence. Perfect health was robbed by sickness; perfect

27

prosperity was robbed by poverty; and eternal life was substituted with death. By faith, man could once again see his perfection and therefore begin to manifest the healing, prosperity, and eternal life that encompassed his original nature in God.

Although we have only been given glimpses into this man's journey, we are convinced that his experiences, both on earth and in heaven, are a testimony to the other-worldly reality of faith. We are made aware that he communed with God, and he was destined to prophesy about many things. He spoke prophetically through his son's name, concerning a new age that would be ushered into the world by the Flood. He spoke concerning the Second coming of the Son of God before there was even a First. He lived his life seeing beyond natural vision, beyond the mortality of man. He was able to do this, because he had received the faith of God – the same faith that created the worlds out of nothing. And as a result of this faith, he passed through the veil of eternity without ever experiencing death.

# CHAPTER THREE

# NOAH

*"By faith Noah, being warned of God of things not seen as yet, moved with fear, prepared an ark to the saving of his house; by the which he condemned the world, and became heir of the righteousness which is by faith." - Hebrews 11:7*

By the ninth generation from Adam, the entire known world was in moral chaos. The Bible tells us that the wickedness of man was great upon the earth and that every imagination of man's heart was continually evil. Man's lifespan was shortened by God in this Antediluvian Era, so that those born would only reach one hundred and twenty years of age. Humanity had, in nine short generations, reached its most decadent point away from God. In all of the thousands and possibly millions of people alive at this time, there was only one man who caught the attention of God. Through the power of this man's faith, mankind would transition from one age of human history to another.

Noah was the son of Lamech, the ninth generation of Adam, whose name was based upon Lamech's prophecy. We read in Genesis

5:29, "And he called his name Noah, saying, "This same shall comfort us concerning our work and toil of our hands, because of the ground which the LORD hath cursed." It is powerful to note that names transmitted from fathers and mothers to their children can be a prophetic indication of God's destiny for the child's life. As were many of the Biblical fathers, Lamech was moved by the Holy Ghost to name his son "Noah" which literally means "rest."[1] He did this foreseeing what the Lord had planned for the whole world. Our destiny in life may very well be identified by the names we are given, which is expressed most significantly in the name of *Jesus* – meaning "Jehovah is Salvation"[2] – who was destined to save humanity from the grip of sin and death.

*"But Noah found grace in the eyes of the Lord." – Genesis 6:8*

Now in the midst of a corrupted world, we are told an extraordinary truth, that a man "found grace in the eyes of the Lord." This verse – "But Noah found grace in the eyes of the Lord" – does not mean that Noah had discovered grace as a result of his own seeking. Scripture clearly portrays the grace of God as a gift, and not something that can be obtained by man's own initiative. If man could obtain it by his own efforts, then it would no longer be grace. The Greek word for "grace" is *charis* which means "the divine influence upon the heart and its reflection in the life."[3] The grace of God is His distinctive presence which blows through a person like a gust of wind, enabling that man or woman to express the divine nature of God to the world around them.

31

In Hebrew, the word "found" is *matsa* which actually means "to be found, to be encountered, or to be discovered."[4] When we combine both the Greek and Hebrew together, this verse could be better translated as "But the divine influence of God's presence discovered Noah." The fact is that Noah had encountered God, and through this encounter, he discovered God's grace which was fully fixated upon him. Our understanding deepens as we look at this next verse.

*"These are the generations of Noah: Noah was a just man and perfect in his generations, and Noah walked with God." - Genesis 6:9*

The word "generations" is the Hebrew word *towledah* which means "history."[5] The history of Noah is this: he was *just*, *perfect*, and he *walked with God*. First, Noah was described as *just*. In order to be called "just," one must live in compliance with laws that have been set by a government. The Divine Law in the Ten Commandments had not been revealed to Noah, therefore we know that he was not considered lawful based upon his obedience to the Mosaic Law. The law which Noah lived by was even higher than the Ten Commandments – that law was the *law of faith*. This is not to say that one law is any more holy than the other; the difference is that the dispensation of the Law given by Moses could not make anyone perfect. All the Law of Moses accomplished was to reveal to mankind that he, by his own efforts, could not keep that law! The law of faith is *higher* in that it does not require the palsied efforts of man but rather the perfection of God, which is conferred upon a man so that he may be called "just" in God's

32

heavenly society. The apostle Paul speaks of this law in Romans 5. Hear his words:

*"Being justified freely by his grace through the redemption that is in Christ Jesus: Whom God hath set forth [to be] a propitiation through faith in his blood, to declare his righteousness for the remission of sins that are past, through the forbearance of God; To declare, [I say], at this time his righteousness: that he might be just, and the justifier of him which believeth in Jesus. Where [is] boasting then? It is excluded. By what law? of works? Nay: but by the law of faith. Therefore we conclude that a man is justified by faith without the deeds of the law."*
*– Romans 5:24-28*

Now, Jesus had not been revealed yet, however the faith of Jesus Christ has *always* existed. Noah was tapping into the eternal work of Christ thousands of years earlier. By faith, Noah could be justified in the eyes of God simply by receiving the faith which God gave him.

The second description of Noah in Genesis 6:9 describes him as having a *perfect* history. This does not mean that he was morally perfect; no man has ever perfectly obeyed the moral law of God. The perfection spoken of here was the perfection conferred upon the individual who lives by faith. Hebrews 10:14 states that the perfection of man is the work of God. In the same way that the New Testament believer is "perfected forever" by faith in the finished work of Christ, Noah was "perfected" by his faith in the Lord.

The third characteristic of Noah is that he *walked with God.* As we have seen from the life of Enoch, to "walk" means to "live." By faith, Noah had legal access into the realm of God, was made perfect by that faith, and therefore lived in the presence of the Almighty. Noah was truly a shining light in the midst of such wickedness! That Noah could be morally imperfect, yet his history called "perfect," reveals that his perfection was rooted in God's power to save him. It was through the agency of faith that Noah was even able to see the grace of God, in the eyes of God Himself, as it were, Who had fixated His almighty presence upon him.

*"By faith Noah, being warned of God of things not seen as yet, moved with fear, prepared an ark to the saving of his house..." - Hebrews 11:7*

Through the eyesight of faith, we are made aware of events that have not yet happened. Because of our natural inability to see beyond our present moment, God will give us faith to perceive when we are in danger, imparting the wisdom necessary to avoid catastrophe. We see this faith operating in Noah's relationship with God. He was "moved with fear" at the divine warning. The literal "moving" within Noah's heart happened "by faith." It is true that we cannot generate the least amount of reverence toward the word of God, if the faith of God has not energized that reverence within our hearts. For example, the Lord Jesus has told us that apart from Him, we can do nothing (John 15:5). This means that the outworking of any form of godliness can only come as a result of God initiating it through us. It is senseless for us to command people to "fear God" if God has not given those people His faith. Furthermore, Solomon describes the fear of the Lord as "to hate evil" (Proverbs 8:13). Since Hebrews 11:7 says that the moving of godly fear occurred "by faith," we may conclude that the source of the hatred of evil is *faith*. In other words, it takes experiencing God through the spiritual lens of faith before we can be moved to hate what is evil. Now, the fact that Noah was "moved with fear" tells us that he must have hated the evil in his environment. This is apparent through our study of his life. And yet, it is clear that the world around him did not hate what was evil, but rather indulged in it. Here we see a clear line drawn between those who have faith and those who do not. Faith releases the motivation to not only hate what is evil, but to reverence God's word through some act of obedience.

Now, Noah's greatest task would require heroic obedience. He was ordered to build an ark that was four hundred and fifty feet long, seventy feet wide, and forty feet high. We are not told who assisted Noah in this project, but we may assume that the building crew consisted of his family. Some believe that it took anywhere from fifty-five to seventy-five years to build this ark. There were four parts to this test: mental, physical, emotional, and spiritual. The mental test was the literal absurdity of such a task, as it had never rained, and therefore the concept of such a vehicle was completely unprecedented. The physical test was the actual constructing of this enormous wooden ship. Decades of hard labor would have taken a serious toll on Noah's body. The emotional test was dealing with the mockery that must have come from friends and family, not to mention the hostile world in which he lived. He must have become a notorious figure in the eyes of all those who heard of the wooden monstrosity that he was building. The spiritual test was whether or not Noah would continue to believe God through the decades of building. Recent archaeological and geological discoveries have revealed to us that Noah *did* possess the faith to believe God, passing all of the other tests as well Although faith does not need physical proof to validate the events in the Bible, when discoveries are made through science, it does validate these events to otherwise unbelieving people.

*"...by the which he condemned the world, and became heir of the righteousness which is by faith." Hebrews 11:7*

When studying the life of Noah, we see two opposing forces held in tension – righteousness and unrighteousness. Righteousness gives a person the status of being "legal" in God's kingdom, whereas unrighteousness is the state of being "illegal." Because of man's self-imposed separation from God, he was excluded from the benefits of the divine kingdom, and therefore became "unrighteous." In order to regain access, man would need God's faith to begin experiencing his legal rights in that divine realm. This "experiencing" of heavenly realities is a direct result of the outworking of righteousness in one's life. Only those who are righteous, or "legal," have access to the privileges in God's kingdom, in the same way that only a citizen of the United States has access to the country's constitutional rights. The transference of a legal status from God to an individual begins when

God releases His word to that person. Then there will be a corresponding faith that goes with that word, which will penetrate the heart, allowing admission into the divine privileges of God's kingdom. The response of the individual toward the Lord is exemplified in Noah's case: a remarkable demonstration of trust. Now, one of the chief experiences of being legal with God is salvation from death. Noah would be saved from the cleansing flood of God's wrath as a result of his righteousness. In essence, Noah's legal status with God gave him divine immunization from the death that would consume the whole world.

In the verse above, the word "condemn" is the Greek word *katakrino* which means, "by one's good example, to render another's wickedness the more evident and censurable."[6] This was a hallmark of Noah's life. He exposed the wicked works of the world around him. Although this is true for all those who live righteously, we must know that the exposing of wickedness is a secondary consequence of being righteous. We are not to tell people how sinful they are, rather, we are to let the good works proceeding from our lives testify of God's righteousness. When a wicked person sees the goodness of God through a righteous life, the stark contrast between the two lives will convict the wicked one of his or her sin. The "condemnation" which Noah's life exposed was the aftereffect of his righteousness in the Lord. All we need in order to expose the corruption of the world around us is to hear the voice of God and allow His faith to move us into action.

*"And spared not the old world, but saved Noah the eighth person, a preacher of righteousness, bringing in the flood upon the world of the ungodly." - 2 Peter 2:5*

The apostle Peter describes Noah as a preacher. Whether he preached vocally or by his life we do not know. But one thing we do know is his message: righteousness. As we have already said, this word is not a spiritual word as much as it is a legal one – used in a court of law. A criminal is a violator of law in a civilization, according to the laws which that civilization has enacted. Criminality is considered unrighteous action within a sphere of governance. Conversely, one who upholds the laws of the land is considered "righteous" or "in right standing" with those laws that are set up by the society. By the time of Noah's day, the entire population was living in unrighteousness. In other words, *there was no faith in God*, therefore no righteousness conferred, and no heavenly benefits given to mankind. Just as the salvation came to mankind by the living Word, we are to preach nothing other than that Word – Jesus Christ; for it is in the preaching of Christ that His faith is released, and those who are living in unrighteousness can receive the faith of the Word and experience their deliverance from death.

Noah was a man who stood in the gap between two realities: heaven and earth. His life preached of a righteous God in the midst of sinful people. If the world around him believed as he did, they would have been saved. However, the life of faith has always been a life of controversy to those who live in unrighteousness. Amidst the great

38

conflict between the Creator and His creation, Noah's obedience made it possible for all those who entered the ark to be under the protection of the Creator. Because of his faith, Noah was entrusted to be the new head of the human race, as humanity was ushered into an entirely new age. The remainder of mankind was brought into a state of glorious rest, as the waves of God's wrath abated, and a life free from the fear of extermination was restored to mankind. Just as a new creation emerged out of the ark after the destruction was completed, we have emerged from the old life of sin and death as a new creation created by God. Noah left a legacy of new beginnings, which is a testimony to the life of faith, having the power to produce the new creation realities which emanate from the very life of God.

# CHAPTER FOUR

# ABRAHAM

*"By faith Abraham, when he was called to go out into a place which he should after receive for an inheritance, obeyed; and he went out, not knowing whither he went. By faith he sojourned in the land of promise, as in a strange country, dwelling in tabernacles with Isaac and Jacob, the heirs with him of the same promise: For he looked for a city which hath foundations, whose builder and maker is God. By faith Abraham, when he was tried, offered up Isaac: and he that had received the promises offered up his only begotten son, Of whom it was said, That in Isaac shall thy seed be called: Accounting that God was able to raise him up, even from the dead; from whence also he received him in a figure." - Hebrews 11:8-10, 17-19*

In the land of Haran, the Lord got for Himself a man. The reason for acquiring this man was to make a nation out of him. It was a simple word that would set in motion a beautifully complex story in which humanity and divinity would walk together. God utters a word to man and gives that man His very own faith to believe and obey what is spoken. In fact, God does nothing in the earth unless He first utters His word. The faith which God gives to the individual is the very catalyst for that word to begin creating the life of God in the earth. Before we look at the specifics of this God-gotten man, let's look at human history and how it centers on our awesome Creator.

The term *history* has been defined many different ways by many different people. We speak of history today as the accumulation of facts about specific people groups, their cultures, and the events that have happened to them over the course of time. However, this view is sterile in the sense that it does not reveal the grandeur of God's purpose in the earth and does not reveal the progression of that purpose in the human race. A true understanding of the history of humanity cannot be based merely in the knowledge of past happenings in specific cultures, but must be founded upon an understanding of the workings of a sovereign Creator. From this biblical perspective, we understand that it was God who spoke all things into existence by His word. He set in motion the first events of history. He started the start. He began time. The context of a true study of all past events – which we define as *history* – can only be understood from the original starting point of God and His word. If we want to know the significance of any event that has happened in history, we must trace it carefully back to the word of God, which has defined not only what exists, but the specific events that would occur in the future.

We can identify many of the nations of the earth today as having begun by the word of God. For example, Mitzrayim was the son of Shem, and grandson of Noah. The name *Mitzrayim* is the Hebrew name for "Egypt." Since Mitzrayim's grandfather Noah was saved from the great Flood, based upon God's word to Him, we know that Mitzrayim's very existence can be traced back to God's word.

41

Mitzrayim's decedents occupied the land that he established, and to this day, the Egyptians have grown and thrived in this place. According to scripture, Egypt was the central hub for provision in the known world about 1716-15 BC. God chose this pagan kingdom to be the place where He would showcase His wisdom and provision through the Hebrew man, Joseph. Like Egypt, each nation serves a different purpose in history, as the Bible reveals.

The nation of Israel today is made up of several million people, with a significance in history that is quite unique, and that significance can be found in each generation going back to Abraham. The origin of this nation can be traced back to the twelve tribes of Israel. The natural origin of these twelve tribes can be traced back to the man Israel – or Jacob – who was the father of each of the heads of the tribes. Jacob finds his natural origin in Isaac, his father. And we know that Isaac finds his natural origin in Abraham, his father. Now it is here, with this man Abraham, that we find the purpose of God and the power of His Word that sets in motion the people and events that will accomplish His ends throughout history. Looking at the origins of this nation, we see the seed of significance found in the word of God which was designed to create an entire race of people, beginning with the man Abraham.

A miracle is considered to be a supernatural intervention or interruption into the natural, material world, bringing about a sudden and dramatic change which science cannot explain. Abraham's life would testify of this supernatural intervention, as the miracle-working word of God came to him with the intention of making him the father of many nations. Whereas Israel's significance was found in the man

42

Abraham, Abraham's significance was found in God and the word that He spoke to him. That divine word interrupted time and the material world, and set this man apart. Before this calling, he was just an obscure part of history. However, God would eventually say, "I have made thee a father of nations," changing his name from "Abram" to Abraham." The miracle of a changed identity brought forth a new destiny, which would forever alter the course of the world. Once again, the significance of the nation of Israel is found within its father Abraham; however, Abraham was literally the result of God's word which changed his identity and thereby defined his destiny as the father of the Israelite nation.

*"Now the LORD had said unto Abram, Get thee out of thy country, and from thy kindred, and from thy father's house, unto a land that I will shew thee: And I will make of thee a great nation, and I will bless thee, and make thy name great; and thou shalt be a blessing: And I will bless them that bless thee, and curse him that curseth thee: and in thee shall all families of the earth be blessed." - Genesis 12:2-3*

Prior to the Genesis 12, we find no record of God ever appearing to Abraham. In fact, according to Joshua 24:2, his father was an idol worshipper, and we may assume that Abraham worshipped these other gods as well. Despite man's upbringing, however, all he needs is one word from God in order for faith to stimulate his heart and produce spiritual life where there was once death. In other words, the word of God will produce God's life – His characteristics and

43

obedience within the hearer. The man who likely worshipped idols, having never had any prior experiences with the Lord, responded to this first word with *immediate obedience*. There is no such thing as delayed obedience, for delayed obedience is actually disobedience. Abraham did not delay but did what the Lord commanded. Faith produces immediate action in the hearer of God's word, a sort of recklessness that will do whatever is spoken, leaving the consequences of that obedience to God. Now, the word Abraham received reveals something typical about God's word to us. Whenever we receive a word from the Lord, the destiny of that word will be both *near* and *far*. The nearness of it is the thing we are to do right now: "Get thee out of thy country"; the farness of it is the thing we will ultimately become or do: "And I will make of thee a great nation." The steps in between now and then are ordered by the Lord (see Proverbs 37:23), yet seldom revealed in the beginning.

Coupled with immediate obedience, another attribute of the life of faith is *uncertainty* in the natural world. In fact, if you study the life of all the great men and women in the Bible, you will find the quality of uncertainty throughout their journeys. Noah built an ark having never seen rain; Joshua was commanded to lead over a million people into a land he had never seen; Solomon was commissioned to be a king having never, in any capacity, judged a nation; Peter was commissioned to preach to the Jews, having no formal Hebrew training; Paul was commissioned to preach to the Gentiles, having had no dealings with the Gentile world prior to his commission. The life of faith transcends cultural norms as well as natural ability, and depends solely upon the supernatural word of God.

44

Abraham built his first altar to the Lord in Canaan, where God said to him, "Unto thy seed will I give this land." (12:7). This is the second word that Abraham received from the Lord. Notice that the initial word did not contain anything about God giving *him* land for his children to inherit. It simply mentioned him being shown a piece of land. But the truth is, each step of obedience makes the image of God's word for our lives clearer. The sacrificial alter was a physical representation of Abraham's heart toward the Lord, which was full of gratitude. Wherever we go, we carry with us a continual altar to the Lord. That altar is not a physical one, but a revelation that upon Christ's sacrificial alter, called the Cross, we were crucified with Him. Romans 12:1 says that we are to "present your bodies as a living sacrifice, holy, acceptable unto God, which is your reasonable service." This is not a command for us to literally kill ourselves. Neither is this a command for us to abstain from certain of life's pleasures out of some sense of religious obligation. The apostle Paul makes this statement right after his previous eleven chapters, explaining in great detail the life lived of under grace of God as opposed to the life lived under the laws of God. The former requires the revelation of Christ's finished work on the Cross, the latter of trying to please God through external acts of service. Paul is saying here that the offering of our bodies to the Lord is simply the recognition that we have been crucified with Christ, and that the life we live in our mortal bodies is lived now by faith in God's eternal work and word to and through our lives, by the Person of Jesus Christ.

Like Abraham's entrance into Canaan, we are continually being led into significant places. And in these significant places, God will often give us clues to what lies ahead in our future. Whether God has called us to California, Canada, or Cambodia, we must allow Him to open our spiritual eyes, so that we may see the divine plan He has for us in these various localities. For example, Abraham was led by God into the Promised Land to see the territory his offspring would inherit almost 500 years later. As he moved about in the land of Canaan, he traveled to the town of Sichem in the plain of Moreh. "Sichem" means "Shoulder Blade"[1] and "Moreh" means "Archer."[2] This is a prophetic clue of what the Israelites would do in Canaan, in their occupation of the land; the Israelites would use archers to thrust their arrows into the fleeing enemy's shoulder blades.

In Genesis 12:8, Abraham moved his tent to the place between Bethel ("The House of God")[3] and Hai ("The Heap of Ruins")[4]. It was there that he built his second alter and called on the name of the Lord. This location graphically represents the tension between the life of faith and the result of a faithless life. We see Abram seemingly straddling these two experiences throughout his life. The former is where we are "housed" by an ever-present reality of God's provision for us, touching both the spiritual and natural part of us. The latter is a life that trusts in our own ability to provide for ourselves, not realizing that we can produce nothing lasting apart from God, who works in and through us so mightily to accomplish His will. This is the first time we see him calling on God. The life of faith involves speaking just as much as hearing. When God speaks, we hear; when we speak, God hears.

Right after the great prophetic word in Canaan, and his communion with the Lord in between Bethel and Hai, we are introduced to the fallibility of this man. Instead of trusting the Lord who spoke such a magnificent word to him concerning his offspring, he feared for the life of his family. As he ventured into Egypt, he decided that lying about his wife Sarah, saying that she was only his sister, would protect her from being taken by the Egyptians. His fear was actualized as Pharaoh took his wife anyway. It should be no surprise to us that the enemy of faith typically comes in the form of fear. What is fascinating here is that when God appears to us, speaks our name, and shows us things to come, we can still be prone to fear! However it is not unscriptural that our faith would receive a trial in order to prove its genuineness. And the genuineness of our faith is seen most evidently through the characteristics of *trust* manifesting as *rest*. A soul at rest is one of the greatest indications that we actually believe God's word. This is why it is folly to continue seeking after confirmation for this or that, when God has already spoken His word – one word is all we need. Our faith is challenged until our trust in God becomes absolute. The goal of our faith is not to arrive at some challenge-less existence, but to never have any doubts as to God's word, in the midst of the challenges. Despite his faltering, Abraham would see the power of a covenant with a faithful God. This is why the apostle Paul declares, "If we believe not, yet he abideth faithful: he cannot deny himself" (2 Timothy 2:13). For Abraham's sake, the Lord would cause terrible signs and wonders to fall upon the Egyptians in order to prove His faithfulness in ensuring the validity of His covenant.

After receiving his first two words, Abraham returned to Canaan and received a third word. In keeping with the first two visitations, he built an alter in the plain of Mamre ("Fatness")[5] which is

47

in Hebron ("Covenant")[6] (Genesis 13:18). Prophetically, the place of *fatness* is in the place of *covenant*. In other words, God's word to us is His covenant with us, producing an inner sustenance which gives us a tangible sense of fulfillment in the midst of our journey. This is why Jesus said in Matthew 4 that "man shall not live by bread alone, but by every word that proceedeth out of the mouth of God." The "bread" here refers to mere physical sustenance, whereas the "word" refers to the spiritual sustenance that is conveyed through the word of God.

*"And there was a strife between the herdmen of Abram's cattle and the herdmen of Lot's cattle: and the Canaanite and the Perizzite dwelled then in the land." - Genesis 13:7*

As we can see in the Scripture verse above, people of faith will inevitably come into direct conflict with those closest to them. It is true that as there are physical principles in the natural world, there are similar principles governing the realm of the Spirit. We can observe one rule of physics in this relational problem which states that, no two objects can occupy the same space at the same time. When God calls a person to do something, His plan is so specific that it will only work according to the spiritual physics of His word. In Abram's case, the conditions were total separation from his past – whether that was his relatives, friends or business (see Genesis 12:2-3). Yet, he was trying to fit his past and his future into his present moment. Lot represented Abraham's past. What many people tend to forget is that Lot was never supposed to leave Ur with his uncle. God told Abraham to get up and

48

leave his city, away from *his kin* and his *father's house.* Any time we allow what God has not, we will jeopardize the peace of our mission, and also delay divine revelation for the future. The first problem here was that two men were trying to realize their destinies in the same geographical region. God's master plan for Lot entailed a different destiny then that of Abraham's, and therefore a different physical region to inhabit. The second problem was that Abraham was prohibited from seeing the next revelation concerning his future. When we bring the wrong relationships into our spiritual mission, the result will always be strife. Although our disobedience does not cause the covenant we have with God to cease, it can block revelation concerning our destiny.

*"And the LORD said unto Abram, after that Lot was separated from him, Lift up now thine eyes, and look from the place where thou art northward, and southward, and eastward, and westward: For all the land which thou seest, to thee will I give it, and to thy seed for ever." - Genesis 13:14-15*

As we look at the above verse, it was as if God had said, *"Now that you have separated from those that are not permitted to share your journey, you now have permission to see another layer of your destiny right in front of you."* Amazingly, up until the point of his separation from Lot, Abraham didn't know that he was staring right at his children's future possession. Here is where we remember the initial word: "Get thee out of thy country, and from thy kindred, and from thy

49

father's house, unto a land that *I will shew thee.* " The Lord was able to show him the land which He spoke of now that he was obedient to truly separate from *all* his kindred and father's house, including Lot. Abraham's faith brought him to a partial fulfillment of God's promise, as he now saw the same land his offspring would possess with his physical eyes. This leads us to another truth about faith. We are led to partial fulfillment after partial fulfillment until every last word that God uttered to us is *completely* fulfilled. This leading occurs in stages until we reach our destination. As we continue to trust God in each stage of our journey, He will unveil another part of our destiny.

Soon after his separation from Lot, another conflict would ensue in Abraham's journey. Lot was taken, along with all his goods and his family, by the armies of Chedoralaomer.

*"And when Abram heard that his brother was taken captive, he armed his trained servants, born in his own house, three hundred and eighteen, and pursued them...And he brought back all the goods, and also brought again his brother Lot, and his goods, and the women also, and the people." – Genesis 14:14 & 16*

It takes a visionary to commission hundreds of men, lead them into battle, rout an enemy and return not only the stolen goods but all the stolen people. And this did Abraham, having no recorded military history. A life of faith is not disconnected from the natural conflicts that arise in our lives, but is the catalyst which causes vision and

50

strategy to be born, bringing redemptive solutions to the problems of others. Like Abraham, we will at some length, go to war with the natural and demonic entities that seek to bring harm to our loved ones and our own well-being. Some of the greatest men and women of faith were those who advocated for the civil rights of different races, the abolition of slavery, and the end of the sex trafficking industry. Our faith in God will be translated into a real currency which will afford the natural and spiritual well-being of those we are called to help.

After this great rescue, Abraham departed for the city of Sodom. Upon journeying to this city, an extraordinary thing took place, which would become a monumental event in his life. This visionary man was about to encounter one of the great mysteries of the Old Testament in the person of Melchizedek. The first time we see Melchizedek, he is bringing some bread and wine to the battle-weary captain who had just liberated a host of his people and their goods. The Bible states that Melchizedek was the king and high priest of Salem. The name *Melchizedek* means "King of Righteousness."[7] The city of his rulership was *Salem* which means "Peace."[8] His spiritual role was that of the high priest ministering before the Lord. His prophetic function in this account was to offer bread and wine to God's covenant man – Abraham – and to bless him with a prophetic word. Melchizedek had no known genealogy, which is almost unheard of in the Hebrew culture, known for meticulous attention to detail when it comes to chronicling genealogies. He has no record of a beginning or of an end, nor father and mother. Let's look at what the writer of Hebrews says of this mystical figure.

*"Without father, without mother, without descent, having neither beginning of days, nor end of life; but made like unto the Son of God; abideth a priest continually...And it is yet far more evident: for that after the similitude of Melchisedec there ariseth another priest, Who is made, not after the law of a carnal commandment, but after the power of an endless life."- Hebrews 7:3, 15-16*

The word "similitude" here is the Greek word *homoiotes* which means "likeness."[9] The prefix "homo" means "the same, or equal." Similarly, we find the word "likeness" in Genesis 1:26, used to describe the identical nature of the man God created, and that of God Himself. In Hebrew, the word "likeness" is *demuwth* which is translated "similitude."[10] The idea behind this Hebrew word conveys a sense of identicalness, in the same way that an armchair manufacturer would manufacture two identical armchairs. The idea that "another priest" would come "after the *similitude* of Melchizedek," means that this other priest would be of the same spiritual priesthood, or spiritual order as Melchizedek. When the writer of Hebrews says "another priest" he was referring to Jesus Christ. In fact, Melchizedek was a *type* of the coming Messiah. Jesus was made after the *likeness* of Melchizedek. He is continually a priest (Hebrews 4, 7 & 10). As man, was born of a virgin, but as God has *no beginning nor end.* Jesus' title is *Righteousness* (1 Corinthians 1:30). He is the *Prince of Peace* and presides over His kingdom with a *government of peace* (Isaiah 9:6); His role is our *High Priest* (Hebrews 4:14); His earthly function was to offer up His *body* and *blood* as the Divine Substitute for God's chosen people, which was also represented in the *bread* and *wine* that was

52

offered to His disciples during Passover (Matthew 26:26-28). It is here that we find a startling comparison between the king-priest of Salem, and the Christ who was yet to be revealed in human form. That Melchizedek, the king-priest, was called away from his kingdom to serve and bless a complete stranger, is one of the closest representations in the Old Testament of the coming Messiah, Who would likewise leave the glory of heaven to bless humanity with His own body and blood on the Cross. Abraham could see in Melchizedek the very type and shadow of the Man who would come out of his own physical lineage four thousand years later! Faith truly brings the substance and evidence of what we have been promised into the present moment.

*"After these things the word of the LORD came unto Abram in a vision, saying, Fear not, Abram: I am thy shield, and thy exceeding great reward. And Abram said, Lord GOD, what wilt thou give me, seeing I go childless, and the steward of my house is this Eliezer of Damascus?" - Genesis 15:1-2*

From these two verses, we find two important statements. The first is that God thought it necessary to tell Abraham "I AM your reward." The second is that Abraham, seemingly unsatisfied with what the Lord had just said, replies with "Lord God, what wilt thou give me?" In other words, the Lord said, "I *AM* your reward," to which Abraham replied, "Yes Lord, but what will you reward me *with*?" The Lord's word to Abraham indicated His intention on bringing him satisfaction from His very Being – a *supernatural, spiritual form.* Abraham's response however reveals the human need for the blessing of God to take on a *natural, physical form.* God did not despise his reply, but rather affirmed it by then revealing His plan to give him a son. How then do we reconcile these two ideas, that God *is* our reward, and that God gives us *a* reward? The truth is, our reward is both *spiritual* and *physical*, *supernatural* and *natural*. God is the reward and the rewarder at the same time, to satisfy both His desire to meet our spiritual satisfaction, and the need for God to meet our natural satisfaction. God does not want us to see His gifts as separate from Himself, but that all natural gifts proceed from the Lord. Faith is what allows us to receive the natural blessing from the spiritual source, just as Abraham would receive a natural son by the Lord's supernatural power.

In verses 4 and 5, The Lord goes on to prophesy His plan which would allow a natural child to come forth from Abraham and Sarah. That seed would become the physical reward for Abram. Now, the divine word, when spoken to us, always has two applications: the first is natural and the second spiritual. We often only see the first application of a word – how it will bless us naturally, physically – and rarely see how it will bring the spiritual impact upon us, the world around us, and the Lord who gave the word. A natural son was the ultimate blessing a father could have, and seeing how Sarah was barren, it would be all the more special to Abraham. His reward would be to have a son to whom he could pass his legacy. God, on the other hand, would view Abraham's son through eternal eyes, seeing thousands of years into the future at *His own Son* being birthed through Abraham's natural lineage. In essence, Abraham's reward of a natural son, would allow for the spiritual Son of God to have a physical heritage in which to be born - that He might redeem all mankind back to His Father. Abraham would be initially blessed, God would be ultimately blessed, and the world would be blessed as a result of the first two blessings. In all three cases we find that the reward ultimately centers on the same blessing, which is the spiritual Son who would manifest in physical form. Jesus Christ was the incarnate blessing of God, satisfying God's love for mankind, and mankind's love for God.

By this we see that God's plan is much greater, much more complex, and certainly more far-reaching than we realize. We may be waiting for the fulfillment of some word in our lives, something tangible that will satisfy us, but God is looking at the bigger picture. In the meantime, our waiting is not supposed to be some "dark time" of the soul; our waiting is anchored in illumination and excitement as we expect God's word to be revealed in the most creative way, in God's own timing. God sees much further in the future than we do. His eyes span limitlessly into eternity. He sees the beginning of time just as He sees the end, and beyond. He will not only bring us to our desired end, but will cause His eternal plan to come forth through us which extends beyond our natural life on earth and into the lives of generations to come.

As we briefly stated earlier, a common theme of God's prophetic words in Scripture is that they address things near and things far away, of the here and now and things that concern future events. Daniel was given words for his specific time in history, and then was told prophecies for later times yet to be revealed. Jesus shared many things with His disciples, and yet, still other things were saved for a later date. Paul revealed things hidden from the beginning of Creation, and yet concealed certain events that were of a futuristic nature. Many of us live a life with either near sighted vision, or far sighted vision. *Nearsightedness* is a condition where "light entering the eye is focused incorrectly, making distant objects appear blurred...you have trouble seeing things that are far away."[11] Spiritual nearsightedness is a result of our focusing too heavily upon what we see and hear in the present, missing the bigger scope of God's plan for the future. *Farsightedness* on the other hand is where there is "greater difficulty seeing near objects than distant objects...It may be caused by the eyeball being too small or the focusing power being too weak."[12] Spiritual farsightedness is when we are more concerned with what God is doing in the future, and we lack concentration on what God is saying and doing in the present. A mature faith is both focused on the present moment, and the future, finding godly fulfillment in both. The emphasis of Abraham's vision was incorrectly focused on his present situation. We will see this as his journey continues.

*"And, behold, the word of the LORD came unto him, saying, This shall not be thine heir; but he that shall come forth out of thine own bowels shall be thine heir. And he brought him forth abroad, and said, Look now toward heaven, and tell the stars, if thou be able to number them: and he said unto him, So shall thy seed be." Genesis 15:4-5*

Abraham is told to look up into the evening sky. Instantly his perspective began to change at the sight of such a brilliant expanse! What with billions and billions of stars shining forth like diamonds over the horizon of Canaan, his heart made the connection between this physical sight, and the spiritual sight of faith, based on the word given to him. He began believing that this great Being who spoke with him was in fact able to do exceedingly, abundantly above all that he could

56

ever ask or think. God will often give us a word concerning our future that can be understood through some visible, natural created thing. What followed was one of the most profound happenings in the history of mankind.

*"And he believed in the LORD; and he counted it to him for righteousness." - Genesis 15:6*

There are two words that are most important in the verse above: "believed" and "righteousness." The word "believed" indicates a condition of the heart that results from hearing God's word. To *believe* in God requires two ingredients: hearing and faith. We sometimes call it "the hearing of faith," however it is two parts nonetheless. Faith comes by hearing, and believing is the result of what we have heard. When a man believes God's word, that man instantly comes into a covenant with God Himself. A "covenant" literally means a contract between two parties. Under the Old Covenant, man was not able to keep his end of the contract, and therefore was condemned under that system of Law. However, this covenant the Lord was making with Abraham actually foreshadowed the Messianic Covenant that would be implemented after the period of history when Law and the Prophets were fulfilled. Abraham was called "righteous" before he even sacrificed to the Lord, indicating that this covenant would not be based upon man's works, but upon faith in God's word. Now after Abraham heard that he was "righteous," the Lord required a detailed sacrifice to be made so that the covenant could be established. And so,

57

Abraham brought the necessary animals, killed them and arranged the pieces in the right order. After this, a "deep sleep" fell upon him and he was not able to finish the ceremonial sacrifice by walking in between the bloody pieces. Instead, we see a "smoking furnace" and a "burning lamp" passing between each hewn piece, while Abraham was under this divine sleep. What's fascinating is that the Lord is the One who walked through the sacrifice, fulfilling what Abraham could not do in his stupored state. In this way, God revealed that the performing of His word would be *His* responsibility, not Abraham's. In other words, faith in God's word was all that God required of Abraham in order to fulfill his end of the covenant. The good news is that, even the faith of Abraham was supplied in God; for faith is not a work of the flesh, but a gift given to man by the Lord (see Ephesians 2:8).

In the fullest sense of the word, *righteousness* is a legal term, not a religious one. A person is deemed *righteous* who has been absolved of committing a crime, or acquitted of any accusation of committing a crime. Faith in God makes a man legal in God's realm, in His heaven. In other words, faith is the access point to all that God has, and is the means by which the divine life becomes accessible to a man. Abraham was made righteous because he trusted in God, believing that what God said would come to pass. This one act of faith set a precedent for the entire fallen world, that a man could be right with the Lord, not by any self-willed work, but by belief in the Person of God. In the same way that Abraham was made righteous by faith in God's word, we are made righteous, as we believe in God's ability to perform His word to us. Instantly we get a divine word, our spiritual vision is corrected, and we begin to walk in the light of what we see.

Oftentimes, after we receive God's word, we undergo a test that is designed to prove the power of the word which we received. Adam received God's word concerning the tree of life and the tree of the knowledge of good and evil; after this, the serpent came to test Adam and his wife to see if he could catch them in unbelief. As we fast forward to the Last Adam, Jesus Christ, we see the Father commending Him based upon His life up until that point, calling Him a well-pleasing Son. Immediately after He received this word, He was led into the wilderness to be tempted by the devil to prove the strength of His faith in His Father's commendation. Faith in the word we have received empowers us to pass the test, just as Jesus passed His test.

*"Now Sarai Abram's wife bare him no children: and she had an handmaid, an Egyptian, whose name was Hagar." – Genesis 16:1*

Abraham and Sarah's servant Hagar is representative of anything or anyone that presents a short-cut to our destiny. Hagar appealed to Abraham as a quicker way to realize the word of the Lord for his life, who had become impatient after years of waiting. And so, he married her and consummated the marriage upon Sarah's request for a child. This action produced a twofold consequence: the wrong woman conceived, and the right woman was despised. As a result, Hagar was cast out of the house, and Sarah blamed Abraham (what a mess!). The truth is, there is no short cut to our destiny. In the natural world, we may arrive at a geographical destination several different ways. In the context of our spiritual journey however, we must realize that God has a path designed specifically to produce within us the kind of character, wisdom, and knowledge that is essential for our future. It is on each of our unique roads that we will discover who we truly are in light of all that God has said about us. Ultimately, when we arrive at our destination, we will have been so transformed by the journey that we will be perfectly fitted for the destination ahead.

*And when Abram was ninety years old and nine, the LORD appeared to Abram, and said unto him, I am the Almighty God; walk before me, and be thou perfect. And I will make my covenant between me and thee, and will multiply thee exceedingly. – Genesis 16:1-2*

Years after the occurrence with Hagar, the Lord was about to make a covenant with Abraham, stating the conditions that he was to fulfill. The first condition was that he "walk before the Lord." As we have seen with Enoch, the word for "walk" here means "to live." This was the first requirement that a covenant with God entailed, to live in a realized communion with Him. The second condition was that he "be...perfect." The word "perfect" is the Hebrew word *tamiym* which means *upright in conduct*, or *blameless*.[13] Tamiym denotes *righteousness*. We've already learned that in order to "live" with God as Enoch, and be "righteous" with God as Abraham was righteous, one must possess the faith of God. Abraham would only be able to accomplish this by faith, which is true for us today. Abraham was before the Law of Moses, therefore the covenant God made with Him was not based upon his ability to keep the Law of God, rather in God's ability to provide him with faith. This was, and is, a superior covenant to that of the Law, for only by faith is it possible to remain in constant communion with the Lord, living in the supreme reality of righteousness with God.

At this point we may be thinking, "But I thought in order to live with God and walk righteously before Him, one needs to be born again?" Although we must see a clear distinction between the Old and New Covenants, we must always see that divine faith transcends all ages and covenants. God's provision for the new birth – the life, death and ascension of His Son – would destroy the old nature of man, giving mankind a new nature that could be received by faith. Abraham's sinful nature did not change when he was called "righteous," however he was still given legal access into the kingdom of God. We can use citizenship versus a visa as an analogy to understand this concept more clearly. To become a permanent citizen of a country, one must complete all of the documents, financial obligations, and fit the requirements of the United States government in order to gain citizenship. However, if one wants to simply visit, or work in the U.S., they will need a temporary visa. Those who are official citizens have full access to everything that the U.S. offers, whereas temporary visitors are limited. However, both have access to the country of the U.S. Similarly, the New Covenant Christian has full access to all that is in the kingdom of God, because a revelation that was hidden before Christ was revealed, especially in the writings of the apostle Paul. And that revelation is this: our evil conscience was cleansed once and for all by the blood of Christ. Furthermore, there is nothing separating us from the life of God and of His eternal kingdom. However, the one who lived under the Old Covenant as well as the one before the Old Covenant only had partial access due to the limited understanding of God's grace, and an awareness that their sinful nature was still in effect. And although it is true that prior to the Old Covenant which was established with Moses, mankind was not made aware of their sin – the Law of the Old Covenant exposing that sin – man was still living without the mature revelation that through the Messiah, a completely different consciousness would exist in everyone who possessed faith.

*As for me, behold, my covenant is with thee, and thou shalt be a father of many nations. Neither shall thy name any more be called Abram, but thy name shall be Abraham; for a father of many nations have I made thee." - Genesis 17:5*

The next significant thing to happen in this man's life, was that the Lord changed his name from "Abram" to "Abraham." The former means "exalted father"[14] and the latter "father of a multitude."[15] Although Western culture has tended to reduce the use of names to convenience and a sort of audible pleasure, the Hebrew culture placed a much greater significance upon a name. The Lord added a letter into the middle of "Abram." The fifth letter of the Hebrew Alphabet is *hay*. In the Talmud, it is said that "the breath of God's mouth" refers to the sound of the letter h*ay* – the out-breathing of Spirit.[16] This letter, when being pronounced, gives off a breathy sound. By inserting the *hay* into Abram's name, the Lord was setting in motion the destiny that awaited him. Psalm 33:6 declares, "By the word of the Lord were the heavens made; and all the host of them by the *breath of his mouth*" (emphasis added). This verse reveals that God's word to us is not merely giving us the right perspective on our future, but is literally creating that future! The prophet Isaiah says, "Declaring the end from the beginning, and from ancient times the things that are not yet done, saying, My counsel shall stand, and I will do all my pleasure" (46:10). God speaks those things that have not yet happened, and establishes them as a fact. Faith simply agrees with what God has declared as fact in our lives.

It is interesting to note that in the entire seventeenth chapter of Genesis, the Lord says the words "I will" a total of eight times, and the words "thou shalt" only once. The emphasis of this covenant is clearly on what the Lord would do, as opposed to what Abraham was required to do. Similarly, in the New Covenant, "it is God who works in us both to will and to do of His good pleasure" (Philippians 2:13). If God is the one who *works, wills* and *does*, what is left for us to do? The truth is, Christ eliminated the false idea that there is an *I* that coexists with Christ. The apostle Paul says in his letter to the Galatians that "I am crucified with Christ: nevertheless I live; yet not I, but Christ liveth in me: and the life which I now live in the flesh I live by the faith of the Son of God, who loved me, and gave himself for me." Notice how Paul does not entertain the idea that we and Christ are separate entities. It is the life of Christ that lives so mightily through us, accomplishing His purposes in the earth. If we have been called to do anything, it would be to trust in Christ and His operation through our lives. Many people today are trying to fulfill God's word to them by trying to drum up more will-power. However, faith is not based in man's ability to will something into existence. God rules out our own will-power by revealing the superior way of living – seeing Christ as the One who lives through us, *as* us. When we trust in God's word, we are trusting in His ability to perform that word. The New Testament Christian recognizes that although they may be doing what God has ordained, it can only be done in the strength of Christ's Spirit within them.

In chapter 18, we find that Lot is in trouble again. The first time he was taken captive during the wars of Chedarolamer, and this time he was surrounded by utter immorality in the city of Sodom. The Lord appeared unto Abraham, along with two angels, in order that they might destroy that wicked city and all that lived there. In this instance, Abraham does not receive a mere spiritual vision or word, rather, is physically visited by the Lord Himself. The Lord says,

*"I will go down now, and see whether they have done altogether according to the cry of it, which is come unto me; and if not, I will know. And the men turned their faces from thence, and went toward Sodom: but Abraham stood yet before the LORD." – Genesis 18:21-22*

Now, Abraham was already in covenant with the Lord. He believed the divine promises, and was faithful to continue his journey toward the promises that awaited him and his family. The Lord (many believe this to be the Second Person of the Godhead) came to the earth in physical form with two of his angels, in order to "see whether they (the Sodomites) have done altogether according to the cry of it, which is come unto me; and if not, I will know." In other words, the city of Sodom was so wicked that their wickedness produced what is described as a "cry" – some audible sound that warranted one more divine glance before a divine judgment came. Here we find the Lord appearing in person, which is an unusual occurrence in the biblical record. This is significant for we know that the Lord did not *need* to be on the earth physically in order to ascertain the moral status of Sodom. He could have easily sent His two messengers into the city to report its condition. But we find the Lord physically involved in this passage. This mysterious visitation is understood most clearly when we consider our relationship with the Lord and the faith which gives us access to Him. Faith does not abstractly connect us with God's kingdom and His awesome presence; faith is the life-line between a man and God, by which all things are created and are sustained. The faith that God imparted to Abraham operates the same way when imparted to us, and can be likened to a string. The Lord ties one end to His own heart, and the other end to the heart of the person. Each feel the other's movements. Man cannot move in faith without involving God, and God cannot move through a man's life without involving that man in His own movements. Abraham's family was in Sodom, and therefore, God could not destroy that city without personally including Abraham in the decision making. In other words, the decision to destroy the city would be an act of faith on the part of the Lord, whereas the decision to halt judgment to any degree would be an act of faith on the part of Abraham. The result of the Lord and Abraham's conversing about this matter presents us with a clear picture of God's faith becoming man's faith.

*"And it came to pass after these things, that God did tempt Abraham, and said unto him, Abraham: and he said, Behold, here I am. And he said, Take now thy son, thine only son Isaac, whom thou lovest, and get thee into the land of Moriah; and offer him there for a burnt*

65

*offering upon one of the mountains which I will tell thee of. And Abraham rose up early in the morning, and saddled his ass, and took two of his young men with him, and Isaac his son, and clave the wood for the burnt offering, and rose up, and went unto the place of which God had told him." - Genesis 22:2-3*

Notice the similarity between this command, and the one that was first given him in Genesis 12. "Now the LORD had said unto Abram, Get thee out of thy country, and from thy kindred, and from thy father's house, unto a land that I will shew thee: And I will make of thee a great nation, and I will bless thee, and make thy name great; and thou shalt be a blessing: And I will bless them that bless thee, and curse him that curseth thee: and in thee shall all families of the earth be blessed." Both commands involved the idea of leaving familiar surroundings, going to a location without specific detail, and taking those with whom he held dearest to his heart. Both cases also show Abraham obeying the word quickly. The first time, God told Abraham that He would make of him a great nation. The second time, God required the son who was supposed to produce that great nation. This may seem grossly unreasonable; however, when we consider Abraham's life thus far, having often received the word of God, having seen the physical representation of the Son of God, having been delivered from foreign enemies, and divinely protected throughout each foreign land, a monumental test such as this was not beyond the scope of his faith. In fact, his faith gave him the vision of God, and therefore the confidence of knowing that God would make good on His promise of making him the father of many nations. He saw Isaac as the

66

promise, and believed that the promise was based upon a living word that could not be killed off before it had accomplished its intended purpose.

*"And Sarah died in Kirjatharba; the same is Hebron in the land of Canaan: and Abraham came to mourn for Sarah, and to weep for her." – Genesis 23:2*

From the time that the Lord called Abraham, to the time of his arrival into his destination, there were many years of waiting and hoping for the fulfillment of God's word. He endured much hardship traveling constantly throughout foreign lands. He endured the fears of large empires threatening his family's welfare, a barren wife, casting out his first born son from the family, and the prospect of losing his second son. Now, in the wake of a great victory of faith on the mountain of Moriah, his wife dies in the land of promise. It was there that a tribe of Canaanite men called "the sons of Heth" heard of Abraham's loss, and went to offer a sepulcher for his wife.

*"Hear us, my lord: thou art a mighty prince among us: in the choice of our sepulchres bury thy dead; none of us shall withhold from thee his sepulchre, but that thou mayest bury thy dead." – Genesis 23:6*

It is significant that these men called Abraham "a mighty prince among us," for this is the third time we read of strangers speaking forth the magnificence of Abraham and his God. The first was Melchizedek, king of Salem, who announced, *"Blessed be Abram of the most high God, possessor of heaven and earth."* The second was Abimelech, king of Gerar, who said, *"God is with thee in all that thou doest."* (see Genesis 21:22). The third was the sons of Heth, recognizing Abraham as a *"mighty prince among us."* The world around Abraham recognized the awesome favor, power, and pleasure that his God had toward him. These recognitions came parallel with the hardship of his nomadic living, the sting of rejecting family members, and the death of loved ones. Many times, people around us will be strangely aware of the Lord working in and through us, while we may only be conscious of our present hardships. This is because the life of faith allows the world to see God's own life in us being worked through us, even though we may be treading through our most painful moments.

Abraham died forty-three years after his wife's death, and was buried with her in Canaan. Remarkably so, he did not want his son to have a Canaanite wife, yet was very particular in wanting to be buried with his wife in Canaan. The reason for this apparent contradiction is twofold. He knew that his lineage were to remain pure and therefore would require them to be separate from the Canaanites. He also knew that his seed would eventually possess the land of Canaan. Thus, being buried in the land of Canaan was a prophetic act of faith, in which his offspring, as living seeds, would be planted in the same land that their descendants would one day occupy. As the writer of Hebrews states, Abraham really did die in faith!

Through studying the life of this great patriarch, it is apparent that the majority of his journey was spent living as a nomad. He moved his family from place to place, living by the inspiration of every word and visitation revealed to him by the Lord. He did not see the nations that were to be born through him, nor the kings that would rule in his lineage. He saw the stars of heaven above him each night, but only one little star – his son Isaac – would be visible by the time of his death. However, he saw with the eyes of faith, the very substance and evidence of God's word to him, the multiplied millions which would come forth from his descendants. Abraham not only received the seed of God's word, but became a living seed which, when planted, produced a tree with many branches, from which, fruit grew and continues to grow. Because he believed God's word, the entire world is still eating the fruit of this man's faithful life.

# CHAPTER FIVE

# SARAH

*"Through faith also Sara herself received strength to conceive seed, and was delivered of a child when she was past age, because she judged him faithful who had promised." - Hebrews 11:11*

It has been said that behind every great man is a great woman. This could never be truer than it was for Abraham and Sarah. Abraham was considered by the Lord to be the "father of many nations" and a "friend of God." Next to this patriarch of faith, Sarah may appear like a blade of grass beside an oak tree. But it was in the shadow of greatness that she was used as the vessel through whom God's promise would come to pass. She married a man of earthly substance who was called to be the father of a royal kingdom. Sarah was first called "Sarai," which is the Hebrew word for "princess." Although her name implied royalty, companied with her marriage to a man of material wealth, she faced a poverty that no amount of money could assuage - the poverty of a barren womb. In light of the divine promise given to her husband, and the fact that she was an inadequate vessel to produce that promise, she faced an immovable mountain of fear. It was not until she saw what God saw, that the mountain of fear was removed, turning the physical fact of barrenness into a fiction. She would learn that the faith of God was all she needed for the birthing of God's word.

*"And I will make of thee a great nation..." - Genesis 12:2*

When the Lord spoke this word to Abraham, an eternal plan was set into motion. Time and space began to conform to the invisible workings of that word, and the mechanics of the invisible future began clicking into place – and it is the word of God which causes the mechanics of *our* invisible future to begin clicking into place. God releases His faith whenever He desires to create something, and likewise, that faith is released for a man or woman in order for them to see the creative work of God in their lives. Faith is the bridge between heaven and earth which allows us to connect with what God is saying, and see what God is doing. We already know that Abraham had received faith to connect with God and His righteousness, for the Bible says "...and Abraham believed, and it was accounted to him as righteousness." In the same way, we know that Sarah probably had an equal opportunity to believe this word, as Abraham undoubtedly told her what the Lord had promised.

Now, Abraham was destined to become a natural father of a physical nation. He would eventually have a son, who would have sons, and so on. The rapid increase in population would eventually become large enough to require a government with laws, thereby leading to the development of a nation. He was also destined to become a spiritual father to a spiritual nation. The apostle Paul says this of Abraham, "to the end the promise might be sure to all the seed;

71

not to that only which is of the law, but to that also which is of the faith of Abraham; *who is the father of us all*" (Romans 4:16, emphasis mine). Here we see the physical nation and the spiritual nation defined by Paul. When he says "not to that only which of the law," he is speaking about the natural nation of Israel who were governed by the Law of Moses. When he says "but to that also which is of the faith of Abraham" he is speaking to all those who would be included into God's divine promises in Christ. Paul is declaring that the faith of Abraham was available not only to the Jews but the Gentiles as well. Now, the spiritual aspect of God's promise to Abraham was brought about by faith. Abraham believed God, became righteous, and the spiritual father of all who would believe God and become righteous in the same manner. The physical part of the promise – a nation of Hebrews – would also come about through faith in God's word. Although it does not take faith for two people to have a child, it does require faith when both the man and woman are physically incapable of having children, as were Abraham and Sarah. Therefore, both the physical and spiritual parts of the promise to Abraham required the same faith.

*"...and Abram went down into Egypt to sojourn there; for the famine was grievous in the land." - Genesis 12:10*

There was a grievous famine in the land of Canaan, and so Sarah and her family journeyed to Egypt. It was here in Egypt, a place that would become known for testing the Israelites, that a test would be provided for Abraham, centering on Sarah's physical beauty. Upon entering Egypt, they encountered a contingent of Pharaoh's army who immediately noticed Sarah's attractive appearance. Because Abraham was a foreigner and evidently powerless to resist the Egyptian army, he and his family were taken by the Egyptians and brought to Pharaoh. God blessed Sarah with physical attraction, even in her old age. However, she did not use her beauty to manipulate or to seduce, but was submissive to her husband, which is apparent by her willingness to obey his word and pose as his sister. Because of this, Sarah was caught in the middle of a precarious situation. On the one hand, she had a husband who was afraid and untrusting of the Lord's protection, and on the other, a foreign nation whose intentions would separate her from her family for the rest of her life. Yet, in the midst of this, there is no record of her displaying fear or a lack of trust in God, in contrast to her fearful and untrusting husband. Unaware of the consequences of his actions, Pharaoh claimed her as his own. Since Sarah was part of a family who was ordained by God to bring about His promise, Pharaoh would reap great destruction as the result of a powerful curse – the entire Egyptian palace was plagued because of her! The reason for this curse stems from the prophetic word given to Abraham which is where the covenant of blessing and cursing started. To this day, that word still holds the same potency as it did then. When people bless the Israelite nation, they come under a powerful blessing; when they manipulate or bring harm upon Israel, they come under an equally powerful curse.

*"And the LORD plagued Pharaoh and his house with great plagues because of Sarai, Abram's wife." - Genesis 12:17*

Egypt was cursed for Sarah's sake. As a result of this awesome display of supernatural power, Pharaoh knew that he had interfered with a bloodline that was rooted in a power greater than his own! Sarah was released from Pharaoh's house, and with her release the plagues ceased. Because of the covenant God made with her husband, Sarah was surrounded by an invisible aura of supernatural authority. Here we find an amazing parallel between the life of Sarah and the life of the Christian. Before Sarah's marriage to Abraham, she was not a partaker of the divine covenant. In the same way, prior to faith in Christ, we were not a partaker of God's covenant administered through Christ. Her marriage to Abraham is like our marriage to Christ. By faith we became partakers of all that He possesses, naturally and spiritually, in the same way that Sarah was a partaker of all that Abraham possessed. Sarah is to us a type of Christian, barren without the supernatural release of God's word. Jesus said "I can do nothing of my own." In essence, He was saying "I am barren without the power of my Father working on the inside of me." Sarah was vitally joined with the covenant between God and her husband, and therefore was shielded by the same protection, provision, and leadership that Abraham obtained.

*"Now Sarai Abram's wife bare him no children: and she had an handmaid, an Egyptian, whose name was Hagar." - Genesis 16:1*

Up until the Law of Moses, there were no hard and fast rules for women who were not physically capable of conceiving, and yet desired to have children. In these ancient Middle Eastern cultures it was accepted that a wife unable to conceive could offer the maid-servant to her husband, and if the servant was able to have a child, she would render the wife as the mother of that child. We are not told that

74

barrenness was the result of God's disapproval with a woman, but rather as one of the detrimental effects of the Fall. Still, the pressure that was on any woman who was not fertile would have been crushing. Before Sarah was given her name, she was called "Sarai" meaning "princess"[1]; yet the nobility of being a princess in this royal family was undoubtedly stripped. Hagar represented Sarah's chance to be a mother, and so Abraham took Hagar because of his wife's desperate plea. The book of Genesis says that when Hagar had conceived, she "despised" Sarah. The word that is used here means "lightly esteemed."[2] Compounding the reality of her barrenness, Sarah was now living with the taunt of her Egyptian servant. Her plan completely backfired. Although we may possess outward beauty, physical possessions, and a tight-knit family we will still have no ability to produce the promises of God any more than Sarah. We may possess great talents, and yet our talented attempts at fulfilling God's word will always lead to disappointment.

It is on the journey to our destiny that we will face great temptations. These temptations come in the form of opportunities that present a quicker way to achieve God's promise. It is interesting that the name *Hagar* means "flight,"[3] as her name implies speed or quickness. Her life symbolizes anything that offers us a seemingly quicker route toward our destiny, instead of the path which God has ordained. There is no substitute for waiting upon God's word to manifest. Quick fixes, whether they be new relationships, changes in occupation, or personal resolutions will not last; rather, they will ultimately lead us into oppression. After the Lord reveals his word to us, He may purposely keep our minds mystified as to how the divine

75

promise will actually manifest. By doing this, He is teaching us that the promise is not something to be figured out intellectually, but rather is something that will manifest spontaneously through the wisdom God births within our hearts. The word that God gave to Abraham would be literally activated from *within Sarah*; her womb would become fertile apart from any mental assent.

It is essential to know that God's promise is *not* some sort of addendum to who He made us to be – that promise *is* essentially who we are! The apostle Paul reveals this stunning truth: "Now unto him that is able to do exceeding abundantly above all that we ask or think, according to the power that worketh in us" (Ephesians 3:20). Notice that the thing God does which is beyond our expectation is according to *the power that works in us*. In other words, what we are destined to become is not something that God creates in the future, nor is it something He does outside of us; rather, it is so vitally connected to us that it proceeds out from us! According to God's word, Sarah was destined to become a mother. In essence, the word that was spoken which formed Sarah's destiny began to form something physical within her. The word she received was literally forming her identity as a mother by creating a womb that was physically capable of bearing children. In essence, she would not only receive that word, but she would *become* that word. Similarly, the Christian realizes that his or her existence is the direct result of God's word. Speaking of the New Covenant believer, the apostle James declares, "Of his own will *begat he us with the word of truth*, that we should be a kind of firstfruits of his creatures" (1:18, emphasis mine). Likewise, the apostle Peter says in his first epistle, "Being born again, not of corruptible seed, but of incorruptible, *by the word of God*, which liveth and abideth for ever" (1:23). Both James and Peter are declaring that we as believers are words from *the* Word! We have our spiritual DNA sourced in God Himself. Therefore, the destiny that lies before us will be an outworking of the word we have become based upon the will of God, who spoke us into existence.

It was not until thirteen years after Hagar conceived, baring a son, that the Lord spoke again to Abraham concerning his wife Sarah.

*"...As for Sarai thy wife, thou shalt not call her name Sarai, but Sarah shall her name be. And I will bless her, and give thee a son also of her: yea, I will bless her, and she shall be a mother of nations; kings of people shall be of her." - Genesis 17:15-16*

Over the course of many years, the Lord had been appearing to Abraham concerning his offspring. Although she was contending with her bodily impotence as well as her old age – she was nearing ninety – Sarah must have heard of these encounters and pondered them. In the above verse we see the Lord appearing along with two angels, while Sarah was in the tent. He spoke of four prophetic events to Abraham:

*1.   I am changing your wife's name from "princess" to "noblewoman"*

*2.   I will bless her with a son of your own*

*3.   I will make her a mother of nations*

*4.   Kings will come out of her.*

Although spoken to her husband, all four of these words directly pertained to Sarah. We will look at the impact of each of these words beginning with the first. *"As for Sarai thy wife, thou shalt not call her name Sarai, but Sarah shall her name be."* As we have already seen, the name *Sarai* means "princess." A princess is part of a royal family whose primary duty is to produce an heir. Since the producing of children is fundamental in the continuance of any kingdom, a fertile womb would be the greatest asset a princess could offer. And so, for a woman in this position, not being capable of conceiving would become the greatest hindrance in keeping the royal bloodline intact, for generations to come. Sarah was not able to conceive a child because she was barren. The result was that her nobility as the wife of Abraham came under fire. Similarly, we may find ourselves in a unique position where we are required to produce something that contributes to those around us. And like Sarah, we may have some form of debility that prohibits us from producing what is required. The first thing that God does in these dilemmas is to *reveal our true identity*, oftentimes before He releases the miracle that changes our situation. God first changed Sarah's name, from *Sarai* to *Sarah*. The name *Sarah* means "noble woman."[4] By changing her name, the Lord was restoring the image of her true identity. The nobility that was stripped from her through natural impotence would be restored back to her through the Lord's supernatural omnipotence. In the same way, the image of our identity is restored to us through who we see ourselves to be, in the Person of Christ. Regardless of whatever false identity we formerly had – uneducated, divorced, addict – God reveals who really are, as *perfect replicas of Jesus Christ*. We have been made to be God's anointed ones, who through the miracle of

78

salvation are transformed into an entirely new species (see 2 Corinthians 5:17). We may stutter like Moses, have no education in speaking like Jeremiah, or have fear like Timothy; however, God's word will transform our identity to the point that omnipotence begins to manifest in our impotence.

*"And I will bless her, and give thee a son also of her."* After God reveals our true identity, we see that God's will for our lives is vitally connected with our deepest desires. The most intimate desire of newly named *Sarah* was to give Abraham an heir. Although Sarah did not have the ability to have a son, God's word would give her that ability. It is essential to understand that God's word can create a life where there is no life, a reality where there is none. When we understand the creative power of God's spoken word, we will see the utter foolishness of continuing to look at our inabilities to measure our capabilities – we are capable of whatever God says! Paul was able to "glory in infirmities," because he understood that "where I am weak, He is strong." If God says it, no force on in heaven or in hell can stop what He has said. Notice that the Lord *told* Abraham that He would give him a son, without first consulting with him or with his wife. God doesn't need to consult with anyone but Himself when determining what will and will not be!

*"And she shall be a mother of nations."* When the Lord speaks, His word has a way of expanding the very borders of our understanding, giving us a vision that was previously far beyond our comprehension. All Sarah wanted was to have a child; however, we know that God does above and beyond all that we could ever ask or

79

think. Not only did she receive a new name, she received the promise of a son; and now she is told that her child will be the beginning of an entire nation of people.

*"Kings will come out of her."* Now, once Sarah's identity changed, she was able to reproduce the seed of promise. That seed, when full grown, would produce a whole orchard of fruit, and the substance of that fruit would be royal – kings would be raised up. The progression of God's word to Sarah was to first reveal her identity as a noble woman. Second, He spoke of the immediate desire within her heart, which was to have a son. Third, He revealed multiplied millions of sons that would eventually come forth from the initial child. And fourth, He revealed the role that these sons would have in the earth – to rule and reign. When all of these things were spoken, divine faith was imparted. In essence, it was faith in Sarah's heart that would keep each prophetic word energized until the time of their fulfillment.

*"Through faith also Sara herself received strength to conceive seed, and was delivered of a child when she was past age, because she judged him faithful who had promised." – Hebrews 11:11*

The Greek word for "strength" here is *dynamis*, which means "inherent power, power residing in a thing by virtue of its nature, or that which a person or thing exerts and puts forth."[5] This word literally implies the exerting of explosive power upon a person's soul for the purpose of manifesting a miracle. As soon as Sarah heard the word of the Lord, the faith of God was given to her. At the moment that faith was received, an explosion of divine power energized her reproductive ability. What is significant about the above verse is that Sarah did not "receive strength to conceive" until "she judged him faithful who had promised." Sarah did not judge the word, but the One Who gave it! Only when she looked at the Person giving the word did she receive strength in her weakness. Some may say, "How can we judge God?" The word "judged" means "to consider, deem, or account."[6] The idea here is that we consider all that God is, accounting for all that He has done, both in eternity and in time; therefore we deem Him faithful to perform the word He has spoken to us. Many times we grow impatient and even angry with God because our situation does not seem to be changing. The fact is, we are not judging Him faithful, but rather maybe gripped by cynicism as to whether or not He will fulfill His word. Cynicism is actually a fruit of unbelief, and we know that it is faith that pleases God, not unbelief. This is a sure way to stay in a weakened and unfruitful condition. The Lord will suspend every physical law in the universe to manifest His word to us; however, it is through faith that those physical laws are superseded by the divine intervention of God's word.

In the eleventh chapter of Hebrews we are told that those who approach God must believe two things: the first is that "He is" and the second that "He is a rewarder of them that diligently seek Him." The first part deals with God's character. When we survey all that God has said and done throughout eternity, there is an assurance which convinces us that He is God. The second part deals with God's intent to bless all of creation with Himself. The Greek word for "rewarder" literally means "one who pays wages."[7] Now, according to Romans 6:23, we know that "the wages of sin is death"; therefore, we may confidently say that the wages of God is *life*. This life which God gives

81

is His very own. For Sarah, the wage she received from the Lord was the gift of God's life, which recreated her reproductive system so that she could give birth to the promised son. It was God's life in Sarah that created new life in her womb.

*"And the LORD visited Sarah as he had said, and the LORD did unto Sarah as he had spoken. For Sarah conceived, and bare Abraham a son in his old age, at the set time of which God had spoken to him...And Sarah said, God hath made me to laugh, so that all that hear will laugh with me." - Genesis 21:1-2, 6*

Sarah's destiny of motherhood arrived at the exact time foretold by the Lord. When the manifested promise was birthed through her womb, the scriptures declare that she laughed. This laugh was the spontaneous response of a woman who had just experienced the long awaited arrival of God's word. We know that it was God who made Sarah laugh, indicating that the physical promise she waited for was intrinsically connected to the spiritual characteristic of joy. In other words, the destiny that awaited her was the point at which she experienced her greatest pleasure. The child born was named *Isaac* which means "laughter."[8] Because Isaac is a representative of God's promises, we may confidently expect great joy when our own destiny is revealed. Now, if we go back to Genesis 18:12, we find Sarah laughing at the initial word which was spoken by the Lord, indicating that she would bare a son. When we compare Genesis 18:12 with

Genesis 21:6 we find this wonderful truth: Sarah laughed when she first heard the word of the Lord, and then again when that word became manifest. It is therefore significant that we see the word of the Lord and the joy of the Lord as vitally connected at the beginning as well as at the end of our journey. Since faith connects the initial word with that word's destiny, we see that the joy of the Lord is to *fill* our entire journey. According to Nehemiah 8:10, it is the joy of the Lord which gives us supernatural strength. Here we find supernatural joy releasing divine strength into the moment when we receive God's word. Both laughter and strength are fruits of God's joy. Sarah "received strength to conceive seed" when she heard the initial word, and laughed with the laughter of joy; therefore, strength was given to birth that word. Sarah prophetically declares in Genesis 21:6 that "...God hath made me to laugh, so that all that hear will laugh with me." In other words, not only do we laugh *with* Sarah at the miraculous intervention in her womb, but we will laugh *like* Sarah at the miraculous intervention in our lives. Sarah is prophesying here of the joy that is experienced not only in the beginning of our journey, but all throughout until we arrive at our destination.

As we survey the scriptures, we find eight barren women specifically listed in the Bible: Sarah, Rebekkah, Rachel, Samson's mother, Hannah, Michal, the Shunammite, and Elizabeth. All these were barren up until the time that God supernaturally opened their wombs. Since Sarah is the first one mentioned, we may consider her the matriarch of barren women. Her life would be a sign and wonder to every woman that felt as though they lost a part of their identity and destiny because of their physical impotence. If God could bring a

83

supernatural conception to Sarah's womb – by faith – then God could do it through any women who had faith in His word. Not only is her life a sign to women, but to all who suffer from barrenness – whether physical or spiritual. Many of the governments in nations overrun with crime feel barren in their ability to produce peace. Likewise, many of the governments in nations full of disease feel barren in their ability to produce cures for their people. The man who is not able to take care of his family financially because he has been laid off feels barren in his ability to provide those things necessary to keep his family alive. In the barren condition that we may find ourselves in, all we need is a word from the Lord. One word, mixed with faith, will produce omnipotent power in our lives and will cause the barren womb of our situation to open and flourish even as Sarah's womb opened to a son.

In the beginning of our study of Sarah's life, we found two of the most important details recorded: she became Abraham's wife and she was barren. Although God's word to Abraham was "I will make a nation from your seed," Sarah did not possess the ability to give her husband that seed. This divine paradox is seen in all who are called of the Lord. God created Adam and Eve and then told them to populate and take dominion over the entire earth. Jesus sent His disciples out to feed the multitudes with only one boy's lunch. The angel Gabriel appeared to a virgin and told her that she was chosen to have a child outside of intercourse. And yet, in each of these instances God would reveal that His purposes would only be achieved by faith. In the midst of her barren condition, Sarah heard God's word and trusted in it, reaching her destined moment of motherhood as she gave birth to the son through whom the entire world would be blessed.

84

# CHAPTER SIX

# ISAAC

*"By faith Isaac blessed Jacob and Esau concerning things to come." -*
*Hebrews 11:20*

We have all likely seen nights when the sky is as black as pitch with a million shining stars, like diamonds scattered across a dark canvas, pulsating and singing their silent symphony. One could spend all night watching those shimmering lights which reveal the splendor and majesty of their Creator. Other nights, we may see only one star, alone and barely visible contrasted with millions of darkened miles of empty space. That one, shimmering star, becomes a reminder to us that there are millions of others hidden, waiting to be unveiled on a another clear night. Abraham was promised a clear night sky, full of stars stretching across the blackened expanse. Just before he died, however, he could see only one shining star visible in the universe. That one solitary star was Isaac. The course for this boy's journey had already been set, already been fitted for him. As a result of his parents' unique calling to be the beginning of a new race of people, accompanied by their faith in God's word, Isaac's life would be the fulfillment of prophecy spoken years earlier. His birth signified the beginning of that new race. Though he was only one, he was destined to be the first of millions of stars in the universe God was making on the earth.

The Bible declares that the things seen were created by things unseen; in other words, the visible is representitive of the invisble. The universe full of stars was the natural representation of a nation that would populate the earth, and the people through whom God would produce the Messiah – mankind's redeemer. As the unseen, invisble word of God pierced through eternity and into time, a plan was set in motion that would cause the Incarnation to manifest in the earth. That word was spoken to Abraham, who received it by faith, which caused a miraculous child to fill the womb of his aged wife. Isaac's very blood had the DNA of divine destiny written into the coding of each cell. He was a nation in seed form, and a child set apart for a special purpose.

What was it like being this long awaited son, on whose shoulders the weight of the world seemed to rest? Surprisingly, the Bible paints an obscure picture of his life, as he repeats his father's nomadic and enigmatic journey throughout the Middle East. Much like that lonely star in an overcast evening sky, his shine is hard to make out in the pages of Genesis. Given the impact that his destiny would have on the world, we are tempted to desire something more of Isaac on a grander scale as we read what is written about his life – some extraordinary feat of strength, or some brilliant undertaking to give his life meaning. Despite whatever impressions we may have had about his account, the record reveals that he reached the objective in God's kingdom-plan for man: he walked by faith and fulfilled his purpose, because he believed God's word.

The Bible declares that faith is born when a person hears the word of God. That word may come from an angel, a prophet, someone in the Body of Christ, or the Lord Himself. Whichever way God chooses to give someone His word, the means by which it comes is entirely up to His own creative wisdom. What is certain is that the hearing of that word releases God's faith into the heart of people, enabling them to walk in the destiny of that word. We also know that the word of God is ageless, and can have the same impact on one generation as it does the next. Regardless of the generation that hears a word from God, the same faith can be inspired in whomever hears and believes that word. However each generation's faith will be determined by the exact word that God speaks to the people.

For example, we teach on the revivals of the past, and the words that past generations received that sparked revival. But teaching on those revivals and the words which the people received does not necessarily cause that revival to come to us today. However if God speaks to the next generation, they can see the same revival manifest in their midst. It is also possible that subsequent generations can walk in the word given to former generations if God intends to perptuate a particular move of His Spirit through time. (The next generation would be under the prophetic canopy of that initial word and would thereby have the embers of revival still burning for them to stoke.) Similarly, we may assume that the first word Isaac heard that inspired faith within him was the prophetic word passed down from his father, which he received when he was ninety nine (see Genesis 17:19 & 21). Although Isaac was not present when the word was given to his father, the word pertained directly to his life and the lives of those that would come from his lineage. Thus, the embers of Abraham's prophetic word were still hot when Isaac was born, which would be stoked throughout Isaac's life.

It is significant to mention here that many aspects of Isaac's life have set precedents in the Scriptures, establishing faith in God's dealings with man for generations to follow. We see many "firsts" in Isaac's experience with God. Webster's defines "precedent" as "prior in time, order, arrangement, or significance." In other words, a precedent is a thing that has already been produced by someone or something, upon which others will base their actions. Abraham set a precedent of moving geographically based upon a word from God. Therefore this act of faith is a model to all those who may be called by God to leave their familiar surroundings and travel into the unknown. We will begin by looking at Isaac's name.

The name "Isaac" was given to him by the Lord in Genesis 17:19, which in Hebrew means "He laughs." Both his father and mother laughed when they heard that they would have a son in their old age. The fact that God gave Isaac his name carries great significance, for it is the first time we find the Lord naming anyone's child in the Bible. By God naming Isaac, he was naming the firstborn of a new nation. The Hebrew word for "laugh" is *tsachaq*.[1] The first time the word *tsachaq* used is Genesis 17:17. The Lord told Abraham that his wife would conceive and have a child, to which he *tsachaq*, or, he "laughed." The second time we find this word is in the case of Sarah, who declared that "God hath made me to *laugh*" (Genesis 21:6). Both Abraham and Sarah are the first two cases of laughter being expressed in the Bible in regard to the birth of Isaac. We tend to associate laughter with times of joy. According to the apostle Paul, Joy is a significant experience of the Kingdom of Heaven (see Romans 14:17). In the Book of Proverbs, laughter is portrayed as highly valued in our human expereince, being compared to medicine. It is therefore signifcant that Isaac was not only the first person *named* by God himself, but also the person with whom the idea of *laughter* is first

89

conveyed in Scripture.

We also see that God was establishing Isaac as a type of His own Son, the Christ. In the Book of Matthew, the angel Gabriel appeared to Joseph and told him the name that the Child was to be given. His name would be called JESUS, symbolizing His role as deliverer. Through the meaning of his name, God was establishing a unique destiny as one who would bring great joy to his father and mother. Similarly, we know that Jesus would bring great joy not only to the world, but also to his Father, by making a way for all mankind to come into the the kingdom of Heaven. Isaac was a manifestation of joy for his father, who spent most of his life wandering the earth, hoping for an heir. Isaac's destiny was to bring joy to his parents, and ultimately health to the entire world through the Son of God who would be born through Isaac's lineage.

The next precedent set through Isaac's life was concerning his wife. It was Isaac's father who sent out a servant to find him a suitable wife. Abraham knew that Isaac must take a wife from his own blood, and not from the blood of the Canaanites. So he sent Eliazar out on a mission to find the right woman for Isaac. This is the first time in Scripture that a father selected a wife for his son. In a prophetic sense, this act of a father on behalf of his son symbolized God the Father's choice of a bride for His Son, which is the Church. The fact that Isaac trusted his father to find him a bride was a prophetic act of submission pointing to Jesus, who would be submitted to His Father's will; the Father sent the Holy Spirit into the world to receive Jesus' bride, just as Abraham sent out Eliezar.

The fourth precedent seen in Isaac's life concerns his father's legacy. Typically, fathers are more concerned about their son's legacies, but Isaac was invested in his father's legacy even more than his own. Isaac was faithfully submitted to that which his father built on the earth. Abraham's servants dug three wells, which would have been a source of sustenance for Abraham's family and their livestock. The Philistines came and "stopped" the wells by filling them with dirt. Isaac re-dug each well, naming them Esek, Sitnah, and Rehoboth. The first two wells were not an easy task, for the Philistines contended with him over the water supply beneath the ground. However, Isaac prevailed and reestablished the same supply of water that his father used to sustain the family. Isaac's unselfish fight to keep his father's legacy alive was a product of faith. It is true that faith will give us an eternal perspective on temporal matters, and will inspire us to do things that have an impact upon our future. That Isaac was concerned about his father's legacy is clear in his contending with the Philistines over the three wells. And by protecting his father's legacy, he was investing into his own destiny; for the water supply would bring sustenance to Isaac and his family. And so, we see Isaac's destiny and his father's legacy intertwined. One pertained to the past of the father, the other to the future of the son. And this is the nature of faith, as it not only reveals the eternal impact of past and future events, but brings about divinely inspired acts which harmonize God's eternal purpose with man's present moment (we will look more closely at this fourth precedent later).

When studying the life of Isaac, we are bound to see a theme emerge from the record: an unusually unwavering trust in the authority figures of his life. More specifically, we see this trust most dramatically in relation to the will of his earthly father. The very essence of trust *is* faith. Isaac trusted his father because *he believed* in the word his father received from God. He believed that he was the son of promise, which translated into a life of trust even in the face of possible death. We can find no biblical evidence that Isaac ever questioned his father's reasoning or motive behind each of his instructions. From this son-to-father trust, we gain a great picture of the true nature of faith, which produces an unwavering trust in God's word. When we trust someone, we are literally investing our life – spirit, soul, and body – into their care. This can be dangerous if the other person is not trustworthy. When talking about "trusting in God," we must realize that God does not have personality liabilities, dishonesty or deceit; in other words, His perfection rules out any possibility of Him being untrustworthy. He gives us His word, and we can trust perfectly in what He's said. Since faith operates in us based upon the word we've heard, we cannot have true faith without true trust in God's character – in the perfection of His character to perform His word to us.

*"And it came to pass after these things, that God did tempt Abraham, and said unto him, Abraham: and he said, Behold, here I am. And he said, Take now thy son, thine only son Isaac, whom thou lovest, and get thee into the land of Moriah; and offer him there for a burnt offering upon one of the mountains which I will tell thee of...And they came to the place which God had told him of; and Abraham built an altar there, and laid the wood in order, and bound Isaac his son, and laid him on the altar upon the wood." – Genesis 22:1-2, 9*

The years between Isaac's birth, and what would transpire on Mount Moriah is shrouded in mystery. The only event that is recorded took place at eight days old, when he was circumcised by his father. We are propelled ahead to the mystical morning when, being awakened by his father, he was told about a three-day journey into the mountains of Moriah. The purpose of this early morning rendezvous was not clear, however, something was said about a sacrifice to the Lord. He did not know that his own life would be required at the end of this journey. Whether by divine design or because Abraham did not have the heart to tell Isaac what was ahead, Isaac did not know that his obedience would lead him to a high mountain where his life would be taken. This gives us a clue as to the life of faith: it is a life of profound *mystery*. Without mystery, there would be no need for faith to operate. 1 Timothy 3:9, the Bible speaks of "the mystery of the faith." The word "mystery" here comes from the Greek word *mysterion* meaning "a hidden purpose or counsel; secret will."[2] When God speaks his word to a person, two things become certain; the first is that what He says is spoken in no uncertain terms – it will come to pass exactly as He has said it; the second is that a mystery forms as to how that word will be fulfilled, and what will be necessary on our part to see that word come to pass. With each word, we know in part, for the Lord only reveals part of the picture to us. In a sense, faith is necessary to solve the mystery of the word, by revealing the part we need to connect the word with our destiny. We are not sure how this particular prophetic word will come to pass, but we've seen into the future in part, and the vision created by the word will lead us to our destination. Yet, the mystery remains for now. The only thing we are left with is faith, which is demonstrated through obedience. We see this in Isaac first in Genesis

22, one of the most monumental passages of Scripture in the Old Testament.

Studying this account in Genesis 22, we see one of the main keys of faith – *obedience*. There are two ways to look at the concept of obedience. The first is that of man doing what God commands him to do. The man hears the word of God and sets out to accomplish that word. We see this idea of obedience when we study the dispensation of Law, beginning with Moses. Under the Law, the ability of man to obey God was flawed. In fact, God gave the Law to man knowing that he, in his attempts to obey each command, would utterly fail. Man does not have the ability to perfectly obey God's Law, and therefore any system that requires man to obey what God commands is a flawed one. This is why Hebrews 8:7 says that the Old Covenant contained *fault* simply because it was based upon man's ability to keep God's Law. The second concept of obedience is that of God *Himself* fulfilling His own word in each person. Under the dispensation of grace, we understand that it is not a man's own ability that carries out God's will in the earth, but it is God's ability through man that accomplishes the divine plan. Paul calls this type of obedience, "the obedience of faith" (Romans 16:26). Another word for obedience is *submission*. Submission is not a decision to work with God, rather, a decision to let God work through us. It is God's will that carries out God's work in our lives. Not only does God *will* to do something, but He desires to be the one who does it. Obedience is the fruit of trusting in God's ability to fulfill His own will in and through us.

Obedience to God – allowing God to fulfill His own word through us – gives us a sort of invincibility against anything that stands as a potential threat to our destiny. If God is working His word out, then we can be confident that no human agency or supernatural entity can stop Him. When Abraham said to the servants, "I and the lad will...come again to you" Isaac believed that he would return with his father based upon God's word. When his father said "My son, God will provide Himself a lamb" he believed that God would provide a substitute based upon God's word. When Abraham bound Isaac to the wood of the offering, Isaac believed that his father's instructions were based upon God's word, and therefore to be followed to the letter. When Isaac looked up at his father, whose outstretched hand clutched a knife, and whose determination to slay his son was burning in his eyes, he still believed in his father's word. Obeying his father without question was the natural result of Isaac's faith, making him invincible to the death that awaited him as he walked up the mountain.

*"And Isaac intreated the LORD for his wife, because she was barren: and the LORD was intreated of him, and Rebekah his wife conceived." - Genesis 25:21*

Isaac made supplication to the Lord concerning his barren wife. The word declares that after Isaac "entreated" the Lord for Rebekah, the Lord was "entreated" of him, and she conceived. The Hebrew word here is *athar* and denotes the idea of burning incense to a god, or to smoke with perfume.[3] Isaac's prayer for his wife was as incense to the Lord. In fact, when God heard Isaac's voice, it was a familiar fragrance to Him – it was as if He was hearing Abraham's voice too. The father had a barren wife, and so did the son; both prayed and both were given a miracle. In the Hebrew language, the name *Rebekah* literally means "ensnarer"; in Arab it is translated to mean "a rope with a noose."[4] This was not an unfit name for a woman who could "ensnare" men with her beauty. Her beauty aside, she was still not able to produce a child, just like her mother in law, Sarah. It was by the faith of Isaac that Rebekah conceived, even as it was by the faith of Abraham that Sarah conceived.

God heard Isaac and answered his supplication. This is the *reward* of faith spoken of in Hebrews 11:6 which says, "...for he that cometh to God must believe that He is and that He is a rewarder of them that diligently seek Him." When a person prays in faith, God hears and God responds with supernatural power. It is a "laughing" faith that believes God to do the impossible. It is "laughable" because of the hilarity of naturally impossible circumstances, turning around supernaturally at the word of God. Since Isaac was a product of his father's faith, he shared the same faith that opened barren wombs.

We will now look at a significant passage in the life of Isaac, and break it open to find God's revelation for us today.

*"And there was a famine in the land, beside the first famine that was in the days of Abraham. And Isaac went unto Abimelech king of the Philistines unto Gerar. And the LORD appeared unto him, and said, Go not down into Egypt; dwell in the land which I shall tell thee of: Sojourn in this land, and I will be with thee, and will bless thee; for unto thee, and unto thy seed, I will give all these countries, and I will*

*perform the oath which I sware unto Abraham thy father; And I will make thy seed to multiply as the stars of heaven, and will give unto thy seed all these countries; and in thy seed shall all the nations of the earth be blessed; Because that Abraham obeyed my voice, and kept my charge, my commandments, my statutes, and my laws." Genesis 26:1-5*

1. *"And there was a famine in the land..."*

The Bible is a book of many thousands of themes, each one revealing a different revelation about the Lord. One of the most important and common themes in the Bible is conflict-resolution. With every conflict in biblical lives, there was always a resolution. Although the conflict is usually different in each case, the resolution is always the same – the word of the Lord. With the death of his father, the barrenness of his wife, and now the famine plaguing his land, Isaac needed a word from God. Without a divine word, no faith can operate in the heart of a person; and without faith, no power is released into the circumstance to see the miraculous take place. It is often in the midst of some outward deprivation that we will have profound encounters with the Lord. These encounters are designed to teach us that God's power, personality, and personal desire for our lives is sourced in His divine word.

2. *"And the LORD appeared unto him"*

This was the first time that God appeared to Isaac. Interestingly, the Lord appeared to Abraham right when a famine was plaguing the land, in which he and his family sojourned. The word to him was quite similar to the word given to his son. Both were words reaffirming the greatness of God's plan for them as individuals, his blessing on their lives, and the land they would possess. Abraham was told to sojourn in Canaan, the land that his descendants would one day occupy. Isaac was told to sojourn in Gerar, the land that his descendants would occupy, also part of Abraham's inheritance. These two places are modern day Israel, and Palestine, both of which were spoken of by God, thousands of years prior to their occupation. The word of the Lord, which we need in times of conflict, may come in various forms – God may appear to us physically, in a vision, or send an angelic messenger. In whatever form His word is delivered to us, it will set in motion the events that will lead to our possessing the land of our inheritance.

3.  *"Go not down into Egypt; dwell in the land which I shall tell thee of: Sojourn in this land, and I will be with thee, and will bless thee..."*

The famine led to a divine appearance unto Isaac, which revealed the word of God to him. The word was a command; in essence, it was the specific strategy of God for Isaac in the midst of the tension of opposing circumstances. What if Isaac chose not to stay in Gerar, but used his situation as an excuse to pick up and move? Would he still have been blessed by God? To an extent he would have still been under the general covering of God, however, he would not have been able to reach his destination had he moved to a place with more external comforts. We should never do anything based upon physical circumstances. We must always receive a fresh word from the Lord so that we do not miss our opportunity for miraculous provision.

4.  *"Sojourn in this land, and I will be with thee, and will bless thee; for unto thee, and unto thy seed, I will give all these countries, and I will perform the oath which I sware unto Abraham thy father; And I will make thy seed to multiply as the stars of heaven, and will give unto thy seed all these countries; and in thy seed shall all the nations of the earth be blessed..."*

Notice the "I wills" in the line above. God is the narrator of each one of these "I wills." The fact is, if God does not say "I will" to us on any particular thing, we can never say "I will" or else we will ourselves doing something by our own initiative, and we will not have any help from the Lord. Whatever God does not "I will" in our lives, cannot and must not be initiated by us, even if the way seems good to us. When God says "I will," our only responsibility is to believe, and then do whatever He says. We are called to simply live a life joined to the initiatives of God in every area of our lives. We live this way by the faith that He gives us, which energizes His plan in us and through us, until every part of that plan is completed.

5.  *"Because that Abraham obeyed my voice, and kept my charge,
    my commandments, my statutes, and my laws."*

All of God's blessings to Isaac were a result of his father's
obedience. And here again we find that the obedience of a man to the
word of God will open a supernatural pathway into the future for the
blessings of God to come upon future generations. Isaac would walk in
a supernatural overflow of his father's faith, and find sustenance
through famine and war, all because he believed as his father had.

Isaac's wife was barren like his father's. He lived through a
famine like his father. He was appeared to by Jehovah just like his
father. He faced losing his wife and his own life at the hands of foreign
kings, like his father. We see this man going through the same testing
that his father went through. We should see by now that Isaac most
certainly lived a life that mirrored his father's, much like Jesus Christ
mirrored the movements of His heavenly Father. We live by the same
rule: the faith of those who have gone before us, we follow.

*"Then Isaac sowed in that land, and received in the same year an
hundred fold: and the Lord blessed him." - Genesis 26:12*

Isaac teaches us a lesson here. When we are facing any form of
economic challenge, the best thing to do is to continue to give out, to
sow freely of our lives and not withhold. We see this principle with
Elijah and on Mt. Carmel, who poured out twelve barrels of water

around the altar, in a time when Israel was experiencing a drought. We see this again when Elijah told the woman of Zarephath to feed him out of the very last bit of food she had to live on. In the first case, God released Israel from its devastating drought; and in the second, God provided a miracle of constant provision for the poor woman of Zarephath. We cannot manipulate the harvest; rather we can simply sow seeds in faith, believing for a return from God. Some have taught that "we should not give to get." However the Bible teaches the opposite. A farmer sows seed *because* he knows that a harvest will come. In the same way, we are to always live a life of faith, one that expects the future reality of God's miraculous harvest coming into our circumstances. We may not see our breakthrough instantly, but by faith, it is as good as done. Isaac received a hundredfold return of the seed he sowed in the same year that he sowed it. It was by faith that Isaac sowed, for it takes faith to believe for a harvest when everything in the natural realm appears to contradict the provision of God.

Many people begin following the Spirit of the Lord, until He begins to lead them through "the valley of the shadow of death." This valley can be seen as some major obstacle, such as the famine which Isaac lived through. Once the pressure of circumstances begins, these same people allow fear to paralyze them, and as a result, no seeds are sown. Some of those who submit to fear will envy those who have trusted the leading of the Spirit and have reaped a glorious harvest. Every good harvest that we reap in life is the result of obeying some law that God has established. If we sow generosity, we'll reap generosity. The same principle can be seen most obviously through natural seed. For example, in order for an apple tree to grow, an apple seed needs to be sown. How ridiculous it would be to expect an apple tree to grow, having not sown an apple seed, or, having not sown anything at all! In the spiritual realm, it takes faith to sow a seed, and faith to continue patiently for that seed to grow into an apple tree. In other words, we must first believe that the seed contains everything necessary to produce after its own kind. Secondly, we must believe that, through patient waiting, we will see that seed transform into its predestined form. Seed-time and harvest is about having faith that our seed will grow in the time necessary, and become exactly what is contained within that seed.

The Bible declares that God has determined by the spoken word the end of the age of man, and He has spoken it from the beginning of time (see Isaiah 46:10). This means that God *knows* the end from the beginning, simply because He has spoken it. God may know for certain that what he says will come to pass, simply because He has faith in His own word. He is confident that what He has said will come to pass. We must carry that same confidence in order to see what God has said come to pass in our own lives. When we begin to act in faith concerning our future, we are in essence doing as Isaac did – sowing seed – and we may expect to receive the harvest of our actions, whether the times and environment we are living in are favorable or not.

*"And the man waxed great, and went forward, and grew until he became very great: For he had possession of flocks, and possession of*

*herds, and great store of servants: and the Philistines envied him." -*
*Genesis 26:13-14*

In the midst of national wars, economic recession, moral famine, or any other type of crisis, God gives us His word and imparts His faith in order to give us spiritual eyes to see our way out of the situation. Like Isaac, we begin to move forward despite the opposing forces that would keep us in a state of inertia. This forward motion is the result of comprehending what God has already said about our future. Once we see what God has said – for example, that we will be great men and women of finance, miracles, or missions – we can wage war against every conceivable threat to our progress. Those threats may include the envy of others, even as Isaac was envied by the Philistines.

We have already briefly discussed the account of the three wells of Abraham, which the Philistines had covered over. Now we will look more in depth at this stage of Isaac's journey, in order to see a greater aspect of the life of faith, in a moment of great opposition. The Philistines were inhabitants of Gerar, a city within the land of Canaan, and were descendants of the man, Canaan, Noah's grandson. Thus, it was not unusual for the Philistines to have lived in the land of their ancestors. However, what is remarkable is that God's promise to Abraham – that He would give him the land of Canaan – explicitly implied that everyone living in that land prior to Abraham receiving it, would be completely uprooted at the appointed time, in order for the destiny of this word to come to pass. In short, God's word creates an immutable precedent in the earth that cannot be altered, trumping cultural, ancestral, and even national establishments. The fact that He spoke of Canaan as Abraham's inheritance, meant that anyone dwelling in Canaan – even the Philistines who were the actual descendants of the man, Canaan – were considered only temporary occupants of that land. Isaac had only to believe God's word and take possession of his rightful inheritance.

The name *Philistine* means "immigrant," and the name Gerar means "lodging place."[5] Indeed, the Philistines were lodging as immigrants in the land that Abraham had been promised. We must realize that they were immigrants, not because they had just moved there temporarily, or because they were living in the territory of another kingdom. The Philistines became immigrants in their own land because God literally re-deeded that land to Abraham, while they were still living there!  Here we see a principle of reaping physical blessings – in this case it was land – and is demonstrated so well in Proverbs 13:22 which says, "…the wealth of the sinner is laid up for the just." In other words, the blessing in store for a righteous man or woman may be in someone else's possession, at the moment. From a natural standpoint, we may find the Philistines' anger to be justified, since their land was being encroached on by a people neither of their ethnicity nor nationality. However, from God's perspective, every people group on earth must yield to His sovereign plan to bring His will to pass. Furthermore, the righteous are always anointed with favor and protection wherever they go, and to resist them is to resist the very hand of God.

*"For all the wells which his father's servants had digged in the days of Abraham his father, the Philistines had stopped them, and filled them with earth." - Genesis 26:15*

The three wells which Abraham dug were significant as they were not only a physical means of bringing sustenance to his family, but prophetically represented the three generations of faith – Abraham, Isaac, and Jacob – who would all occupy this land. These wells were not merely for the physical need of water, but for establishing three landmarks that future generations would have as a sign of God's covenant with Abraham, Isaac and Jacob. Abraham had pioneered three wells which provided a supply for each generation. It is interesting that Isaac, the second generation, uncovered the three wells only after he had his sons Esau and Jacob, who both represented the third generation. Here we see Isaac not only "reopening" his father's legacy, but establishing that legacy for his children to partake of. By this, we see that Isaac represents Christ, who brought spiritual regeneration to the world, and revealing the supernatural sustenance from the Father, to the sons.

A well of water may also be symbolic of other important truths besides marking the legacy of three patriarchs. Isaiah speaks of water wells as a place where salvation dwells: *"Therefore with joy shall ye draw water out of the wells of salvation."* Solomon speaks of the well as the mouth of man, through which words proceed: *"The mouth of a righteous man is a well of life."* And again, Solomon speaks of a well as a lover, who is *"a fountain of gardens, a well of living waters."* Jesus refers to the inward part of man – his spirit – as a well where living water is *"springing up into everlasting life."* Similarly, Jesus

105

says that to those who believe in Him, *"out of his belly shall flow rivers of living water."* We get the idea that a well is most symbolic of the person, or more specifically the *inward* part of that person, such as their soul or spirit, whereas water is symbolic of what flows *out from* that person, be it words or actions. Now, Faith is the divine substance that comes from within a man's spirit, and is released through man's mouth in the form of a confession. It is a point of fact that whatever we believe becomes our confession. The Bible declares that "out of the abundance of the heart the mouth speaketh" (Matthew 12:34) Likewise, "Keep your heart with all diligence; for out of it are the issues of life" (Proverbs 4:23). It is in the inward part of man – his heart and spirit – that becomes the well, housing the divine contents of faith. This is why we must make sure that the well of our heart remains free from the contamination and covering of the enemy, who seeks to stop the confession from proceeding out of our mouths, and through our lives.

In an effort to oppose the Israelites, the Philistines came to pour dirt into each well, to stop the flow of water. Notice that the enemy could not remove the water supply for Abraham and his family, they could only *bury* it. This is a clear picture of how the enemy works even to this day. When a person steps out in faith to cooperate with God's purpose in the earth, that which has been stopped up and covered over by religion will be released and revealed, allowing many to come and draw spiritual life from that spiritual well. For example, Charles Finney, one of the great revivalists of the 19th century, labored in Upstate New York for many years, and saw hundreds of thousands of souls revived, along with supernatural signs and wonders confirming what the Spirit of God was doing there. Years later, that powerful movement began to wane, and it was as if the enemy targeted the same region that was once ablaze with revival. Many religious cults such as Mormonism, along with many spiritist movements began to appear in the same region. The Philistine's were attempting to inhabit a land that was ordained by God for Abraham's seed.

*"And Isaac digged again the wells of water, which they had digged in the days of Abraham his father; for the Philistines had stopped them after the death of Abraham: and he called their names after the names by which his father had called them." - Genesis 26:18*

Isaac named the first well *Esek* which means "contention."[6] The second he named *Sitnah* which means "strife,"[7] and the third, *Rehoboth* which means "wide places."[8] Two of the most dangerous enemies of the flow of faith are contention and strife. James 3 says "For where envying and strife is, there is confusion and every evil work." The Philistines envied Isaac, and caused contention and strife with him over his father's legacy in the land. In keeping with the comparison of the three wells and the generational line of Abraham, Isaac, and Jacob, the first and second well represents Abraham and Isaac. They both had to contend and strive in order to take the ground of Canaan from the Philistines. The third well, however, represents Jacob, for by the time he became a man, he would not have to contend nor strive with the Philistines. God made room for him and his seed –

"a wide place" – because two generations before him fought to make his destiny a reality.

Faith is an eternal substance, the very divine energy of God behind all that God does, and therefore is not bound by time. Hence, a life of faith considers what has been and what will be, when determining what to do in the present moment. Isaac was determined to contend for the wells in Gerar, so that Abraham's legacy would not be marred and Jacob's future would not be in question.

The conflict between Isaac and the Philistines ended in the physical reward of three reopened wells, and the spiritual reward of a divine encounter with God.

*"And the LORD appeared unto him the same night, and said, I am the God of Abraham thy father: fear not, for I am with thee, and will bless thee, and multiply thy seed for my servant Abraham's sake." - Genesis 26:24*

The life of faith is continually experiencing God-realities. When we experience these realities, we are typically moved to express what has been made real to us. Like his father, Isaac built an altar there where God appeared to him. Practically speaking, we may not be led to build a physical monument in the places that we encounter God, however, writing about spiritual events is one way to capture the essence of what occurred, for ourselves to be encouraged in the future, as well as for others to be enriched who may read of our experiences.

In fact, writing was one of the main reasons we have these phenomenal accounts of the men and women of faith, recorded in the Bible.

*"And Isaac said unto them, Wherefore come ye to me, seeing ye hate me, and have sent me away from you? And they said, We saw certainly that the LORD was with thee." - Genesis 26:27-28*

The king of Gerar had more than one encounter with the famed son of Abraham. He may not have known the reason that this man's path was full of supernatural victories and awesome feats of determination, but he had a reverence for him and for his God nonetheless. He came to seek a peace agreement between them, and to ask Isaac to leave Gerar on good terms. However, not before making the powerful statement *"We saw certainly that the LORD was with thee."* The Philistine king recognized the Divine Presence upon Isaac's life. The reason for this recognition was two-fold. First, when God appears *to* a person, He ends up appearing *through* that person, and all who make contact become strangely aware of the supernatural aura that envelops him or her. We can see this in Moses life, whose face shown with glory in front of the Hebrews; the life of Stephen, whose face shown like that of an angel in front of the Pharisees; and Jesus, whose entire countenance was transfigured upon the mountain top in front of Peter, James and John.

Second, when God chooses to speak a word to someone, faith enters the heart resulting in supernatural boldness to go and do extraordinary things, such as in the case of Isaac, who uncovered his father's wells in a land that was clearly being occupied by another nation. This was a "gutsy" thing to do. It was a faith-move. The heathen king Abimilech recognized these two aspects of Isaac's life, resulting in an amicable covenant with Abimelech culminating in a big feast between these two men and their families. A life of faith is a life that pleases the Lord, releasing God's favor thus fulfilling the Scripture: *"When a man's ways please the Lord, He makes even his enemies be at peace with him"* (Proverbs 16:7).

*"By faith Isaac blessed Jacob and Esau concerning things to come." -*
*Hebrews 11:20*

We are told by the author of Hebrews that at the end of Isaac's life, he prophesied over his two sons – Jacob and Esau – "by faith." We know, according to Romans 12, that it takes faith to prophesy. Since faith is substance and evidence of that which is unseen and unknown to the human mind, a prophetic word is therefore the unveiling of what was previously unknown or hid from a person's understanding. Now, Hebrews tells us that Isaac "blessed" his two sons by the means of faith. In other words, God revealed to Isaac what he had previously not known about his two sons. When Isaac spoke those words of blessing, they released the plan of God for his sons. If we are moved by the Holy Spirit as Isaac was, we will be inspired by God's faith, and speak what He wants to say to people. That God's word is "inspired" means that His word has been breathed into, or upon someone. Many times, we try to formulate intellectually what to say to people, but if we are led by the Spirit of the Lord, the prophetic word will come forth spontaneously without our intellect inhibiting it.

The blessing Isaac transferred to his sons was done "by faith." In biblical times, these were serious pronouncements meant to evoke and fulfill the will of God. Today, many believe that a blessing is simply a nice thing for one individual to express to another, such as the well-known saying, "may you live long and prosper." In our culture a blessing has been reduced to powerless slogans, feigned words, and cheap greeting card verses. But the Bible says that the blessing with which Isaac blessed his sons required the supernatural ability of God, known as *faith*. Therefore, if a blessing is to be more than feigned words, we must allow God's word to come into our hearts, inspiring His faith within us, so that we may truly speak the blessing that is in line with God's will for that person. The blessing Isaac spoke over Jacob and Esau was "concerning things to come" indicating that the blessing was equal to a prophecy – that special grace which reveals something supernaturally concerning an individual. As a conduit for the power of faith, Isaac was *not* basing his blessing upon the natural order of things; the eldest son would have received the greater blessing if that were the case. This fact alone is proof that his motive was inspired by the Lord. God blessed Jacob, not because of his age or his integrity, but because it was part of God's sovereign will to bless Jacob with the greater blessing. Isaac blessed both Jacob and Esau by faith, and set in motion the course of two nations by this last prophetic act.

From the sacrifice of Mount Moriah and the conflict in Gerar, to the blessing of two future nations, we see faith as the common thread that binds these events together. It is clear to see that Isaac lived at a specific time in history to fulfill his role as a bridge between two of the most important generations – Abraham and Jacob – which would define not only a new nation of people, but would become the center piece of all humanity: Israel, through whom God's plan of salvation would be birthed. Perhaps the greatest legacy that Isaac produced was that his existence foreshadowed the life and purpose of the Messiah. Like Isaac, Jesus came from His Father and bridged the gap between the divine life of God and the sinful soul of man. Perhaps no other figure in the Old Testament displayed the submission, trust, and supernatural faith of the Messiah as did Isaac.

# CHAPTER SEVEN

# JACOB

*"By faith Jacob, when he was a dying, blessed both the sons of Joseph; and worshiped, leaning upon the top of his staff." - Hebrews 11:21*

There was a stir inside of her womb, with two brothers competing for birth. As Rebecca witnessed her elder son coming out first, with the younger close behind him, something startling occurred. The younger grabbed a hold of the elder's heel with the tenacity of a man straining toward some invisible finish line, foreshadowing a life-long struggle to obtain his inheritance. What this tenacious youngster, Jacob, was unaware of at the start of his journey was that he would receive that inheritance quite apart from his own efforts. It is here that we begin another journey in the life of faith.

First, let's take a look at the significance of his royal bloodline. Although Abraham was never specifically mentioned as a king, we know that he was a royal man by virtue of his covenant with Jehovah. When the Lord chooses a man or woman to enter into a covenant with Himself, that man or woman becomes royalty, as they become unified with the "King of kings." The kingly nature of God is then imparted to that person, pervading every aspect of their life. The result is that they become partakers of the eternal kingdom of the King. Under the Old Covenant, The Lord told Moses that the Israelites were a "kingdom of priests" (Exodus 19:6). Likewise, Peter describes those who have entered into the New Covenant as a "royal priesthzood" (1Peter 2:9). Both the nation of Israel, and the Church of Christ, are described as "kingdoms," which implies a people with a royal status. Each are "kingdoms" in the sense that they both have a government, a territory, and a family, in the natural and the spiritual sense, as well as a King ruling over them. Essentially, each of these two orders – Israel being a natural order and the Church a spiritual order – exist because of the covenant God made with them.

The Hebrew nation officially began with God choosing the man, Abraham. The name *Hebrew* is thought to have come from Abraham's ancestor *Eber*, which is translated as "the region beyond."[1] Indeed, Abraham had crossed over into a supernatural kingdom where galaxies, stars, planets, and nations are created. Because Abraham was promised a physical government, territory, and a family, he would be the divinely appointed head of a new kingdom, a new order, a new race of people. All who came from the natural line of Abraham would inherit his royal covenant, as contracted by God Himself. Thus, his family would be royalty – a kingdom of priests – and would become the greatest physical nation of all the nations ever created. Jacob was fourth in line in this royal family, surpassed only by his elder brother, Esau.

Like those people who are called by the Lord to do something great and are faced with opposition as a result, Jacob met with conflict at an early age; in fact, he had not even left the womb of his mother when his first battle began. The conflict was between the two seeds in Rebekkah's womb that would grow into two nations, both of which were prophesied to Rebekkah by God. He even told her that the elder would serve the younger. We are not told who began this early battle, however our initial reaction may be to assume it was Esau; after all, he was the elder of the two. The elder brother has typically been the one to initiate conflict or insurrection in the Bible. Cain slew his younger brother Abel. Eliab, along with his 6 older brothers, mocked his younger brother David on the battlefield. The Pharisees criticized Jesus for the inferiority of His age – they being some 20 to 30 years older than Him. However, judging by the life that Jacob would lead, it may be more likely that he was the instigator of the conflict. Since this is the earliest record of what occurred in Jacob's life, we know that the struggle in the womb was a precedent-setting event revealing two things to us. First, it establishes the type of life Jacob was destined to lead, one of inner conflict. This conflict would reveal the power of inferiority in his own conscience. Second, it reveals something profound about the life of faith, more specifically, the external "fight of faith" that aggressively pursues what has been promised by the Lord. Both of these themes will be revealed in greater depth throughout this chapter.

Turning to Esau, we see that he became an expert hunter, and a "mighty man in the fields." He was a crude man with a warrior disposition and was favored by his father. Jacob, on the other hand, was described as a "plain man," and spent most of his time working in and around the family tents. The Hebrew word for "plain" is *tam* which means "whole" or "upright," indicating someone who possessed a calmer and steadier disposition than that of someone like Esau, who possessed a more ferocious character.[2] He was clearly favored by his mother. Being favored and apparently raised predominately by Rebekkah, working in the tents and tending to the household duties, it easy to see that Jacob possessed a more domestic personality. In fact, it was the servants or the women who served the men when they came back from a long day's work; we find that it is Jacob taking care of his brother upon his return from a long hunting outing.

It is important to remember that a person's significance in life is determined by the Lord. In Genesis 25:22-23, we read *"And the children struggled together within her; and she said, If it be so, why am I thus? And she went to enquire of the LORD. And the LORD said unto her, Two nations are in thy womb, and two manner of people shall be separated from thy bowels; and the one people shall be stronger than the other people; and the elder shall serve the younger."* Rebekkah already knew that Jacob was destined to become a great man, even greater as a nation than his brother. Likewise, we may relate to this, for instance, if we have been given a word about who or what we will become. Yet, we are faced with our "plainness" every time we look in the mirror. That plainness may not be physical, but might be our ordinary day-to-day experience. And, like Jacob, we may not have attained to any great standing in our occupations or arrived at a status that reflects our culture's standards of success. In our insecurity, we despise our position and grow despondent. Our despondency turns into covetousness, and eventually, we find ourselves doing and saying things in order to get to our destination without going through the God-ordained process of time and testing. But God only blesses what has been tested by Him through time and experience. Anything that shortcuts God's timing hinders divine appointments and ultimately prolongs the time it takes for us to arrive at our divine destination. Jacob did not quite understand that his destiny was not to be had through covetousness and manipulation, but through faith in God's word. Any life that is not lived in faith will ultimately yield to some form of deception.

*"And Esau said to Jacob, Feed me, I pray thee, with that same red pottage; for I am faint: therefore was his name called Edom." -*
*Genesis 25:30*

Jacob was boiling red soup when his brother came in, desiring to eat. Jacob had an idea, that had no doubt been simmering in his mind, just like the stew he was about to serve Esau; a business transaction was about to take place. Jacob knew the state of his eldest brother, having been out in the field all day, and physically exhausted. This exhaustion would have undoubtedly caused him to be weakened mentally. The deal would be simple and boldly underhanded: a pot of soup for a birthright. Now, the average person would not compromise something as valuable as his birthright for a bowl of soup, but Jacob must have known that his brother was not an upright man. If he were, than Jacob never would have offered such a deal. Yet, through a verbal oath, Esau did not hesitate to swear over his birthright for a pot of red lentils.

*"Then Jacob gave Esau bread and pottage of lentiles; and he did eat and drink, and rose up, and went his way: thus Esau despised his birthright." - Genesis 25:34*

There are two things apparent by this business deal. The first is that Jacob had placed great value upon his brother's birthright, something that Esau evidently failed to do. Esau clearly committed the greater sin, as he sold his inheritance instead of protecting and valuing it. We are reminded of the story which Jesus gave to his disciples about the shrewd business man who went about undermining his former boss by lowering the debts which were owed him. Jesus commended this man as having done wisely. Jesus used this example to illustrate the wisdom of the world. Jacob exhibited a shrewd mind for business as he offered an underhanded trade to a man he knew was physically exhausted and hence vulnerable, but more importantly, void of integrity, having disdain for what was rightfully his. However, as clever as the world's wisdom is, it can never replace our utter dependence upon God's sovereign ability to bring to pass our destiny. This leads us to the second revelatory truth: Jacob was trying to obtain this blessed inheritance by his own efforts. *He did not yet have a revelation of God's grace.* He would soon discover that every attempt to obtain his promise through means other than God's ordination would only produce strife.

After the incident at birth when he grabbed his brother's heel, and the buying of his brother's birthright, we find a third instance of significance between Jacob and Esau. As Isaac was becoming old and waning in life, he desired to bless his eldest son, Esau. It was customary for the father to pronounce blessing on his children, the greatest portion going to the eldest. Rebekah favored Jacob even as the Lord favored him above his brother, and it was with Jacob that God would establish His covenant. Knowing this, Rebekah concocted a scheme through which Jacob would receive the pronouncement of favor from his father. It is at this point, that we recognize Jacob as the "supplanter" for which he was named. However, it is important to note that Rebekah, not Jacob, was the one who insisted on him doing this deed, cloaking himself in a goat's skin, and pretending that he was Esau. Jacob simply submitted to his mother's request.

Now, at the end of his life, Isaac blesses Jacob with the blessing intended for Esau. Amazingly enough, Isaac prophesied the blessing all the while thinking he was prophesying to Esau! That God could bypass Isaac's natural understanding, using the word intended for Esau, to bless Jacob, is one of the mysteries of God's sovereignty. This reveals to us that our destiny may in fact be realized through circumstances that are beyond our understanding. God will use other people to facilitate our destiny through words and actions, even though they are not intending to bless us.

We can infer that Jacob had been shaped by his own internal wrestlings with his father and grandfather's reputation of greatness and the pressure to become like them. Isaac did not seem to have a big role in Jacob's life, unlike his mother's influence upon him. This made

Jacob's ascent toward his destiny out of reach to Jacob, at least by his own efforts. And Rebekah was vying for Jacob to do whatever was necessary to fulfill the divine prophecies about his life. But Jacob was about to encounter God Himself. God would show Jacob that, although His intention was to bless him, Jacob would not ultimately obtain those blessings by his own cunning craftiness as a good businessman or clever operator; it would be because of the sovereign plan of God for his life.

*"And God Almighty bless thee, and make thee fruitful, and multiply thee, that thou mayest be a multitude of people; And give thee the blessing of Abraham, to thee, and to thy seed with thee; that thou mayest inherit the land wherein thou art a stranger, which God gave unto Abraham." – Genesis 28:3-4*

The word of God to Abraham in Genesis 12 was spoken again to Isaac, recorded in Genesis 26, and now is spoken to Jacob. It is a fact that the word of God transcends every generation of man. Each generation from Abraham heard the same word as previous ones, and it is the gift of faith God gives to each generation that inspires men and woman to move toward the destiny of the word. Every word that God speaks has the supernatural ability to supply the hearer with faith. After hearing the word of God, we are tested, just as Abraham and Isaac was tested in their lives over the promises they received by the Lord. The test is not meant to frustrate us, but to reveal the very essence of God's faith working in us, which produces a manifestation of the word we have received. We gain a great revelation when considering Jesus' disciples on that memorable stormy evening. They would not only be tested, but would showcase the three-part progression we have been studying in this book – the word of God, the faith of God, and the destination revealing all that God has promised. We read:

*"Now when Jesus saw great multitudes about him, he gave commandment to depart unto the other side...And, behold, there arose a great tempest in the sea, insomuch that the ship was covered with the waves: but he was asleep. And his disciples came to him, and awoke him, saying, Lord, save us: we perish. Then he arose, and rebuked the winds and the sea; and there was a great calm." - Matthew 8:18, 24-26*

The disciples were given a word by the Messiah, "We're going to go to the other side." This is the word of God to us. He brings a clear word to us about something in the future. "There arose a great tempest." The storm came, not coincidentally, but in direct proportion to the word that had just been spoken. The storm came and the disciples' faith in Jesus's word was put to the test. Next, we find our Messiah sleeping: "The ship was covered with waves...but he was asleep." While we are in the journey between the word and our "other side," it may appear as though God is absent, or maybe with us yet asleep. Much like Abraham who received the word of God and then fought the birds off until the dawn, the disciples had to fight off the demons of fear in the form of wind and waves: "The disciples came to him and awoke him, saying, Lord, save us: we perish." Before we become too judgmental with their response, we might compare this instinctive reaction of the disciples to the response that comes out of us in many of our crisis moments. We run to the Lord in a panic and actually accuse Him of negligence. "Don't you care that we are perishing here?" In response to their indictment against His character, Jesus gets up and rebukes the wind and the waves, and commands them to be still. What we must understand is that *Jesus was to them the manifestation of the word of God.* When He spoke the word "We shall go to the other side" He embodied that word, and so was Himself its fulfillment! Their failure to see Jesus and His word as one made it impossible for them to believe that they would make it to the other side. In the same way, when God speaks to us, He personally goes with us to guarantee the fulfillment of that word. In the Book of Isaiah, God speaks prophetically out of the mouth of His prophet saying, *"So shall my word be that goeth forth out of my mouth: it shall not return unto me void, but it shall accomplish that which I please, and it shall prosper in the thing whereto I sent it."* God is personally invested in His own word. When that word is attached to someone's life, the God of that word will be ever-present, working in the life of the believer, ensuring its success.

As Jacob journeyed away from his parents, he came to Haran, the home of his grandfather. It was here in the mountainous regions of Mesopotamia that Jacob dreamed a dream.

*"And he dreamed, and behold a ladder set up on the earth, and the top of it reached to heaven: and behold the angels of God ascending and descending on it. And, behold, the LORD stood above it, and said, I am the LORD God of Abraham thy father, and the God of Isaac: the land whereon thou liest, to thee will I give it, and to thy seed; And thy seed shall be as the dust of the earth, and thou shalt spread abroad to the west, and to the east, and to the north, and to the south: and in thee*

123

*and in thy seed shall all the families of the earth be blessed. And, behold, I am with thee, and will keep thee in all places whither thou goest, and will bring thee again into this land; for I will not leave thee, until I have done that which I have spoken to thee of." – Genesis 28:12-15:12-15*

Dreams are night visions given by God to reveal His purpose for our lives. When we dream a dream that is from the Lord, it is known as a "prophetic" dream. The word "prophetic" simply means *divinely inspired*. Notice, God spoke to Jacob in a dream, and would eventually speak to his eleventh son, Joseph, primarily in dreams. After he awakes from his dream, Jacob does something significant. He took the rock that was beneath his head and anointed it with oil and set it as a pillar, or monument, unto the Lord. He then called the name of that place *Bethel*, meaning "House of God."[4] The monument was erected as a sign of God's word to Jacob, and would become the central location for the birth of the Messiah hundreds of years later. Our prophetic dreams can signify and shape future events, as these God-inspired visions reveal His eternal word to us concerning our destiny. God may even inspire us in our dreams for the future manifestation of His word, just as Jacob anointed the rock after being inspired by his dream. This anointed rock was a symbol of God's own Son who would be anointed to take away the sins of man, as the "Rock of Ages."

After he erected the pillar to the Lord, Jacob vowed to give a tenth of all that he would gain, to the Lord. Giving should be a consequence of receiving revelation. Today, many are told *what* to give instead of being encouraged to give by revelation out of our oneness with God. As a result of this mystical union we find that it is God Himself that is giving through us as He pleases. We are told by the apostle Paul that our giving must not be out of "necessity" (see 2 Corinthians 9:7). Our giving is "out of necessity" when we are told to give a specific amount. However, we know that Abraham gave a tenth of his goods to Melchizedek not because he was commanded to by a law, but because God revealed His nature to him through Melchizedek. In the same way, we must see that revelation of God and His will should always precede our giving.

When Jacob left his family, he began to hear the word of the Lord for himself. Prior to that, he heard the word through his father and probably his mother. But now he was dreaming dreams from the Lord. As he stepped out of his familiar surroundings in the way that his grandfather did, the veil between him and God seemed to be lifted. The conflict at home propelled him into a new season. The season he was now in was that of marriage. Upon entering the fields of his uncle he came face to face with the woman who would become his wife. He immediately went to her, kissed her and wept. When God reveals a provision for our destiny we receive an inner witness that transcends our understanding. Jacob knew that this woman was there by God's design, and like Jacob we will have a certainty and great joy when He reveals significant parts leading to the fulfillment of our destiny.

*"And it came to pass, when Laban heard the tidings of Jacob his sister's son, that he ran to meet him, and embraced him, and kissed him, and brought him to his house. And he told Laban all these things.*

*And Laban said to him, Surely thou art my bone and my flesh. And he abode with him the space of a month." – Genesis 29:13-14*

Laban was a business man, and a crafty one at that. He owned a business which was run by his sons. Being "flesh of his flesh and bone of his bone," Laban would not have his nephew work in the business without pay. Jacob thought of the best payment he could possibly receive from his uncle: a wife. The woman he chose was Rachel, the one who came out into the field to meet him. Jacob worked a long and arduous seven years for the woman he loved. In the process of time, Jacob completed his end of the bargain – seven years of dutiful work; it was now time for Laban to fulfill what he had promised. However, because Laban intended that his first born daughter would marry before his second, he underhandedly gave Jacob Leah instead of Rachel. We may assume that Jacob had not seen much of Rachel in seven years and that Leah resembled Rachel, for Jacob took Leah to be his wife under the assumption that it was in fact Rachel. The morning after the wedding night, Jacob realized he had married the wrong woman, and was outraged at his uncle. Jacob was so busy working seven years for his would-be wife, that he did not even realize this woman was not Rachel! Whether attempting to precede his brother at birth, the shrewd business deal of acquiring his brother's birthright, deceptively posing as his brother in order to get his brother's blessing, or laboring seven years for a wife, we see Jacob attempting to earn his destiny by his own efforts.

Now, as the Lord promised to be with and to bless his grandfather and his father, Jacob was also blessed. In fact, all who came into contact with him received the blessing that was on his life. Listen to Laban's words,

*"And Laban said unto him, I pray thee, if I have found favour in thine eyes, tarry: for I have learned by experience that the LORD hath blessed me for thy sake." - Genesis 28:27*

Because Laban had Jacob participate in his family and business, both spheres were blessed. When God speaks a word to us, the covenant blessings that come to us as a result of that word will overflow onto anyone who comes in contact with our life. We saw this with Jacob's grandfather, who left the land of Ur with Lot his nephew. When they went out together, Lot was blessed because of the blessing that was spoken directly to Abraham. Even though Lot and Laban ultimately caused strife for Abraham and Jacob, they were still blessed abundantly as a result of their relationships. A man or woman of faith is good for anyone's business or enterprise! After fourteen years, Jacob finally married Rachel.

After their marriage, we find another reality of faith: faith works by *love*. Because of Rachel's infertility, Jacob petitioned the Lord on her behalf because he loved her. As a result of this petition, joining with the cry of Rachel's heart for a child, God answered and caused her to conceive. Anything we do motivated by love gives us a

127

good indication that faith is at work. The name given this child was *Joseph* which means "Jehovah will add."[5] Through the motivation of love, the working of faith will cause great addition to our lives. The addition occurs when God reveals some external blessing during the course of our journey, something essential for our destination.

After the birth of his first son, Jacob desired that he and his new family would be released from service to his uncle Laban. In order to do this, he would first need sufficient provision for him and his family to live off of. He devised a test in order to gain the best cattle of Laban's livestock. First, Jacob took rods of green poplar and of the almond and chestnut trees, peeled strips off them exposing the white which was in the rods. Second, he caused the cattle to breed in front of the various rods. Third, he separated the feebler cattle and only caused the stronger ones to face the rods, so the outcome would be a stronger and healthier flock for himself. The result was that the new offspring came out spotted and speckled, and they multiplied greatly. If they had come out without spots and speckles, then Laban could accuse him of stealing his son's cattle. But God was with Jacob and caused him to prosper supernaturally, as there was no reason in the natural – either biologically or chemically – that the cattle should have come out with streaks and speckles by simply breeding in front of speckled and spotted rods.

In doing this, Jacob demonstrated another great characteristic of faith. When we begin to trust God for favor in an area of our life, He will give us supernatural wisdom in order to produce supernatural results. Jacob modeled a supernatural way of doing business! In this instance, he found a specific method for producing the "cream of the crop," which activated his faith. Wisdom and faith always work together. When once we see what God has said about our future, we receive wisdom to do a specific work in order to see that word manifest. The work will always vary and can never be made into a formula. God wants us to prosper, and gives innumerable ways for us to walk out that prosperity. The key is doing whatever God's wisdom shows us to do.

*"And the man increased exceedingly, and had much cattle, and maidservants, and menservants, and camels, and asses. And he heard the words of Laban's sons, saying, Jacob hath taken away all that was our father's; and of that which was our father's hath he gotten all this glory." Genesis 30:43; 31:1*

This is the first time we see the word *glory* in the Bible. Through working out his faith with the wisdom of God, Jacob produced more "glory" than Laban and his sons. The Hebrew word for "glory" here is *kabowd*, which refers to *honor*, *abundance*, and the idea of *weightiness*.[6] We find here a revelation about the Originator of this glory. The concept of *glory* can be understood by seeing it in three parts, for there are 3 parts to God's glory. The first is that of His person, the person of His *Son*. The apostle John said that when the Word of God became flesh, we "beheld His glory" speaking of the physical Person of Jesus Christ, whom the world was able to physically touch (John 1:14). The second is that of His spiritual *presence*. We can understand this aspect of "presence" by considering

129

the priests of Solomon's Temple who ministered in the presence of the Lord. God's physical person was not evident, but his spiritual presence was so evidently manifested that the priests could no longer stand to minister. The third is that of His *possessions*. We see this aspect of glory in Genesis 30 as Jacob's possessions are considered to be "glory" by Moses, the writer of Genesis. That the physical possessions of Jacob would be considered glory is substantiated by the fact that the physical earth is considered to be a manifestation of God's glory. The prophet Isaiah heard one angel say to another, "The whole earth is filled with His glory" (Isaiah 6:3). Over and over again the psalmist says that the glory of the Lord is over the whole earth. It is important to understand that, although each aspect of God's glory is essentially part of Himself, He has ordained mankind to share in His glory, making it an inclusive experience for all humanity. In the New Covenant, we have access to all three dimensions of God's glory: His Person, His Presence, and His Possessions. By faith, we walk in all three, as we have the Person of the Holy Spirit within us, His divine presence flowing through us, and all of His divine possessions filling the earth around us. Jacob's glory was greater than Laban and his sons, because the "glory" of God's possessions – the earth and the fullness thereof – belongs not only to God, but to those with whom He has covenanted through His word. Jacob was a partaker of this glory. Remember, God promised Abraham that the physical land of Canaan would one day be his descendant's possession. This physical land was and still is part of God's glory, as it was created by God's word.

It must be noted that in the journey of Jacob's faith, he had to continue onward despite the unpredictable opposition of those close to him – his own family. For instance, Laban hired Jacob with the intent to use him deceitfully. He changed Jacob's wages 10 different times, deceived him by giving him the wrong daughter for marriage, and caused him to work 14 years for the woman he loved the most. However, God allowed Jacob to go through this season, in part to show Jacob the deceitfulness of his own actions in his early years. Jacob cheated his brother out of the paternal blessing of Isaac, and was therefore cheated out of wages 10 times along with being deceived into marrying the wrong woman. Through this time of trial and deception, his character would grow greatly. His patience was tested through 14 years of waiting for Rachel; his love was tested, as he served an underhanded uncle who dealt unfairly with him; his faith was tested, by the word which God spoke to him in Bethel concerning his destiny.

*"But the God of my father hath been with me...God suffered him not to hurt me." - Genesis 31:5 & 7*

At the conclusion of this season, Jacob's testimony points back to God and His omnipresence in all His dealings throughout a tumultuous fourteen-year period. This serves as a reminder to us, that God never leaves us, but is invested in our success. Despite all adversity that seeks to divert us from our destiny, God makes sure that His word to us finds safe passage toward its destination.

*"And it came to pass at the time that the cattle conceived, that I lifted up mine eyes, and saw in a dream, and, behold, the rams which leaped upon the cattle were ringstraked, speckled, and grisled. And the angel of God spake unto me in a dream, saying, Jacob: And I said, Here am I. And he said, Lift up now thine eyes, and see, all the rams which leap upon the cattle are ringstraked, speckled, and grisled: for I have seen all that Laban doeth unto thee. I am the God of Bethel, where thou anointedst the pillar, and where thou vowedst a vow unto me: now arise, get thee out from this land, and return unto the land of thy kindred." - Genesis 31:10-13*

The season changes in our lives when God speaks a new word to us. God's method of speaking to us may take the form of a dream or special visitation, however, the point is always to bring us revelation of some new thing God desires us to know. In the same way that Abraham was instructed to depart from his nephew Lot in order to receive a clear revelation of his destiny, Jacob was told by God to depart from his uncle in order to continue on toward his next phase of the journey. When we come into the knowledge of God's will about another season, it inspires a fresh application of faith and causes us to draw on the wisdom of God in order to do the necessary work required.

A study of Jacob's life reveals the same continual traveling that we find in his father and grandfather's lives. In fact, Abraham serves as the first example, from which we see thousands of physical location-changes through the lives of a plethora of people throughout the first five books of the Bible. In the same way that Abraham moved away from his family to a strange land, Jacob traveled away from his own family, Joseph was relocated to Egypt, Moses journeyed to the backside of the desert, and the Israelites traveled through Sanai. We live with constant changes. Faith reveals the invisible story that is unfolding all of the time through a thousand events strung together.

Now, Laban had heard of Jacob's exodus, along with his new found family and their property; he became so enraged that he wanted to overtake Jacob and do him harm. In the midst of devising a vengeful plan, Laban was warned in a dream by the Lord not to touch Jacob. This sounds much like God's word to Abimelech, who was admonished by the Lord in a dream, warning him of his corrupt dealings with Abraham. Laban heeded the word of God, and when he finally overtook Jacob he made a covenant with him instead of fighting against him. Jacob named the place of their meeting *Galead* which means "witness heap,"[7] and also *Mizpah* meaning "watchtower."[8] These two names would have significant meaning later on, as both would become significant dwellings for key people like the prophet Samuel.

*"And Jacob went on his way, and the angels of God met him." – Genesis 32:1*

It is a primary function of angels to watch over God's people, primarily when God releases a word to them about their destiny. Psalm 103:20 declares that angels are "hearkening unto the voice of His word." Not only are angels attentive to God's word, but will manifest in the lives of those whom God has called. Joshua had angels meet him, Elijah was taken up by angels, and Elisha asked the Lord to open the eyes of his servant to see the chariots of fire and the angels surrounding them. Do the angels of God still meet us in our journey? Absolutely! But they do not appear unless there is divine reason for them to do so. Sometimes, it is so that we can believe in God's plan for our lives. Other times, it is to bring comfort to us because of the season we are about to walk into. Jacob was about to face a great test of epic proportions, and would need both faith and comfort to succeed. He was about to meet his brother Esau.

*"And Jacob was left alone; and there wrestled a man with him until the breaking of the day." - Genesis 32:24*

Right before the monumental meeting between the elder and younger brother, we find a monumental meeting between man and God. Jacob encountered the Angel of the Lord, and wrestled with him all night long to obtain a divine blessing. It is here that we see one of the chief weaknesses of this man's life: inner strife. In the womb he was wrestling with his brother. At birth he was striving to grab his brother's heel. As a young man he was manipulating his father for the blessing intended for his elder brother. And now, we see Jacob wrestling with God Himself! It would seem that Jacob had lived under the assumption that he needed to strive violently in order to gain acceptance, identity, and ultimately his destiny. Jacob had a *nature* problem that the Lord needed to correct before the blessing could be imparted. The nature problem is revealed in his name: *the supplanter*

134

or *the deceiver*. It was in this natural tendency to supplant or deceive, that Jacob believed to be his strength.

*"And when he saw that he prevailed not against him, he touched the hollow of his thigh; and the hollow of Jacob's thigh was out of joint, as he wrestled with him. And he said, Let me go, for the day breaketh. And he said, I will not let thee go, except thou bless me. And he said unto him, What is thy name? And he said, Jacob." - Genesis 32:25-27*

This mystical conflict ended by the Angel of the Lord dislocating Jacob's hipbone. The hip, being one of the strongest areas of man's physical body, can in this instance be seen representing Jacob's dominant disposition of strife. His striving was a result of a strong desire to obtain his destiny through any means necessary including deception. Following the all-night struggle the angel asks Jacob for his name. By doing this, the angel causes Jacob to confront his nature. As we have seen in Scripture, a man's name may be directly connected with his destiny. God said that Jacob would be a great nation; but God does not bless deception, manipulation, and control. And so, the question was put to Jacob: "What is your name." Upon the recognition of his name "Jacob" - "supplanter" and "deceiver" - Jacob received a new name. From that time forward Jacob limped, symbolizing the weakness and futility inherent in man's sinful nature, and his attempts to gain his life apart from yielding to the Lord. The truth is, we will only "wrestle" with God when we have not come to terms with our new nature in Christ. When once we rest in His word for our lives, we will immediately walk in the peace and assurance that what God has said about us is true, and that His purposes will come to pass.

*"And he said, Thy name shall be called no more Jacob, but Israel: for as a prince hast thou power with God and with men, and hast prevailed." – Genesis 32:28*

By changing his name from "Jacob" to "Israel," God was revealing that this man was now able to walk in his destiny, as a prince and not just a man. In the same way, we as Christians are given a new identity through the death and resurrection of Jesus Christ. Like Jacob, the Lord touched our old identity and destroyed it, and has given us new identities in Christ. He literally changed our identity from sinners to saints. Once we received a change in identity, we entered into a new destiny. We were all *deceivers* who learned to go through life obtaining our objectives in our own strength, by our own devices. Now we have become Princes with God, and have inherited God's kingdom through the destruction of our natural, human strength.

*"And Jacob asked him, and said, Tell me, I pray thee, thy name. And he said, Wherefore is it that thou dost ask after my name? And he blessed him there. And Jacob called the name of the place Peniel: for I have seen God face to face, and my life is preserved." - Genesis 32:29-30*

Right after this divine visitation, Jacob would be ready to meet his brother. We gain a great revelation when looking at this part of Jacob's journey, his post-divine encounter.

*"And Jacob said, Nay, I pray thee, if now I have found grace in thy sight, then receive my present at my hand: for therefore I have seen thy face, as though I had seen the face of God, and thou wast pleased with me." - Genesis 33:10*

Like Jacob, something happens to our vision when we have an encounter with God. We begin to see those things around us differently. Jacob once feared to see his brother; in fact, he probably never wanted to see him again. But he had seen the face of God which transformed his greatest fear into something beautiful. Upon looking at Esau's face – though it was the face of his enemy – it was as though he were looking at the face of God. Seeing God at work in our lives revolutionizes our perspective. Immediately, we have confidence in the face of our worst fear, because our faith gives us the ability to see God where we once saw our greatest enemy. Jacob not only had courage to meet Esau, he was completely reconciled to his elder brother.

Upon leaving this extraordinary experience, Jacob journeys to a place where he would build his home and set up booths for his cattle. Jacob named this place "Succoth" which means "booths."[9] These tabernacles or booths are symbolic of the spiritual tabernacle that our faith becomes for future generations. For example, Paul tells Timothy to look at the legacy of faith provided by his mother Lois and his grandmother, for spiritual inspiration (see 2 Timothy 1:5). Wherever a person of faith goes, there will they leave a legacy that future generations can walk in. For the descendants of Jacob, Succoth would become a place where the Israelites would go to escape Egyptian captivity. This is where the "Feast of Tabernacles" originated, which to this day is celebrated in remembrance of their faith in God's provision in the wilderness.

*"And he dreamed, and behold a ladder set up on the earth, and the top of it reached to heaven: and behold the angels of God ascending and descending on it. And Jacob rose up early in the morning, and took the stone that he had put for his pillows, and set it up for a pillar, and poured oil upon the top of it. And he called the name of that place Bethel: but the name of that city was called Luz at the first." – Genesis 28:12, 18-19*

Throughout Scripture we find that names of places have a prophetic significance pointing to future events that will take place there. Jacob named the place in which he received the divine dream, *Bethel*, where the Messiah would be born. He named the place of covenant with Laban *Mizpah* and *Gileed* which would be home of great prophets such as Samuel. We then find him naming the place of his divine wrestling, *Peniel* – "the face of God"[10] – and would represent the place of mystical encounters with the divine presence of God. The Patriarchs of Genesis were always making visible the invisible moves of God in their life through the construction of monuments and alters. They also demonstrated the sovereign intervention of God into human affairs through inspiration of the Holy

Spirit, by naming places that would have significance to future generations. Jacob did not know at Succoth that, hundreds of years later, his descendants would build shelters there in the wilderness upon their exodus.

One of the last great acts of this man of faith occurred right before his death. Jacob, now called Israel, prophesied over each of his 12 sons in the land of Egypt. After he had done this, he turned to Joseph's two sons, and placed his right hand on Ephraim, Joseph's second born, and his left on Manasseh, Joseph's first born. The right hand was typically reserved for the first born, as it signified preeminence and greater authority. Yet, Jacob prophetically foresaw that the second born would produce a greater size nation. This was the word of the Lord, and it set in motion the destinies of Manasseh and Ephraim, as well as their individual lineages. The elder would be subservient to the younger.

What is significant here is that the Bible declares in Hebrews 11, that Jacob blessed Joseph's two sons *"leaning upon the top of his staff."* Here we have the picture of an old man who was also physically impaired since the day the Angel of the Lord dislocated his hip. The image of Jacob as a God-dependent man leaning upon his staff while prophetically blessing his children speaks of a life that has been made most useful to the Lord and to people through the breaking of the sinful nature. Jacob leaning on his staff symbolized a life that was surrendered to the will of God. A man or woman who recognizes their utter weakness apart from the life of Christ will be better able to move under the anointing of God and demonstrate the strength of Christ's life in the earth.

As we reflect upon this monumental figure in the Bible, we find a young man who valued the sacred birthright intended for Esau. We see a man obedient to his mother's prompting to seize Esau's blessing. He was a man of great passion, as he worked seven additional years for the woman he loved in spite of the deceptions of an underhanded uncle. He was a man of intense desire, wrestling with the Angel of the Lord for a divine blessing. He built alters and offerings to the Lord. He changed the name of his son from Ben-oni to Benjamin, thus changing his destiny from "Son of my sorrow"[11] to "Son of my right hand."[12] He went to Egypt by the word of the Lord. He blessed Joseph's sons on top of his staff while worshiping God. This was a man who epitomized the old nature of sin, seen in his manipulation and fear, but also prophetically of the new nature of Christ, as he was given a new name, identity, and a lineage from which would come perhaps the greatest people-group in the history of the world.

# CHAPTER EIGHT

# JOSEPH

*"By faith Joseph, when he died, made mention of the departing of the children of Israel; and gave commandment concerning his bones." - Hebrews 11:22*

Joseph was a dreamer. He had dreams from the Lord beginning at the early age of 17. Contained in those dreams was the very source of this man's faith – the word of God. Job said that God speaks to man "in a dream, in a vision of the night, when deep sleep falleth upon men, in slumberings upon the bed." If God truly speaks to a man in dreams, then it is possible for man to be given faith in that dream. When we dream, our consciousness is asleep, but our subconscious is awake. We are unaware of physical realities, but made aware of creative spiritual realities. If God imparts a dream to a person, He is inviting them into the theater of His own mind, to gain some insight into their life. If we are not careful, we will misunderstand the dream given us, and seek to exalt ourselves in light of the great thing God has shown us. But the design of God showing the dream to us – even if there are decades before its actual fulfillment – is to inspire faith in the heart of the dreamer, and it is by faith that we will see a manifestation of the dreams that God has given us.

God chose to create Adam's helpmate when Adam fell into a deep sleep. He established a covenant with Abraham while Abraham fell into a deep sleep. And He gave Jacob a dream while sleeping in the place he called "Bethel," that would ultimately foretell of the coming Messiah. In like manner, Joseph would receive a dream that would actually define his destiny. What he did not understand after he awoke, however, was that the dream would require faith to lead him to its fulfillment. It was after the dream was given, that Joseph would be launched into one of the most grueling tests recorded in Scripture.

God spoke two very specific words to Joseph in the form of two dreams. The first depicted Joseph, who was the youngest brother, and his older brothers, as sheaves – the latter bowing in worship to the former. The second depicted the sun and moon and eleven stars worshiping Joseph; the symbolism of the sun referred to Jacob, the moon to Leah, and the eleven stars to his brothers. Because of these dreams, in addition to a special multi-colored coat given to him by his father, Joseph's brothers hated him and could not live peaceably with him.

We then find Joseph going out into the fields to find his brothers.

*"And they said one to another, Behold, this dreamer cometh. Come now therefore, and let us slay him, and cast him into some pit, and we will say, Some evil beast hath devoured him: and we shall see what will become of his dreams. And Reuben heard [it], and he delivered*

143

*him out of their hands; and said, Let us not kill him." - Genesis 37:19-*
*21*

Right in the middle of this heinous plan to kill their own brother, Reuben, who was the eldest of them, stood up and forbade them to carry out their malicious plot. Note the language of the brothers, "...we shall see what will become of his dreams." Of course, what they did not realize is that it wasn't Joseph's dream, but God's dream *for* Joseph. It is not possible that men can kill our God ordained destiny. The Lord has already taken into account all that man will try to do to prevent our success. He has creatively weaved a plan through every evil plot that man has devised against us.

*"Then there passed by Midianites merchantmen; and they drew and lifted up Joseph out of the pit, and sold Joseph to the Ishmeelites for twenty pieces of silver: and they brought Joseph into Egypt...And the Midianites sold him into Egypt unto Potiphar, an officer of Pharaoh's, and captain of the guard." - Genesis 37:28, 36*

Joseph's brothers sold him to the Ishmaelites, who in turn sold him to Egypt to an officer of Pharaoh's named Potiphar. Forced out of the familiarity of family and work, Joseph found himself in the fetters of a foreign people, namely Egypt, a nation that historically opposed Abraham, Isaac, and Jacob. It is interesting that Joseph's enslavement in this foreign kingdom made him the first Hebrew to ever be enslaved to another nation.

144

*"And the LORD was with Joseph, and he was a prosperous man; and he was in the house of his master the Egyptian. And his master saw that the LORD [was] with him, and that the LORD made all that he did to prosper in his hand. And Joseph found grace in his sight, and he served him: and he made him overseer over his house, and all [that] he had he put into his hand...and Joseph was a goodly person, and well favoured." - Genesis 39:2-4, 9*

The Bible says that "the Lord was with Joseph," revealing God's protective hand over His people, more specifically, over the word He gives to them. The prophet Isaiah tells us that the word of God will "prosper in the thing where to" God sends it. Joseph carried the word of God in the form of a dream, and no one – not his family, the Ishmaelites, or the Egyptians – would be able to kill that dream.

Joseph was of a good physical appearance as is evident by the phrase, "...and Joseph was a goodly person, and well favoured." The Hebrew word "goodly" means "shape, form, outline, figure, appearance."[1] Joseph was handsome and was in good health. It is likely that due to his belief in the promised future position of rulership, his faith produced a desire to take care of his physical body. Just like Joseph, our faith will produce accompanying works that demonstrate what we believe. For example, if God spoke to us and said that our destiny is to rule a nation one day, then faith in that word would undoubtedly produce a desire to take care of our physical bodies, so that we are physically fitted for the fulfillment of that word. In other

145

words, faith sees what we look like in the future, and produces works that fit us to that future image.

Just as our faith produces accompanying works, those works, when manifested, will produce favor with men. In short, *favor is the result of our faith in action*. Now, favor is not given to us by God for ourselves, but for the world around us. Because of this, favor has more to do with the natural, visible realm which the world around us can see, than the spiritual, invisible realm which can only be seen with spiritual eyes. Remember God's word to Samuel: "Man looketh on the *outward appearance* but the Lord looketh on the heart" (1 Samuel 16:7, emphasis mine). While it is true that God looks at the invisible heart of a man when considering that person, it is equally true that the world looks on the visible aspects of man to make its considerations. This is why the Scripture uses the phrase, "And Joseph found grace in his *sight*" (verse 4, emphasis mine). Joseph pleased Potiphar in part based upon his outward appearance. Now, the action of our faith which produces favor is not limited to the maintaining of physical appearance; it covers all physical as well as intellectual abilities that we possess, which we use as tools in our sphere of influence. Joseph was not only attractive in appearance, but possessed a degree of administrative savvy in business, as he administered over all that was in Potiphar's house.

Joseph's faith produced great work, which in turn brought him much favor in the eyes of those he encountered. Because of this, he would inevitably face a great test, as he caught the eye of Potiphar's wife.

*"And it came to pass after these things, that his master's wife cast her eyes upon Joseph; and she said, Lie with me."* - Genesis 39:7

When we begin to experience favor with the world around us, we will often see, simultaneously, a work of the enemy in progress. If we are exalted by the Lord through some human instrumentation – as Joseph was through Potiphar – we may face temptations from those in greater authority. The temptation itself may not be different from those in past situations, but the consequences of our disobedience will have a greater impact, since the choices we make will affect more people due to our greater sphere of authority. Joseph was dealing with his master's wife, who carried significant influence in Egypt due to her marriage with Potiphar. Joseph knew that sinning in this way with Potiphar's wife would be sin against God, consequently diminishing his integrity in the eyes of those in the royal household. In the place of temptation, it is helpful to remind ourselves of the divine word which reveals the destiny that awaits us. Joseph's individual word was a creative vision given to him in a dream, where he would become a ruler in great authority, so much so that his own family would bow to him. Although he had not yet seen this vision come to pass, it was there as a continual reminder of where his life was heading. Glimpses of the greatness that lays waiting in our future will give us the faith to say "no" to the pleasures of sin that are presented to us in our journey.

*"And it came to pass about this time, that Joseph went into the house to do his business; and there was none of the men of the house there*

147

*within. And she caught him by his garment, saying, Lie with me: and he left his garment in her hand, and fled, and got him out. And it came to pass, when she saw that he had left his garment in her hand, and was fled forth, That she called unto the men of her house, and spake unto them, saying, See, he hath brought in an Hebrew unto us to mock us; he came in unto me to lie with me, and I cried with a loud voice: And it came to pass, when he heard that I lifted up my voice and cried, that he left his garment with me, and fled, and got him out."* - *Genesis 39:13*

The trap had been set; however, Joseph's tested integrity would not allow him to compromise his moral position with this evil woman. Thus, she conspired against this righteous man of faith and set another trap for him. Although Joseph had been given a great position in the palace, this woman knew that he was still a foreigner and a servant, therefore vulnerable to her accusations. It might seem to most of us that this would be a good time for God to intervene and expose this woman for the liar and adulteress that she was. But He refrained from any intervention, and instead kept silent. Often times God keeps silent during the times we think He should speak the most. These are the times when our faith can go through a fiery trial. If we truly believe that faith is the substance of things hoped for and the evidence of things not seen, then we will also believe that any circumstance whatsoever cannot prevent our hope in God's word from coming to pass. By remaining in faith, Joseph was wrongfully imprisoned for a crime he did not commit.

*"And Joseph's master took him, and put him into the prison, a place where the king's prisoners were bound: and he was there in the prison. But the LORD was with Joseph, and shewed him mercy, and gave him favour in the sight of the keeper of the prison. And the keeper of the prison committed to Joseph's hand all the prisoners that were in the prison; and whatsoever they did there, he was the doer of it. "* – *Genesis 39:20-22*

This is the second time we find Joseph in a difficult place, obtaining the favor of those in authority over him. The first time we see this is when his Egyptian master placed him in charge of all the affairs of his house. The second time is here with the prison keeper. This prison ward placed Joseph in charge over all the prisoners as well as their affairs. Here in the grips of yet another injustice, God was training Joseph in the business of ruling, as the prophetic word about ruling his family was undoubtedly still burning within him.

*"And it came to pass after these things, that the butler of the king of Egypt and his baker had offended their lord the king of Egypt. And Pharaoh was wroth against two of his officers, against the chief of the butlers, and against the chief of the bakers. And he put them in ward in the house of the captain of the guard, into the prison, the place where Joseph was bound."* - *Genesis 40:1-3*

Unbeknownst to Joseph, the butler and the baker were divinely placed into the same prison. God's purpose in this arrangement was not revealed to Joseph immediately; however, these men would become instrumental in the fulfillment of Joseph's destiny. Similarly, there are people that are being positioned right now for an entrance into our

149

lives with a divine part to play in our journey. Joseph was in a pit not knowing that a merchant group of Ishmaelites were on their way to Egypt, and would be divinely inspired to buy him from his brothers. Eventually, he found himself working as a servant in an Egyptian official's house, unaware that his master would hire him for a top position within the palace. And here, Joseph was confined in the inner prison, unaware of the opportunity that would arise from the two prisoners newly sent to share his fate. It is clear that God engineers our circumstances, oftentimes placing us in testing conditions, with a plan to bring us closer to our destinies.

*"And they said unto him, We have dreamed a dream, and there is no interpreter of it. And Joseph said unto them, Do not interpretations belong to God? tell me them, I pray you." - Genesis 40:8*

Both the butler and the baker dreamed dreams, to which they confided in Joseph, hoping to receive an interpretation. It is important to say here, that nowhere between the time of Joseph's two dreams while still in his father's house, and the time of these inmate's two dreams, that Joseph was known as a dream interpreter. It is implicit, however, that Joseph understood dreams to be an avenue through which a divine word could be given, as he received two dreams in his youth indicating his destiny. In the instance of the butler and the baker, not only did Joseph believe that the interpretations of such "night visions" came from the Lord, but that *he* had the ability to explain the meaning of both of them. This confidence demonstrated Joseph's faith

150

in God's ability through him to manifest supernatural knowledge. And his faith in this divine ability brought him the reward of seeing both his interpretations perfectly coming to pass: the butler would be exonerated by Pharaoh, while the baker would be hanged.

It would seem that Joseph had a way out of that dark hole, through such an accurate, supernatural gift of interpretation; however the Bible says, "Yet did not the chief butler remember Joseph, but forgat him" (Genesis 40:23). Likewise, there are moments of opportunity that come into our lives, where we see God doing great things through us. And through those moments, we expect certain things to transpire that will bring promotion in a particular area of our life. Yet, like Joseph, we are not always recognized by the people we think should, though we are used in some supernatural capacity to help them.

*"And it came to pass at the end of two full years, that Pharaoh dreamed: and, behold, he stood by the river." - Genesis 41:1*

Two years after the butler's exoneration, God gave Pharaoh a dream. It is evident that God gave Pharaoh this dream, for it was a dream that would eventually come to pass. It was also the very dream that would become a gateway for the fulfillment of Joseph's destiny. Therefore it was by God's providence that the exonerated butler forgot about Joseph when he did; the young Hebrew was ordained to interpret Pharaoh's dream and thereby fulfill his destiny two years later (we will

151

look at this in depth below). If Joseph would have been recognized by the butler, his destiny would have been subverted. The Lord's timing is unalterably perfect in everything He does and allows in our lives. Faith believes in the perfect timing of God's word, even when everything around us speaks to the contrary. We must not entertain the idea that there are many ways to get to our destination; the Lord is not a waster of time nor of resources, and will lead us only in one direction, down the perfect pathway to that expected end (see Psalm 18:30). The Bible declares, "Humble yourselves therefore under the mighty hand of God, that he may exalt you in *due time*" (1 Peter 5:6, emphasis mine). Because our destiny is held in a specific moment of time, there is a specific opportunity that will provide us with access to that "due time." If left up to us, we would continually take chances on all opportunities that seem good, and would miss the divinely appointed one. But God's success for us is determined by a specific course that has already been laid out by Him. Waiting becomes one of the paramount virtues of the believer's experience. Joseph had learned the art of waiting, and soon, this determined patience would pay off.

*"And it came to pass in the morning that his spirit was troubled; and he sent and called for all the magicians of Egypt, and all the wise men thereof: and Pharaoh told them his dream; but there was none that could interpret them unto Pharaoh. Then spake the chief butler unto Pharaoh, saying...And there was there with us a young man, an Hebrew, servant to the captain of the guard; and we told him, and he interpreted to us our dreams; to each man according to his dream he did interpret. And it came to pass, as he interpreted to us, so it was; me*

152

*he restored unto mine office, and him he hanged." - Genesis 41:8-9,*

*12-13*

Divine opportunities often present themselves in the form of someone else's problem. If we can solve their problem, we gain access into greater spheres of favor. This access allows us to influence more people for God's purposes. Pharaoh was a heathen king in that he did not worship the God of Abraham, Isaac and Jacob. It was God that troubled him with a dream that could not be interpreted by him or by any of his "spiritual" counsel. It is here in the course of Joseph's life that the Lord called upon the exonerated butler to do his part in remembering the young Hebrew two years later.

*"And Pharaoh said unto Joseph, I have dreamed a dream, and there is none that can interpret it: and I have heard say of thee, that thou canst understand a dream to interpret it. And Joseph answered Pharaoh, saying, It is not in me: God shall give Pharaoh an answer of peace." - Genesis 41:16*

Had Joseph been a proud man, he may have egotistically said, "Do not fear, mighty Pharaoh, for I will interpret your dream!" But after many years of testing, having been betrayed, lied about, and forgotten, Joseph learned to give glory to God. He made a clear distinction between himself and the Lord – himself having no ability, and the Lord having almighty ability. God was not only the giver of dreams, but the One who was able to interpret those dreams, and therefore the only One who could provide peace to Pharaoh's troubled mind. Joseph was simply the channel by which the interpretation would come. The single act of interpreting the dream became the hinge upon which the door to his destiny would finally be opened.

*"And the thing was good in the eyes of Pharaoh, and in the eyes of all his servants. And Pharaoh said unto his servants, Can we find such a one as this is, a man in whom the Spirit of God is?" - Genesis 41:37-*
*38*

Pharaoh was moved by more than one man's ability to interpret his dream; in a moment of time he fell under the power of God's eternal purposes for Joseph's life. He was unaware that Joseph had a dream 13 years earlier which propelled him into a journey wrought with inconceivable hardships. He was unaware of the countless moments that this young Hebrew spent longing for his promise, facing unimaginable fears. He was also unaware of the significance that was given to the Hebrew nation – the people group through which the Messiah would come. All Pharaoh could do in light of this divine interpretation was to fulfill God's plan for Joseph by extending to him the arm of Egyptian power. We can be assured that when the kings of the world see the awesome abilities that come through God's people, moments of profound opportunity will be afforded them.

Pharaoh commences to exalt Joseph with this powerful declaration:

*"Thou shalt be over my house, and according unto thy word shall all my people be ruled: only in the throne will I be greater than thou.*
*Thou shalt be over my house, and according unto thy word shall all my people be ruled: only in the throne will I be greater than thou. And*

*Pharaoh said unto Joseph, See, I have set thee over all the land of Egypt. And Pharaoh took off his ring from his hand, and put it upon Joseph's hand, and arrayed him in vestures of fine linen, and put a gold chain about his neck; And he made him to ride in the second chariot which he had; and they cried before him, Bow the knee: and he made him ruler over all the land of Egypt. And Pharaoh said unto Joseph, I am Pharaoh, and without thee shall no man lift up his hand or foot in all the land of Egypt. And Pharaoh called Joseph's name Zaphnathpaaneah; and he gave him to wife Asenath the daughter of Potipherah priest of On." - Genesis 41:40-45*

Joseph was 30 when he stood before Pharaoh. He was exalted to the second highest position in Egypt beneath Pharaoh, becoming the governor over the land and the people. Consequently, he was blessed with a royal wife who bore him two children. The first was named *Manasseh*, which means "causing to forget."[2] The apostle John says, "A woman when she is in travail hath sorrow, because her hour is come: but as soon as she is delivered of the child, she remembereth no more the anguish, for joy that a man is born into the world" (16:21). This picture of child bearing demonstrates what happens after we see the fulfillment of our destiny: there is a supernatural forgetfulness that occurs within us. It's not that we forget all of the events that led up to our present moment, rather, the joy of arriving alleviates the suffering we may have felt in the waiting. The second born was named *Ephraim* which means "double ash heap: I shall be doubly fruitful."[3] Ephraim represented the supernatural increase that came after Joseph's thirteen year journey. Out of the "ash heap" of suffering came a manifestation of fruitfulness in the form of a governorship, a royal wife, and

155

offspring to carry on his legacy. This is similar to the experience of Job who, at the end of his grueling trial, received double of all that was taken from him during the Satanic onslaught against him and his family (see Job 42).

The name which Pharaoh gave to Joseph was *Zaphnathpaaneah*, the Hebrew interpretation of the word which means "revealer of secrets."[4] The psalmist says, "Shall not God search this out? For he knoweth the *secrets* of the heart." Also, the prophet Daniel declares, "But there is a God in heaven that revealeth *secrets*" (2:28). It is apparent here that it is God who knows the secrets of men's hearts, and that He is the one who reveals them. Yet, Pharaoh recognized Joseph as having the ability to reveal secrets. The reality was that Joseph was able to reveal what only God knew because he believed that God was able to communicate those things through him. This belief in God's ability to reveal what is hidden from the minds of men is sourced in faith. And Joseph was recognized by Pharaoh as possessing such a characteristic, which testified to the power of God working through his faith.

When Joseph became the governor of Egypt, the dream of his youth began to be fulfilled. Pharaoh ordered all the inhabitants therein that cried for food to go unto the young Hebrew. The book of Genesis declares that Joseph "opened all the storehouses, and sold unto the Egyptians" and that "all countries came into Egypt to Joseph for to buy corn; because that the famine was so sore in all lands" (41:56-57). Not only was Joseph governing this nation, but he was selling food to nations all over the earth that came there for relief. We know God does

156

abundantly more than we could ask or think. In this case, Joseph knew that he would be ruling over his family; however he did not see how expansive the measure of rule would be. He was ruling in a famine, the nation of his ruling was Egypt, and the scope of his ruling was the ends of the earth. Likewise, God will often give us the main idea behind our destiny, but will hide from us the expanse of that destiny. In other words, we will be doing much more than we presently see.

*"And Joseph was the governor over the land, and he it was that sold to all the people of the land: and Joseph's brethren came, and bowed down themselves before him with their faces to the earth." - Genesis 42:6*

Now, it was a providential thing that this massive famine touched even God's covenant man – Jacob, and his sons. Sometimes, we are touched with various calamities so that God can exalt and promote one of his faithful servants somewhere else in the world (what a thought!). This covenant family had a rift right down the middle of it; however God's plan was to not only bring reconciliation within the family, but to bring other nations into the same covenantal blessings that they experienced.

*"And Joseph's ten brethren went down to buy corn in Egypt. But Benjamin, Joseph's brother, Jacob sent not with his brethren; for he said, Lest peradventure mischief befall him. And the sons of Israel came to buy corn among those that came: for the famine was in the land of Canaan. And Joseph saw his brethren, and he knew them, but made himself strange unto them...And Joseph knew his brethren, but*

*they knew not him. And Joseph remembered the dreams which he dreamed of them." - Genesis 42:3-5, 7-9*

Joseph's faith had taken him from the hatred of his brothers, into a pit; from a pit into a slave trade, from a slave trade into a palace to work as a servant; from the palace to the dungeon falsely condemned as an assailant; then, from the dungeon to the court of Pharaoh, where a dream needed interpretation. From the place of interpretation, he moved to the place of supreme exaltation, where now, not only did all the nations vexed by the famine come to him for aid, but his own family bowed at his feet in desperation. Interestingly, his brothers did not recognize Joseph; however Joseph recognized them. When our faith takes us from a dream to fulfillment, we will be so transformed in the process that we will carry ourselves differently, exuding an authority that only time and testing could have fashioned.

*"Hereby ye shall be proved: By the life of Pharaoh ye shall not go forth hence, except your youngest brother come hither." – Genesis 42:15*

His brothers bowed before him even as the sheaves bowed before the sheaf in his dream as a youth. Yet, Joseph's dream told of *eleven* stars worshiping him; there were only 10 present. And so, Joseph commanded the ten which bowed before him to go back home and bring the eleventh – their youngest brother. The revelation here is that, until *every* part of God's word is fulfilled, the believer's destiny cannot come to fruition. And so it was essential that Benjamin was brought into Egypt. Indeed, not only Benjamin, but his father Jacob

158

and the entire family were brought back to Egypt. Despite the fact that Joseph had the authority to humiliate his brothers, he acted with mercy. The result was that Jacob's mighty seed would be planted in a country outside of their homeland of Canaan, thus fulfilling prophecy. When they were all present, Joseph was granted a request before Pharaoh, who decreed that not only should Joseph's family live in Egypt, but they should have authority over all the cattle in the land. Because of faithful Joseph, who came from the line of faithful Abraham, "all the families of the earth" were being blessed, that came into Egypt during the years of famine.

*"And Joseph dwelt in Egypt, he, and his father's house: and Joseph lived an hundred and ten years. And Joseph saw Ephraim's children of the third generation: the children also of Machir the son of Manasseh were brought up upon Joseph's knees. And Joseph said unto his brethren, I die: and God will surely visit you, and bring you out of this land unto the land which he sware to Abraham, to Isaac, and to Jacob. And Joseph took an oath of the children of Israel, saying, God will surely visit you, and ye shall carry up my bones from hence. So Joseph died, being an hundred and ten years old: and they embalmed him, and he was put in a coffin in Egypt." - Genesis 50:22-2*

The last act of Joseph was to prophesy concerning the children of Israel. Joseph prophetically foresaw the enslavement of his family that would occur years later in the land of Egypt, and thus prophesied to those at his death with these words, "God will surely visit you, and bring you out of this land unto the land which he sware to Abraham, to Isaac, and to Jacob." Along with this prophetic word, he ordered the children of Israel to carry his bones with them into the promise land, when the events of their deliverance from Egypt would transpire. This is truly awesome! In the same way that Joseph's very first dream accompanied him through the years of captivity in Egypt, into the promised place of power, his physical remains would be carried by the Israelites from their place of captivity, to the place of their promise. This is an encouraging word of hope assuring us that God's word, in whatever form it manifests, will go with us until our faith in that word sees the manifestation of its glorious destiny. Furthermore, after we have fulfilled our mission, our lives will continue to speak to future generations

When reflecting on this man's journey, we find another astounding aspect of faith, from the time of his life at home to the manifold journey toward his seat of governance: there is not one record of Joseph complaining about the tribulations that continually beset him. The Scriptures do record David expressing his anguish in the midst of his various persecutions, Moses expressing his frustrations with a bedraggled and obstinate people, and Abraham voicing his fears around foreign nations, even to the point of lying to stay safe. In Joseph's experience, he would not allow his soul to produce negativity to the point of despair, but rather allowed the peace of God to govern his mind, knowing that his arrival into his destiny would occur in God's power, not his own. Likewise, we are not to allow the difficulties that beset us to spill out in despair, as we are being prepared for our destinies. Also, once the door to our destination is opened, our work hasn't ended, but in many ways has just begun. Even in death, Joseph was still "speaking" to the nation of Israel, in the sense that his bones represented the life of faith which inherits God's promises. As a result of his bones, the nation had a physical token to inspire them onward no matter what lay ahead. Here we find the final lesson of Joseph: the life of faith will continue to speak on, as generations yet to be born will benefit from the example that we have set while alive.

# CHAPTER NINE

# MOSES

*"By faith Moses, when he was born, was hid three months of his parents, because they saw he was a proper child; and they were not afraid of the king's commandment. By faith Moses, when he was come to years, refused to be called the son of Pharaoh's daughter; Choosing rather to suffer affliction with the people of God, than to enjoy the pleasures of sin for a season; Esteeming the reproach of Christ greater riches than the treasures in Egypt: for he had respect unto the recompence of the reward. By faith he forsook Egypt, not fearing the wrath of the king: for he endured, as seeing him who is invisible. Through faith he kept the passover, and the sprinkling of blood, lest he that destroyed the firstborn should touch them. By faith they passed through the Red sea as by dry land: which the Egyptians assaying to do were drowned." - Hebrews 11:23-29*

He was more than just a man, he became a symbol of the very Law of God, not only for the nation of Israel, but for the entire world. He was raised up in a time of unparalleled need, on the tail end of a four hundred and thirty year enslavement to the Egyptian people. It is commonly accepted that over the course of his life he authored the first five books of the Bible, which is not only essential to the Christian faith, but became known as the Torah – the basis for the Jewish religion. He is revered as the quintessential deliverer of the Old Testament, and is known for having one of the most dynamic miracle ministries of the Old Testament. The purpose of his life had already been determined and was wonderfully revealed to him through a divine encounter with the word of the Lord. At the point of hearing that word, the purpose to which he was called began to unfold. His destiny would prove impossible to attain through human strength, but was made gloriously possible through the supernatural working of faith that continually inspired his vision, and empowered his ministry. His name was Moses, and his life would become one of the most dynamic accounts of faith recorded in Scripture.

In order to fully appreciate the impact of Moses' life and ministry, we must consider the nation of Israel under the governorship of Joseph. It is a fact that Egypt prospered under the rule of Joseph. Pharaoh knew Joseph, and therefore he and his country were blessed in a critical time of famine due to his alliance with the young Hebrew. After the death of Joseph, there were administrative changes within Egypt's government including a new Pharaoh. This new Egyptian ruler did not know Joseph personally, nor did he have the sympathies for the Israelites that the previous Pharaoh had. Instead, he began a campaign of oppression toward the Israelites because of their massive and threatening growth throughout the Egyptian empire. The Hebrews were seen as a growing threat to the kingdom, even though it was through the Hebrew Joseph that the nation of Egypt was supernaturally provided for in the great famine. And so, the nationalization of enslavement began as brutal task masters were set over the Hebrews, requiring hard labor. This did not have the effect that the new king desired, however, as the Hebrews began to multiply in number even more through their persecution. As such, an edict was issued requiring the midwives of the Israelite women to kill every newborn, male child. The result of this was the slaughter of countless babies throughout the kingdom.

This is the first record of genocide that we find in the Bible. We see this method of genocide again in the days of Josiah, Jeremiah, and also at the time when Jesus was born. Furthermore, we know from history that the Jewish people have faced the threat of extinction from more than one nation, including Nazi Germany and Russia during the Second World War. From these accounts, we see a diabolical plan to destroy the lives of those whom God has set apart through a covenant. Now the covenant God makes is essentially spiritual in nature, as it begins with Him uttering His word to a person. Once that word has been spoken, it enters the heart, which is essentially the spirit. The spiritual heart of man needs a physical body in order for that word to find its fulfillment. By faith, that man transports the spiritual word until it has reached its destination. The point here is that this transportation of spiritual words requires the physical part of man to be alive. This is why we find Satan throughout Scripture and recent history attempting to kill the very people that God has spoken to, in order to destroy the destiny of God's word. It was during this demonic reign that we are introduced to a Hebrew family who did not do what was commanded of them by their heathen masters.

It is important to take note of any individual whose birth is surrounded by acts of faith. An "act of faith" is some kind of response to God's word which can be heard or seen. Although the Bible describes faith as the result of *hearing* the word of God, we know that the concept of hearing is not limited to the audible word. The prophet Habakkuk said "I will stand upon my watch, and set me upon the tower, and will watch to *see* what he will *say* unto me" (2:1). According to this verse, it is possible to *see* God's words which are spoken, and not merely hear them with the ear. The apostle John said of Jesus, "And the Word was made flesh, and dwelt among us, (*and we beheld his glory*...)" (John 1:14). The disciples "beheld" the Word of God that was made flesh in the Person of Jesus. In other words, by seeing the Lord, they were beholding the word of God. Jesus rebuked his followers when He said "How long have I been with you, and you still don't recognize me?" In seeing someone, it is possible to perceive who they are according to God's word. As we have learned in the introduction of this book, it is faith that gives us God's eyesight to perceive His word made manifest before us.

Moses survived his birth at this time of genocide due to the spiritual perception of those around him. The book of Hebrews records that his parents "saw he was a proper child" (11:23). The author is not merely saying that his parents saved his life because he was physically attractive – any father or mother can see beauty in their own child. Furthermore, they would obviously be inclined to preserve their baby's life from a mass slaughter. Something beyond physical appearance and parental love moved his parents to save his life – it was the divine word that they perceived in their child. God had a grand plan for this

Hebrew baby who was scheduled to die along with all the other Hebrew babies in Egypt. God caused his parents to *behold* his tiny form, and *see* the beauty of the living word upon this young one's life; hence, their decision to hide him for three months was act of faith. His parents could not have known the eternal significance which God placed upon their acts of heroism.

There is an infinitely wise purpose that God has for his people, one that stretches beyond momentary events and into the future, affecting not only our lives, but the lives of countless others. We see this by studying the life of Joseph and the life of Moses. Joseph was born in Canaan. It was the land of Canaan that the entire Israelite people were destined to inherit. Through the hatred of his brothers, Joseph was sold as a slave in Egypt. While this event may seem unconnected to the inheritance of Canaan, we find that Joseph, through the course of much tribulation, was promoted in the land of Egypt and was able therefore to bless many nations, including the Israelites who were from Canaan. As the Israelites found a welcoming home in Egypt, they left Canaan and began to live and thrive in this new land. Next, we see Moses, who was born with all the other Israelites in Egypt under a demonic rule. By a heroic act of his parents, he was saved from the slaughter of the land. As a result, he would someday walk in a deliverance ministry focused on delivering his people from Egypt, back into the land of Canaan. Joseph brought the children of Israel into Egypt for a place of refuge from the oppression of famine, and Moses would eventually lead the same people back into Canaan, away from the oppression of enslavement. This is the complex wisdom of God, seen over the course of time, in the lives of different individuals who are most often unaware that they are fulfilling God's divinely engineered plan for humanity.

As a vulnerable baby floating up the river in a basket, Moses was discovered in the reeds by Pharaoh's daughter. Ironically, she was the daughter of the king who oppressed the Hebrews and ordered all Hebrew boys to be put to death! She took pity on him and claimed him as her son, naming him *Moses,* which means "drawn out."[1] It is interesting to note that God's way of positioning His people to fulfill their destiny is quite beyond human engineering. Moses was destined to draw out the children of Israel from the depths of Egyptian tyranny, however it would be necessary to become grafted into Egypt in order to fulfill the divine plan. And so, a heathen princess drew a male baby out of the water, unaware that his destiny was to save the nation of Israel.

Now, Egypt has been made to represent many things by theologians, but one of the most striking symbols that this great nation represents is the *world system* mentioned in John's first epistle. John writes, "For all that is in the world, the lust of the flesh, and the lust of the eyes, and the pride of life, is not of the Father, but is of the world" (2:16). The word *world* here is the Greek word *kosmos*, meaning *worldly affairs; the aggregate of things earthly: the whole circle of earthly goods, endowments, riches, advantages, pleasures.*[2] Ancient Egypt was a nation of prosperity and a land of opulence. Earthly opportunity was ever present. Every desire – riches, fame, power, and pleasure, was available to Egyptian citizens. Right in the middle of this great nation, Moses would grow up as a prince. The magnificence of his position presented great rewards to Moses. As Pharaoh's grandson, he would have been entitled to luxurious living, fine horses and chariots, all the sport he desired, and any woman in the empire he wanted. However, there was a force greater than his will at work upon his life – the plan of God that had yet to be revealed through God's word.

*"And it came to pass in those days, when Moses was grown, that he went out unto his brethren, and looked on their burdens: and he spied an Egyptian smiting an Hebrew, one of his brethren. And he looked this way and that way, and when he saw that there was no man, he slew the Egyptian, and hid him in the sand. And when he went out the second day, behold, two men of the Hebrews strove together: and he said to him that did the wrong, Wherefore smitest thou thy fellow? And he said, Who made thee a prince and a judge over us? intendest thou to kill me, as thou killedst the Egyptian? And Moses feared, and said, Surely this thing is known." - Exodus 2:11-14*

Even before a person is directly called out by God for a divine work, he or she may begin to exhibit aspects of that calling beforehand. It is as if their future bends back into the present moment, to reveal the purpose for which they were created. Moses did not know the awesome task that lay ahead of him. Yet, justice for his fellowman burned in his soul as he saw the evil treatment his brothers received at the hands of the Egyptians. First, by rescuing the Hebrew man and killing the Egyptian, he was performing one part of his calling – to deliver his people from the Egyptians. Second, by intervening into the quarrel between the two Hebrews he was demonstrating another part of

168

his calling – to be the priestly mediator between the Hebrew people and God once they were delivered from Egypt. Notice the language of the man who acted wrongly against his fellow Hebrew; he unknowingly uncovers Moses' identity in his question, "Who made you *prince* and *judge* over us?" The two major parts of Moses' destiny were recognized years before their fulfillment, as he was delivering the Hebrew with the might of a prince and judging over the two who were at odds. It is true that the Lord will allow us to experience the outworking of our destiny in advance, so that the realization of our future is indelibly imprinted upon our consciousness. These experiences confirm the true nature of our calling, settling within us the truth that we will never be satisfied doing anything else. This transcendent knowing solidifies within our own consciousness the conviction and motivation to do whatever is necessary in order that we may fulfill that calling. Moses was a man raised as a citizen and prince of Egypt, however, in light of two profound experiences he knew that his destiny could not be realized in Egypt any longer.

*"By faith Moses, when he was come to years, refused to be called the son of Pharaoh's daughter; Choosing rather to suffer affliction with the people of God, than to enjoy the pleasures of sin for a season; Esteeming the reproach of Christ greater riches than the treasures in Egypt: for he had respect unto the recompence of the reward. By faith he forsook Egypt, not fearing the wrath of the king: for he endured, as seeing him who is invisible." - Hebrews 11:24-2.*

The Bible declares that Moses actually esteemed the reproach of Christ as a greater treasure than all the natural treasures in Egypt.

169

The "reproach of Christ" here speaks of the reproach which Christ received because of His continual denial of the world system, a system by which the religious and non-religious alike strive to attain greatness. That system is based upon human will-power to achieve what is satisfying to the eyes, flesh, and pride of man. Christ not only forsook this humanistic course, but paved a new way for humanity in which the purpose of mankind would not be found in man's independent pursuit of his destiny, but in the union of mankind with God Himself. It was a life of faith which Christ embodied, always conscious of the perfection which awaited all of mankind through man's acknowledgment of his union with God.

The above verses teach us that faith is not based in time, but is an eternal reality, and those who walk by faith experience the unseen and eternal pleasures of heaven at all times. It was by this faith that Moses was able to refuse the world system in Egypt, therefore "esteeming the reproach of Christ" having never seen the Christ physically. We could say that faith *sees* the future; for that which is 'hoped for' is always something in the future. The future is 'unseen' in the sense that it exists from an eternal standpoint, not having been made a reality in the realm of time and space. Faith therefore gives us the ability to see into the invisible, future realm, where what *will be* is seen in the present moment. Moses endured the hardship of leaving Egypt because his faith gave him the ability to see far into the future, and thus created a greater reality within him than the one that was presently before him. It is absolute foolishness to the natural mind that Moses was willing to give up all that he had in Egypt for something he had never physically experienced. However, it reveals clear evidence of the fact that faith was his greater reality. The fact is, a person of faith is not led primarily by what is sensible – that which accommodates natural reason. The works of faith are not based upon physical *senses*, but rather upon spiritual *knowing* and *seeing*. It is therefore true that the knowledge of something in the future, something that God has ordained for us, will impact us in a greater way, causing even the physical pleasures that may present themselves to us presently, to seem insignificant in comparison.

Now, after Moses killed the Egyptian and mediated between the two Hebrews, he fled Egypt as Pharaoh heard of these deeds and sought to kill him. Many of the lives of men and women in scripture were marked by continual confrontation. The truth is that a life of faith creates an atmosphere that attracts conflict. It may be that we are facing the criticism of others, or possibly even our own self-prejudices. Whatever the conflict may be, there will always be a challenge to the prophetic word in our lives. The writer of Hebrews speaks of the fight of affliction we endure. Listen to his words:

*"But call to remembrance the former days, in which, after ye were illuminated, ye endured a great fight of afflictions." - Hebrews 10:32*

After we receive a personal revelation from the Lord, affliction will inevitably follow. The reason that God allows afflicting agents to test us is so that the genuiness of our faith may be revealed. Many believers understand the idea of "testing" what other people say to determine if the source of their words are in fact from God. However, when the word we hear is truly from the Lord, we can be assured that we will not be testing that word – the word will be testing us! Now,

171

God's word will not only bring about faith, but will simultaneously open that faith up to some form of test. The test is described in scripture as a "fire." The apostle Peter declares, "That the trial of your faith, being much more precious than of gold that perisheth, though it be *tried with fire* might be found unto praise and honor and glory at the appearing of Jesus Christ..." (1 Peter 1:7). The fire which refines gold is an agent in the arsenal of the goldsmith, so that over the course of time the gold becomes so refined – without any spot or blemish – that he may see his own reflection on the surface. In the same way, the test we undergo as a result of God's word becomes an agent of God to reveal the very essence of our belief, by creating a spotless image of that word in our minds. Only God knows when our faith in that word is refined. All we know is that the test is continually causing our faith to see that word, until that word has been so clarified in our consciousness that we no longer have even a spot of unbelief. The apostle Peter makes it clear that our *faith* is the subject of the fire.

God gives man His own faith, and we know that His faith is essentially perfect. However man may not yet operate maturely in that faith. To better understand this concept, we may liken faith to a pair of binoculars. Binoculars are viewing instruments that magnify what is seen at a distance. Although the binoculars themselves are completely proficient in identifying objects from afar, if they are not adjusted properly they will not present the one using them with an accurate view. Similarly, we must learn how to see through the lens of faith. An individual operating maturely in faith will see God's word coming to pass without doubting, which will produce a confident expectation of that future, despite present circumstances. An individual operating immaturely in faith will see that word through blurred vision, and will become more easily discouraged by the adversity. It is not as though faith itself is weak, but that our operation of faith is not yet mature. The test comes in the form of anything that seeks to blur our vision. Through experiencing each test we learn to adjust our spiritual vision by agreeing with the word of the Lord. As we agree with that word, what was once a distorted image is made clear.

*"Fight the good fight of faith, lay hold on eternal life, whereunto thou art also called, and hast professed a good profession before many witnesses." - 1 Timothy 6:12*

According to the apostle Paul, faith is a "good fight." By this we understand that faith contains the quality of militancy. Unlike natural militancy, the fight of faith is not based upon the might of one's own will-power to defeat a physical enemy. In fact, to operate in true faith is to see *God* as the One who not only performs His word through us, but empowers us supernaturally to overcome enemy tactics. The fact is, our "fight" is essentially a *passive* one. Our fight is *passive* in the sense that we do nothing in our own strength to make God's word come to pass, and neither do we do anything physical to wage war against our enemy. This is why the apostle Paul declares that "we wrestle not against flesh and blood..." (Ephesians 6:12). That our enemy is not "flesh and blood" reveals that our enemy is not a physical being. Furthermore, since our enemy is not a physical being, we know that there is no physical wrestling required in order to fight the fight of faith. The apostle Paul goes on to say, "For the weapons of our warfare are not carnal, but mighty through God to the pulling down of strong

173

holds; Casting down imaginations, and every high thing that exalteth itself against the knowledge of God, and bringing into captivity every thought to the obedience of Christ" (2 Corinthians 10:4-5). Our fight is actually against *thoughts* and *imaginations*, both of which are intangible, revealing that our warfare is also intangible. Thoughts and imaginations become the enemy's greatest weapons against us, for in planting these intangibles into our minds, his desire is that we abandon our trust in the word of God. We can see this demonic strategy when looking at the fall of Adam and Eve. By submitting to the evil thought that they could become like God through self-effort, *even though they were already like God* – made in His image and likeness – and because of the imagination presented to them of a desirable yet distorted picture of obtaining equal status with God through a means other than faith, they allowed the devil to bankrupt their faith in God. This is the essential and unchanging strategy of the enemy today. And this is why our greatest weapon to combat satanic assault is faith, that simple trust in God's word to us, that what He has said is actually true! This trust in God's word produces a rest that is able to transport us through the difficult times of testing, and into our promised land.

After fleeing from Egypt, Moses made his way to Midian. Upon coming to a well of water surrounded by seven women, he observed that the women were being harassed by local shepherds who prohibited them from drawing water out for their flocks. At this point, the scripture declares that Moses "stood up and helped them" (Exodus 2:17). By this we know that he defended the women until the intimidating shepherds left them alone. This is the third act of deliverance that Moses performed, following the two in Egypt right

174

before his departure. Moses did not know these women, their history, or the land in which they lived. He was in a foreign place surrounded by foreign people. Moses simply did what was in him to do – to deliver those who were oppressed. Taken out of our environment, away from the people we know and the familiar things we've grown accustomed to, we will naturally begin to manifest what God has placed within us. Although Moses was hundreds of miles away from the place of his citizenship, the energy of his calling could not be contained.

So far, Moses' life reveals to us that before we are made consciously aware of the specific thing God has called us to, we may unconsciously manifest that calling in various situations. This *unconscious* manifesting of our ultimate purpose reveals to us that our true calling is eternal, and can manifest at any given time throughout our journey. Although we are waiting for direct revelation from the Lord concerning our future, we may still begin acting and speaking as though we had already been given that revelation. It is through the operation of faith that the future is reeled into the present, showcasing the eternal nature of God's calling in our lives.

As the result of his heroics in defending the seven women, Moses was taken to their father, a Midianite man named Reuel (whose name would later become "Jethro"). He received Moses as a son, and gave him one of his daughters for a wife. It was here that Moses would enter a forty year season as a shepherd, tending the flock of his father-in-law in the desert. Now it is important to see that Moses' forty years in isolation was a precursor to the forty years he would spend in the Wilderness of Sinai, after having led the Israelites out of Egypt. What

175

is significant is that there is a parallel that exists between the time spent in isolation tending sheep, and the time spent walking in his actual destiny. We may better understand these two times in this way: the time of preparing for our destiny involves the *inward* workings of God, whereas the actual time of ministry in our destiny involves the *outward* workings of God. Moses was being prepared inwardly as he tended sheep before he assumed his role as shepherd of an entire nation. This time would have undoubtedly produced necessary qualities of leadership, including patience and humility. In the same way, we see this pattern of the inward and outward working of God in the life of David. He spent an estimated ten to fifteen years preparing for his high calling as king over all of Israel. We know that Jesus spent thirty years of silent preparation for three years of public ministry as Messiah. The Disciples of Christ spent three years in strict submission to the Lord, before they were released into their own apostolic ministries. The apostle Paul spent approximately seventeen years of preparation after his initial encounter with the Lord, till the time of his separation in Antioch where he was sent forth to fulfill his international ministry. Every individual's preparation may look different; however it is clear that there is a set time of intense, inward working within the individual whom God has chosen for an outward expression of His purposes.

*Now Moses kept the flock of Jethro his father in law, the priest of Midian: and he led the flock to the backside of the desert, and came to the mountain of God, even to Horeb. And the angel of the LORD appeared unto him in a flame of fire out of the midst of a bush: and he looked, and, behold, the bush burned with fire, and the bush was not*

*consumed. And Moses said, I will now turn aside, and see this great*
*sight, why the bush is not burnt. And when the LORD saw that he*
*turned aside to see, God called unto him out of the midst of the bush,*
*and said, Moses, Moses. And he said, Here am I.*

On one particular day when Moses was with his sheep on the backside of the desert that he observed a strange spectacle – a desert bush was burning with fire. He observed that while the bush itself was engulfed in a flame, it was not burning up. That the bush was not disintegrating tells us that the fire was supernatural. In fact, the fire was a manifestation of the Lord Himself. In describing God in the book of Deuteronomy, Moses actually calls Him a "consuming fire" (4:24). The writer of Hebrews reiterates Moses' words, attributing the same attributes to the Lord. (12:29). What is fascinating here is that God, being described as a "consuming fire," was manifesting Himself through a bush and yet the bush itself was not being consumed! This is because the nature of that holy fire is different from natural fire. Whereas natural fire destroys whatever it touches, the supernatural fire of God actually *preserves* that which it contacts. The purpose for the preserving power of God's fire is to allow natural creation to personally experience the awesome Creator while being sustained in the presence of His almighty power. The bush that was being burned actually represented *Moses* and his *future ministry*. Moses, being a man, would not be capable of sustaining the ministry that God had for him, no more than the bush could sustain being burned with natural fire. Furthermore, he would not be able to carry the glory of God without the sustaining power of God's fire upon him. He would need the supernatural flame of God to manifest upon his life, which would enable him to reveal God's glory without being consumed. Again, it is important that we understand the consuming nature of God's fire, the purpose of which is not to destroy a man, but that man may exhibit the divine presence of God for the purpose for which he is called.

*"Moreover he said, I am the God of thy father, the God of Abraham, the God of Isaac, and the God of Jacob. And Moses hid his face; for he was afraid to look upon God." – Genesis 3:6*

The Lord identifies Himself by Moses' natural lineage. The reason that these forefathers are mentioned is because each of them represent the successive generations proceeding out of God's word to Abraham. It was for the divine word spoken to Abraham that God was about to deliver the Israelites out of Egypt. The covenant God made with Abraham ensured that his seed would eventually produce the Messiah, and the entire world would be blessed as a result. Moses would soon learn that the Lord was choosing him to go forth as His ambassador of deliverance.

*"And the LORD said, I have surely seen the affliction of my people which are in Egypt, and have heard their cry by reason of their taskmasters; for I know their sorrows; And I am come down to deliver them out of the hand of the Egyptians, and to bring them up out of that land unto a good land and a large, unto a land flowing with milk and honey; unto the place of the Canaanites, and the Hittites, and the Amorites, and the Perizzites, and the Hivites, and the Jebusites. Now therefore, behold, the cry of the children of Israel is come unto me: and I have also seen the oppression wherewith the Egyptians oppress them. Come now therefore, and I will send thee unto Pharaoh, that*

*thou mayest bring forth my people the children of Israel out of Egypt."*
*– Exodus 3:7-10*

Here we find the idea of a *calling* defined sequentially. First, there is a need in the earth requiring divine assistance. Second, through the Lord's awareness of that need, He chooses someone He can use to meet the need. And third, the Lord calls upon that individual in some unique way, revealing to them His divine plan. Notice the language the Lord uses in the verses above. God *saw* the affliction of His people, He *heard* the cry of their voices, and He *knew* their sorrows. God's *senses* were involved as he saw, heard, and knew of the affliction that Abraham's seed received. To the Lord, delivering the Israelites was personal. The Lord is equally as involved in our own callings. It is because God is involved with our future that He calls us for service. He is uniquely aware of the spiritual and natural conditions in the sphere of service that awaits us. The need that presents itself within our calling is made personal to us only because it is made personal to the Lord first. It is interesting that God would personally deliver the Israelites, as He explicitly states "And I am come down to *deliver* them." And yet, at the end of this passage we find Him saying, "Come now therefore and I will send *thee*...that *thou* mayest *bring forth* my people." When we study the Hebrew origins of the word "deliver" and the words "bring forth" we find that the meanings are connected. To "deliver" means to "snatch away, rescue, save, or plunder;"[3] to "bring forth" means to "go out, come out, exit, and go forth."[4] Both ideas are intertwined in that God intended to rescue the Israelites through the ministry of Moses, who would physically bring them out of Egypt.

179

This reinforces the truth that whatever God calls us to do, it is actually God Himself that will do it through us.

It is by the power of the Holy Spirit that we are able to fulfill our destiny. Not understanding this simple truth will cause us to protest God's word after we hear it. Moses was a stuttering man, apparently unable to correct this defect, despite having lived many years as a prince in the modern kingdom of Egypt. Now this would be one of Moses' main points of protest against what God had called him to do. We similarly protest against God's word for our lives when we point to whatever physical or psychological impediments we may have. Moses' reply to the Lord was not unlike many of ours when we are made aware of our destiny.

*"And Moses said unto the LORD, O my Lord, I am not eloquent, neither heretofore, nor since thou hast spoken unto thy servant: but I am slow of speech, and of a slow tongue...And the anger of the LORD was kindled against Moses" - Exodus 4:10, 14*

Moses was actually making a case to legitimize his inability to perform God's word. And yet, it was because of his natural inability that God chose Him! The fact is, *nobody* is able to muster up enough physical and psychological competence in order to manifest a single facet of God's will. It is through faith that heavenly wisdom, creativity, and power is made available for the task assigned to us. In short, God's faith gives us God's ability. When we hear God's word, the faith that comes with that word infuses our natural life with the belief that God's supernatural ability will make the impossible, possible. Moses found out that he was being sent forth with greater equipment than he could

180

ever imagine. He was given a rod that had the ability to change forms, which would also enable him to perform miracles. Furthermore, he was given supernatural ability in his hand for a sign and a wonder, as well as his brother-in-law Aaron, who would become the spokesman to communicate God's word to Moses concerning Pharaoh and the Israelites.

*"And Moses said unto God, Who am I, that I should go unto Pharaoh, and that I should bring forth the children of Israel out of Egypt? And he said, Certainly I will be with thee; and this shall be a token unto thee, that I have sent thee: When thou hast brought forth the people out of Egypt, ye shall serve God upon this mountain." – Exodus 3:11-12*

In the verses above, a startling revelation appears concerning the way in which God's word and man's destiny are connected. The place in which God chose to reveal Moses' destiny was in the backside of the desert, somewhere on Mount Horeb. We know that Mount Horeb is later named *Mount Sanai*, the mountain where the Ten Commandments would be given to Moses and administered to the Israelite people. The divine commission which Moses received was to bring the Israelites out from Egypt, leading them back to the same mountain. The significance of this moment was twofold; not only did God choose to reveal Moses' destiny, but chose to reveal it in the very place where that destiny would manifest. By standing on Mount Sinai, Moses was personally experiencing the most significant place of his destiny! It is the function of faith to make our destiny a tangible reality before we physically arrive. This is why the writer of Hebrews describes faith as "the substance of things hoped for, the evidence of things not seen." Faith substantiates the word we have received by providing a conscious reality of the word that will come to pass. In essence, faith brings tangibility to the word we have believed.

*"And afterward Moses and Aaron went in, and told Pharaoh, Thus saith the LORD God of Israel, Let my people go, that they may hold a feast unto me in the wilderness." – Exodus 5:1*

This was Moses' first of ten attempts to free the Israelites from Pharaoh's iron grip. Because of the hardness of Pharaoh's heart, Moses was instructed to perform a specific sign after Pharaoh denied the Israelites their freedom. Each time Moses went before the king, Pharaoh hardened his heart, and each time his heart was hardened, Moses performed another sign. Although Pharaoh did not believe in the God of Moses, what he witnessed was god-like. The first sign took place as Moses threw down his rod, which transformed into a serpent (Exodus 7:10, 14). The second sign occurred as Moses turned the river into blood (7:17). The third sign happened as the borders of Egypt were smitten with frogs (8:2). The fourth sign manifested as the dust of the earth became lice (8:17). The fifth sign done was to smite all the cattle in Egypt with sickness. (9:3, 6-7). The sixth sign was accomplished when Egypt was plagued with the dust of a fiery furnace (9:8). The seventh sign was to send a rain of hail upon the land (9:18). The eighth sign came as Moses commanded a plague of locusts to cover Egypt (10:14). The ninth sign occurred as darkness covered the land for three days (10:22). And finally, the tenth sign was that the angel of death was released to kill every first born child in Egypt, along with the first born of the cattle in the land (12:29). That Moses demonstrated god-like abilities before Pharaoh is evident in the scripture below.

*"And the LORD said unto Moses, See, I have made thee a god to*
*Pharaoh: and Aaron thy brother shall be thy prophet. Thou shalt speak*
*all that I command thee: and Aaron thy brother shall speak unto*
*Pharaoh, that he send the children of Israel out of his land. And I will*
*harden Pharaoh's heart, and multiply my signs and my wonders in the*
*land of Egypt." – Exodus 7:1-3*

What's fascinating here is that the faith that was given to Moses caused him to act just like God! As Moses stepped into his role as deliverer of Israel, God's word to him began to manifest in signs and wonders which supernaturally amplified this man's ability. The truth is that faith causes an individual to amplify the divine nature of God to the world. Moses was God's image and likeness to the unbelieving Pharaoh; when this hardened Egyptian king beheld Moses, he was beholding God. We must never forget that we *are* God's image in the earth, and it is by faith that we communicate that image to the world. We must not *try* to be like God; for it was Satan's lie in the Garden which spawned the belief that mankind was not already made like his Creator. If we will believe that we have already been made perfect representations of the Creator, we will manifest His nature. Faith makes the reality of our sameness with God evident to the world. For instance, we see this in the Lord's directive to His disciples. He instructed them not to prepare a speech or a performance when brought before kings; the Spirit of God would reveal to them in the same hour

183

what they were to say and do. By faith, the disciples went out and boldly demonstrated the kingdom of God. As they did this, people recognized that they had been with Jesus, for they looked and talked just like Him. We too will represent Christ and His kingdom effortlessly, through faith demonstrating that we are God's mirror image. It is that reflection which will convince the world that we are His ambassadors.

After the departure from Egypt, and the supernatural parting of the red sea, Moses brought approximately 2 million Hebrews into the Wilderness of Sinai. It was here that Moses received his initial commissioning by the Lord – the word which propelled him into his destiny. By studying two verses in the New Testament, one by the apostle James in Acts 15:21, and the other by the apostle Paul in 2 Corinthians 3:15, it is evident that Moses not only gave the Israelites the Law of God on Sinai, but was a physical representation of that Law to the nation. James says, "For Moses of old time hath in every city them that *preach him*, being *read* in the synagogues every sabbath day." We see that Moses is able to be "preached" and "read" in the synagogues, which is actually speaking of the Law that he dictated in the Wilderness. Similarly, Paul says, "But even unto this day, when *Moses is read*, the veil is upon their heart." Again, Moses is able to be "read" by the Jews, inferring that he and the Commandments dictated to the Israelites are one in the same. This is significant when understanding Moses' final phase of his destiny. He had already delivered the Israelites out of Egypt, thus fulfilling that part of the divine mandate. He brought them to Mount Sinai as the Lord had also commanded. The only thing left to do was to bring them to the land of Canaan, which would serve as their inheritance.

Now, we glean from the New Testament that the promised land of Canaan is a type and shadow of the spiritual Promised Land we enter under the New Covenant. That spiritual Promised Land is found in the Person of Christ. Both the physical land of Canaan and spiritual land of Christ can only be entered through faith. This is why Joshua and Caleb were the only two Israelites who entered into Canaan of their generation – they were the only two who possessed a real faith. Similarly, it is by faith that we enter into Christ and His finished works on the Cross. We also know that no one can gain access to God by performing the works of the Law, for it is impossible for anyone to perfectly fulfill that Law. It is not by obedience to laws or rules that we have access into the divine life, but by believing upon Jesus Christ. Since Moses represented the Law, he would not be able to personally experience Canaan, just as the person who tries to fulfill the Law of God can never experience Christ's work of grace. Therefore, as a symbol of the Law, Moses could not enter into the Promised Land, but was destined to die in the Wilderness at the threshold of Canaan. Now, even though Moses represented the Law, as a man, he could not perfectly fulfill that Law. He disobeyed a command given by the Lord, and thus was prohibited from entering Canaan. That he was denied access into the Promised Land does not imply that he had not fulfilled his destiny, but that his destiny was *never* to enter the Promised Land; rather, he was to lead the Israelite nation into the Wilderness, dispense God's Law, and bring them to the doorway of their own destiny.

185

It is astonishing to consider all that this man's ministry produced. The wealth of miraculous events that occurred as a result of his life must be attributed to the life of faith. Through faith, this unlikely deliverer was energized and catapulted into his divine purpose. Born in a time where genocide threatened his existence, he escaped death because of the faith of his parents. Although he was planted in the midst of the Egyptian palace, where his upbringing was that of a prince, he would not be able to continue there in light of the burning desire to see justice done for his own people. His journey would lead him away from the world he once knew, into the solitary life of tending sheep in the midst of the desert. He was used of God to do mighty exploits, however he remained unusually humble. By faith he delivered two million Hebrews from Egyptian tyranny, worked unprecedented signs and wonders, received the Law of God, and sojourned forty long years in the wilderness as the head of an entire nation. Moses faced many challenges to his faith. He had a speech defect which seemed insurmountable when compared with his assignment; however he learned that man's impediments cannot impede God's providential calling. He faced the imminent threat of being killed by Pharaoh as he repeatedly sought the deliverance of his people. Fleeing from the Egyptian army, he found himself and the Israelites trapped against the Red Sea, where the Lord performed one of the most famous miraculous acts in Scripture. He faced the uncertainty of daily survival in the Wilderness. His authority was tested by the mutinous rebellion led by the sons of Korah. He was betrayed by his brother and wife who sought to undermine his authority. And yet, he was a man perfectly fitted for his role as deliverer and shepherd. By all this, we may confidently conclude that

186

God does not need human ingenuity to accomplish His purposes. He chose this man not for his abilities, but to reveal Himself as the ultimate source of success. Moses was a man perfectly fitted for his role as deliverer and shepherd, because he believed in the One who fitted him with the purpose and power necessary to fulfill his destiny.

# CHAPTER TEN

# RAHAB

*"By faith the harlot Rahab perished not with them that believed not, when she had received the spies with peace." - Hebrews 11:31*

The testimony of this next heroine of faith emerged out of a scandalous life, a life that was considered appalling in biblical times and today. To the Israelite mindset, harlotry – or prostitution – was considered a defilement of God's law as recorded in the books of Exodus, Leviticus and Deuteronomy. We read scriptures such as Leviticus 19:29 which says, "Do not prostitute thy daughter, to cause her to be a whore; lest the land fall to whoredom, and the land become full of wickedness." Also, we read in Leviticus 21:9 that "....the daughter of any priest, if she profane herself by playing the whore, she profaneth her father: she shall be burnt with fire." Likewise, in Deuteronomy 23:17-18 we understand that, "There shall be no whore of the daughters of Israel, nor a Sodomite of the sons of Israel. Thou shalt not bring the hire of a whore, or the price of a dog, into the house of the Lord thy God for any vow: for even both these are abomination unto the Lord thy God." These were just a few of the many commands concerning the sin of harlotry in Israel's priesthood and in its people.

Unlike in Western cultures of today where governments create laws that deal primarily with social, political, and economic issues, the Israelite government of the Old Testament combined both spiritual and religious as well as natural laws into their constitution to create one guiding plan for society. A violation against any spiritual law could convict a person just as legally as a violation against a natural law. Harlots were viewed as violators of Israelite law which condemned sexual immorality regardless of the age or sex of the individual involved. If the harlot was a daughter of a priest, she was legally required to be burned to death. Now, as God's treasured nation, partakers of the divine promises which gave them provision and protection, there was a holiness or *separateness* that Israel was required to walk in. That Israel was called to be *separate* implies that the foundation of their society was fundamentally different than those of every other nation in the world. Their separateness was designed to reveal the Creator, so that all other people groups had a living, physical model that represented God's order and His Person. The apostle Paul describes all who were outside of this nation as "aliens of the commonwealth of Israel...strangers from the covenants of promise, having no hope, and without God in the world" (Ephesians 2:12). From this verse, it is apparent that any person who was a non-Israelite did not have the same natural or spiritual benefits that Israel would have had. Furthermore, anyone who practiced harlotry, who was also a non-Israelite, must have been looked at as the basest of people without even the remotest possibility of becoming part of this righteous nation. It is at this point that we turn to one of the most unlikely heroines of the faith, to see how this very thing was accomplished for her.

189

Joshua, the man who succeeded Moses, was given a great commission from the Lord to go and bring the Israelites into their long awaited Promise Land. He was commanded to kill anyone who disobeyed or rebelled against his orders. Before this monumental mission could be carried out successfully, he commanded two men to spy out the land, "especially Jericho." En route to completing this assingment, the two spies found lodging inside the home of a harlot named Rahab. Now it is interesting that the city of Jericho was, and still is the geographically lowest permanently inhabited place in the world, and one of the oldest continuously inhabited cities on earth. What's significant is that in the lowest habitable place on earth, we find these two spies lodging with a woman occupied in the most immoral profession known to the Israelites. Both the natural and moral altitude of her situation signifies the sheer poverty of Rahab's existence. However, listen to her words as she speaks to the two men:

*"I know that the LORD has given you the land, and that the terror of you has fallen on us, and that all the inhabitants of the land have melted away before you. **For we have heard** how the LORD dried up the water of the Red sea for you, when ye came out of Egypt; and what ye did unto the two kings of the Amorites, that were on the other side Jordan, Sihon and Og, whom ye utterly destroyed. And as soon as **we had heard** these things, our hearts did melt, neither did there remain any more courage in any man, because of you: for the LORD your God, he is God in heaven above, and in earth beneath." - Joshua 2:9-11 (emphasis mine)*

The very first words out of Rahab's mouth were an affirmation that the Lord had in fact given the Israelites this land. The reason for this affirming word was that Rahab attributed the Israelites' success as a nation to the Lord Who guided them. She began to recall all of the famous battles in which the Lord had given victory to his people. In addition to her recognition of the Israelite's god, we find another insight in the eleventh chapter of Hebrews, which says that "Rahab...received the spies with peace." This indicates that she was *at peace* harboring two men whose intention was not only to spy out the land, but provide military intelligence for their army to come and destroy it. Naturally speaking, she should have been terrified at the thought of harboring two men who represented her nation's destruction. And yet, we are told that she actually at peace in their presence! The fact is that she had received divine faith somewhere between the time of hearing about the great exploits done by the Israelite nation, and the present moment with these two Israelites. As we study her words in the second chapter of Joshua, we find the stunning truth that faith had been administered to her heart simply by *hearing* about the omnipotence of the Israelite God. She was not an Israelite, and therefore was not raised with the intimate knowledge of Jehovah, nor with His laws. And yet, she not only acknowledged the existence of their God, but emphatically states that He is the true "God in heaven above, and in earth beneath." The apostle Paul reaveals to us that "Faith comes by hearing and hearing by the word of God." It becomes apparent that the Israelites were more than just a chosen people, but they were *the physical representation of the word of God.* In other words, God's word was upon God's people, for they came into existence by His word. By hearing of the Israelites victories in battle,

191

Rahab was *hearing* the word of God as it was manifested through those victories. As Rahab considered the greatness of this people, faith began to spring up in the midst of her heart, and she was moved to help the two Israelite spies. She may not have been able to quote one scripture, or one of the 613 laws given to Israel, but she was still qualified to receive the gift of faith, for she had heard of the chosen people as well as the greatness of their Lord, and believed with the same faith that was given to Abraham, Isaac, and Jacob.

Speaking of Abraham, Paul says in his letter to the Romans: "As it is written, I have made thee a father of many nations, before him whom he believed, even God, who quickeneth the dead, and calleth those things which be not as though they were" (4:17). Rahab began to declare what had not yet occurred as though it had already happened. This heathen prostitute woman began to prophesy to the Israelites! She said boldly, "I know that the LORD has given you this land." What is even more fascinating is that along with her receiving God's faith, her prophetic words would be used to inspire the entire Israelite army in their conquest of Jericho.

*"And they said unto Joshua, Truly the LORD hath delivered into our hands all the land; for even all the inhabitants of the country do faint because of us." - Joshua 2:24*

Joshua was a man of great faith, called to lead a nation into their destiny. He was no stranger to the power of God, the workings of the Spirit, and angelic assistence; however, he needed a good report to reassure him before conquering Jericho. Waiting on the other side of

192

his conquest was the harlot Rahab, who had the right word at the right time. Had Joshua and his men known the vessel with whom the Lord would use to encourage, as well as confirm His word to them, they may have had an internal conflict knowing the evils of harlotry and those who were engaged in such a profession. Surely, there might be a stately man like Aaron, or a prophetess like Miriam waiting for their arrival. And yet, God chose a poor harlot to bring forth His mighty word, even as the apostle Paul says that "God hath chosen the foolish things of the world to confound the wise" (1 Corinthians 1:27). Here we see that the only qualification necessary to be used by God is to possess the faith of God. Rahab had neither social status nor religious standing, and yet through her came the prophetic oracle that would inspire the Israelite nation to victory.

Now, Rahab was not only concerned for her own safety, but also the safety of her family. She might have arranged for the Israelites to simply come for her, but she had a burst of courage to ask for the salvation of her entire household. The result of her heroism, not only to help the Israelite spies but also to ensure her family's safety, was a direct result of faith. God's faith produces supernatural courage within us to do what we normally would not do in a given situation. We see this truth demonstrated through the human body's production of adrenaline, which is released during stressful situations. The brain signals the adrenal glands to produce adrenaline which increases the rate that the heart beats. In turn, the increased rate of the heart produces more oxygen for the muscles, putting the body in a heightened state to react. The longer the body produces adrenaline, the more energy the body releases. The brain signaling for the producing of adrenaline is like the word of God being spoken to a man or woman.

Once that word is spoken, the adrenaline of faith is released into the heart, causing a greater flow of supernatural energy to come forth. The result of this "spiritual adrenaline" is that we become capable of reacting to situations with heightened spiritual energy. Rahab had the adrenaline of faith pumping through her heart as she not only delivered the prophetic word to God's men, but confirmed the safety of her loved ones.

The two spies agreed to deal kindly with her and her house, under the condition that she, along with her entire family, stay in the house – the Israelite army was bound to destroy all who ventured into the streets. The sign that would cause the Israelites to know her home apart from all others was a scarlet thread that was to be attached to the window. The color of this thread can be seen in the Tabernacle of Moses, on the priestly garments of the Levites, and ultimately symbolic of the blood of Jesus Christ on the Cross. The color scarlet is a biblical symbol representing a sacrifice made by someone on the behalf of another. The window which was opened to allow the men of God to escape would be the same window upon which the sign would be posted, leading to Rahab and her family's escape. By this, we see that Rahab's sacrifice for the safety of the spies was reciprocated in her own time of need. This is prophetic imagery that details the symbiotic nature of our actions, when done in faith. If we are moved by faith to do something for someone else, we are not only helping them, we are helping ourselves in the same way. If Rahab forgot to tie the scarlet thread to the window, she and her family would have likely been killed. But as the Scripture has said, "faith without works is dead," we know that a living faith will always produce actions that demonstrate what we believe.

*"And Joshua saved Rahab the harlot alive, and her father's household, and all that she had; and she dwelleth in Israel even unto this day; because she hid the messengers, which Joshua sent to spy out Jericho." – Joshua 6:25*

When Rahab harbored the two spies, protected their whereabouts, gave them safe passage, and made sure that they would have little trouble getting out safely, she was not only helping them but the whole nation of Israel. Joshua, the captain of God's soldiers, was the ambassador of God representing the divine will of the Lord for His people. As such, he sowed into her what she had sowed into the nation of Israel – life. Not only was there a safe passage out of the city of Jericho, but a *new* city and nation were opened to Rahab and her family. She was literally translated from one kingdom into another, in the same way that the man or woman who has faith in Christ is translated from the kingdom of darkness into the kingdom of light. Rahab's experience teaches us that by faith, we are translated from one reality into another. Not only did she leave her old nation, but she left her old lifestyle of prostitution as well.

Perhaps the most profound event in Rahab's life after her transition was when she married the Israelite, Salmon (see Matthew 1:5). This man's name means "garment,"[1] which gives us a wonderful prophetic picture of God's love for sinners, removing their nakedness and shame with the robe of righteousness. As quoted earlier, Rahab was as all who are without Christ, "aliens of the commonwealth of Israel, and strangers from the coveants of promise, having no hope, and without God in the world." The rightouessness of God made us legal in His kingdom, even as the marriage between the Israelite Salmon and his wife Rahab, gave her legal rights to the protection and provision within the nation of Israel. She was "covered" by her husband's Israelite heritage, because she had faith in the God of the Israelites. Romans 4:7 describes this blessed state that Rahab had entered: "Blessed are they whose iniquities are forgiven, and whose sins are covered." From her union with Salmon, one of the most remarkable yet little emphasized events occured in all of scripture – Rahab gave birth to Boaz, who became the great grandfather of David. We know that it is from the lineage of David that the Messiah was born. Because of one act of faith, Rahab the harlot, who was hours away from being executed along with her entire city, was not only saved from the ensuing conquest, but was grafted into the most powerful people group on the earth through her marriage with one of its citizens. Furthermore, she gave birth to a son, through whose lineage the Christ would be born. Rahab's account is truly one of the most remarkable stories of transformation in the Bible.

The name *Rahab* literally means "broad" or "wide."[2] Although her beginnings were small and obscure, by faith she was translated into a broad inheritance which culminated in the birth of Christ. How could a woman from the basest of professions, who had no inheritance with the Israelites, find salvation from death along with her entire family? What made it possible for her to live among the most blessed nation on earth and become part of the Messiah's ancestry? In a word: faith. By faith, God takes utter outcasts and changes their destiny from a narrow and empty existence, to a *broad* and *wide* place filled with the blessings and joys of divine approval. Rahab the harlot won divine approval through the recognition of God's word upon God's people, which was revealed to her through the eyes of faith.

# CHAPTER ELEVEN

# BARAK

*"And Deborah said unto Barak, Up; for this is the day in which the LORD hath delivered Sisera into thine hand: is not the LORD gone out before thee?" - Judges 4:14*

After the long-awaited arrival of the Israelites into the Promised Land, they entered into the time of the Judges, a series of God-appointed men and women who judged the nation in order to see righteousness established. After the passing of each righteous judge's administration, there was a predictable backsliding on Israel's part. Upon reading the accounts of the Judges, one may become mystified with the Israelite nation's behavior, as we find a consistent pattern of faithfulness and blessing followed by unfaithfulness and calamity. It was in one of Israel's moral declines that a little-known general would arise, and lead the Israelites to yet another victory over their oppressors. The reason for the oppression was the deep-seated root of rebellion found in the hearts of the Israelites. This rebellion always led to a national cry of repentance, which was answered by the raising up of a judge and the sending forth of a deliverer.

Israel just had a series of heroic deliverances by two famous men, Ehud who slew 10,000 Moabites, and Shamgar who slew 600 Philistines. It is no wonder the nations of the earth feared Israel, for they were a supernatural force to be reckoned with. No nation could stand against the children of Israel when they were in righteous standing with God. One man could rout hundreds, while 10 men could tear down ancient demon strongholds. God was on Israel's side. And so, it is possible to conclude that Israel's worst enemy would ultimately be *Israel* themselves. In times of widespread sin, God allowed the enemies of this chosen people to overcome them. This was the divine strategy to cause Israel to see Her need for God. Once in the grips of some foreign army, they would begin to cry out for the God of Abraham to deliver them. In response, the Lord would send His word through a man or woman in order to remind them of His covenant, and then He would bring the nation through a supernatural deliverance. When they were brought back into right standing with the Lord, the Israelites were placed back under the government of God, where the word of God was meant to govern them. We know that God's word not only brings governmental order, but it also releases faith which provides divine vision for a nation. When people lose regard for God's word, they lose the vision of God for their lives. Proverbs 29:18 declares that "where there is no vision, the people perish." The word "perish" here is the Hebrew word *para* which means "to cast off restraint."[1] In other words, when a nation has no regard for God's word, revelation of God's destiny for them will be clouded; consequently, their restraint toward evil will diminish to the point that they are easily enticed and corrupted by false gods. As far as the Israelites were concerned, they needed continual reminders that only

199

with God's revelation could they succeed as a nation and stay free from oppression. After the deliverance brought by Ehud and Shamgar, Israel needed yet another reminder.

Barak was the son of Abinoam from Kadeshnaphtali, a region that was allotted to the tribe of Naphtali. Although we don't know much about his upbringing, we know that for at least 20 years he and his people lived under the mighty regime of Jabin, the Canaanite king, and Sisera his captain. Nine hundred chariots of iron and a multitude of evil oppressors were a constant threat to the Israelites, and so they cried to the Lord for deliverance. In answer to their cry, Barak was called for a special assignment. His calling would come through the prophet of the Lord and current judge of Israel - a mighty woman in her own right named Deborah. We must see the significance of this woman's life before we look at the details of Barak's calling and his faith in God's word.

Deborah dwelt with her husband under the Tree of Deborah between Ramah and Bethel in the mountain of Ephraim. The Tree of Deborah under which the prophetess lived was most likely close to the oak tree described in the book of Genesis. In the thirty-fifth chapter of Genesis, we read of a tree under which the family nurse of Jacob and Rebecca was buried. This nurse was dearly loved by Jacob and his family. When she had died, they buried her beneath an oak tree which they called *Allonbachuh*, meaning "oak of weeping."[2] Their weeping indicated her familial value to them as not only a nurse but as a mother figure in this family. The site of this tree was in the valley beneath Bethel. It is therefore likely that the prophetess Deborah lived in close proximity. The significance of this is that Deborah was to Israel as Rebekkah's nurse was to Jacob's family. We could say that Deborah represented one who carried spiritual medicine to the nation, nursing them to health in a time of spiritual sickness. Deborah is also depicted as a "mother in Israel" in the prophetic song that she and Barak would sing after the great battle with Sisera (Judges 5:7). As a spiritual mother, she had a passion to see the children of Israel governed by righteousness.

Now, Deborah's prophetic office held this important charge: she was to not only speak God's word but become a living embodiment of that word. It is true that all prophets are *physical representatives* of God's word, not only speaking forth the counsels of God, but representing His will through their actions. Where the prophet goes, the word of God goes too. We see this in the prophet Ezekiel, who was commanded to lie on his left side for three hundred and ninety days to represent each year that Israel was living in iniquity (see Ezekiel 4). Similarly, we see the prophet Isaiah walking naked and barefoot for three years as a sign against Egypt and Ethiopia, indicating that they would be stripped of their dignity by a conquering nation (see Isaiah 20). In the New Testament we are told that the prophet Agabus "signified that there should be a great dearth in all the world" (see Acts 11:28). The word "signify" in the Greek denotes the "giving of a sign." We see this same word used in Revelation 1:1, where the angel of the Lord was sent to John, in order to "signify" through descriptive visions, events in the future. Lastly, we know that the prophet Agabus took Paul's belt, bound his hands and feet with it, in order to demonstrate what would happen if he went into Jerusalem (see Acts

21:11). It significant therefore that we see the carrier of God's word as not merely a mouthpiece, but rather a *living representation* of God's living word.

It was unto the mountain of Ephraim that the Israelites came to be judged by God through Deborah's word. The judgment they were seeking was one of favor – that they could obtain supernatural relief from the oppressive Canaanite enemy. Prompted by the Spirit of God, Deborah responded to their cries and called for a deliverer.

*"And she sent and called Barak the son of Abinoam out of Kedeshnaphtali..." Judges 4:6*

Deborah made her way to Kedeshnaphtali to seek out a man of Naphtali named Barak. The Hebrew name "Barak" means "lightning flash."[3] Indeed, his calling would come much like a *flash of lightning*, giving him little time to reason or to question, for the prophetess had come – the Word had arrived. Even more than this, Barak was called *to be* a "lightning flash" of God. The first place in Scripture the word "lightning" is used is in 2 Samuel 22:15: "And he sent out arrows, and scattered them; *lightning*, and discomfited them." The first place the plural, "lightnings" is used is Exodus 19:16: "And it came to pass on the third day in the morning, that there were thunders and *lightnings*, and a thick cloud upon the mount, and the voice of the trumpet exceeding loud; so that all the people that was in the camp trembled." We know from Revelation 4:5 that "out of the throne proceeded *lightnings* and thunderings and voices: and there were seven lamps of fire burning before the throne, which are the seven Spirits of God." It is apparent from these verses that lightning is vitally connected to the

Person of God. Scientifically, we know that lightning is a massive electrostatic discharge between electrically charged regions within clouds, or between a cloud and the earth's surface. When there is a great enough difference between the static charge in a cloud and that of its surroundings it will discharge a lightning bolt. We may personally experience this phenomenon when we rub our feet on a dry carpet. The friction that results causes our feet to pick up electrons. When we then touch a piece of uncharged metal, the electrons jump to the metal and we feel a shock. Spiritually speaking, the Lord builds His supernatural charge within us most acutely when we experience our greatest conflict with our surroundings. At the point when the conflict reaches its climax, there is a discharge of God's supernatural lightning which is designed to literally "shock" our opposition.

Although lightning does not make a sound, right after a strike, there is an audible thunder that can be heard by all. Thunder is actually a *response* generated from the lightning bolt that is released. We know that any sound which can be heard is made up of vibrations, and those vibrations travel through the air as waves until they reach our ears. This means that lightning must cause some vibrations. When lightning strikes, huge amounts of electricity shoot through the air causing two things to happen; the first is that the electricity passes through the air and starts to vibrate; the second is that the lightning heats up the air around it. Since hot air expands and therefore pushes apart the air particles, the vibrations begin to make a sound – we call this *thunder*. And so, we see that God's word literally supercharges the individual that He has called. Secondly, that spiritual charge becomes so great, that it conflicts with everything in the natural realm until

203

finally there is a discharge of that supernatural power into the atmosphere. The result is that a thunderous demonstration is experienced by all those around. Poignant examples of this are found all throughout the book of Acts. We know that the early Church was birthed into a time in history when there was great opposition, not only from the secular governments of the day, but from the religious sector of society. With each bold conflict came an even bolder display of God's power through His supercharged people. In the midst of Israel's static condition of bondage, Barak would be called to demonstrate the lightnings of God's supernatural deliverance.

*"Go and draw toward mount Tabor, and take with thee ten thousand men of the children of Naphtali and of the children of Zebulun. And I will draw unto thee to the river Kishon Sisera, the captain of Jabin's army, with his chariots and his multitude; and I will deliver him into thine hand." - Judges 4:6-7*

The tribe of Naphtali were warriors, always ready for battle along with their brother tribe of Zebulun. Deborah's word directed them to the winding river of Kishon where the armies of the enemy were. Barak brought his men to the captain of Jabin's army, who led a multitude of soldiers with 900 iron chariots at the helm. Chariots were a specialty of the Canaanites which were symbolic of glory, dominance, and war. They were a means of intimidation to those they meant to conquer. In spite of this great enemy along with all their weapons of war, God said through His prophetess "I will deliver him into thine hand." God expresses supreme confidence without the slightest bit of concern over the size or capability of the enemy. One of the greatest mistakes we can make in our own journey is to see our circumstances *differently* than God sees them. Only through the lens of faith will we see each circumstance correctly. A correct vision will always produce the same confidence in us that was in God when He spoke the initial word. When God said to the Israelites that He would deliver the enemy into their hands, His word was based upon His supreme knowing about Israel's future. In other words, *victory over the Canaanites was God's preordained future for Israel.* When God says that He will do something in an area of our lives, He is saying it already knowing what will take place in the future. Faith is the lens by which we see into God's prepared future for us. If we have received a specific word, it does not matter how large the opposition is to that word – we may be supremely confident in the face of our enemy. Let us remember that David's enemy was a physical giant, Samson's was a thousand Philistine soldiers, Moses' was an evil emperor and his hierarchy of demonized sorcerers, and Paul's was the "beasts" he fought at Ephesus. All of them overcame their enemies, as will we, when we see our future as God sees it.

*"If thou wilt go with me, then I will go: but if thou wilt not go with me, then I will not go." – Judges 4:8*

It is likely that Barak had some military experience before this military conflict, as the Bible does not record him questioning his own ability to lead an army of Israelites. However, he expresses a fascinating reliance upon the prophetess Deborah. We know that women did not fight in Israel's army and therefore were not warriors. Neither did women typically provide military strategy for the men who went to war. Barak placed such a demand upon Deborah's presence as a direct result of recognizing *who* she represented: *she was the embodiment of the word of God.* We are introduced to a great truth here, that regardless of our past experiences, as well as our natural talents and strengths, when we are called out by God for a specific mission, we can depend on none of those things to produce the godly outcome in our lives. Barak realized that the word of God not only gave him faith, but also the supernatural equipment to reach his destiny. He recognized more than just a Hebrew woman standing before him – he saw the word of God which was his greatest ally. He equated the prophetic word spoken to him in Judges 4:6-7 with the prophetic vessel, seeing the two as one, and his victory dependent upon both being present with him in battle. Barak teaches us that the value we place on God's word is the same we are to place on the vessel giving that word. In other words, the manifestation of victory in our lives is dependent upon the clear word of God which comes through the person whom God has chosen to deliver that word. Although flesh can do nothing for us in times of supernatural need, the power of God's word will have the same impact coming through a person as it would through the Lord Himself.

In the Hebrew language, the name *Deborah* means "bee."[4] A bee is a winged insect that flies around to various flowers and plants in order to pollinate them. Pollination occurs when the bee transmits the pollen – microscopic grains discharged from the male part of one flower – into another plant, and thereby causing that plant to reproduce. In the same way, the word of God comes and "pollinates" those who receive it. Barak was like a plant who received the spiritual pollination of God's word through the prophetess, which would cause him to be fruitful in his calling.

And so, Deborah consented to go with Barak, but not before telling him a divine secret:

*"I will surely go with thee: notwithstanding the journey that thou takest shall not be for thine honour; for the LORD shall sell Sisera into the hand of a woman. And Deborah arose, and went with Barak to Kedesh." 4:9*

There were three things made absolutely clear at the outset of this mission: the first was that Barak would defeat his enemy (Judges 4:6-7); the second is that it would be a woman who would kill Sisera; the third was that the Lord would receive the credit for the victory, for it was He who was responsible for the battle strategy and the victory. Any boasting at the outcome of a conflict is eliminated when we realize that God's word is responsible for calling us, equipping us, and producing the victory through us. The truth is that Barak's "role" in his own calling was more passive than he may have realized – his own human efforts were not necessary for victory.

A detailed study of the Bible suggests that it was God's original intention that mankind would live without the consciousness of his own efforts. The very fact that we delineate between God's effort and our own reveals our belief that *ability* has two different sources – one is of divine origin and the other is of human origin. However man was never intended to see his effort as generated separately from His Creator. The idea that man's efforts were

207

somehow separate from God's was not conceived of until after the Fall. Even though God created Adam to live and work on the earth, the *source* of his livelihood and the *source* of his work were both found in God. Now, although Adam was created without any physical limitations, we know that after the Fall his abilities became limited as his body received the blow of corruption, thereby limiting what he could do. That man's abilities became limited implies that he was no longer operating in the limitless power of God, but was living off of the half-life of an *unbelieving consciousness*. Adam *thought* he was separate from God, as demonstrated when he tried to hide from the Lord in the Garden; this foolish act was a manifestation of the false belief that he had become independent from God's nature. Therefore it was after the Fall that the effectiveness or ineffectiveness of man's efforts became the focus of his successes or failures in life. If he was not able to physically accomplish something, he would either try harder or simply come short of experiencing blessing in that area. Some men would see themselves as more successful than others, and therefore pride became a factor in their lives. Since pride is amplified through what man thinks he is able to accomplish, he would become continually conscious of his own efforts as the means by which he obtained those accomplishments. This self-consciousness inhibited man from seeing his very existence as tied to the existence of God, and his abilities as solely made possible by the power of God. Man now thrived on what he could achieve in his limited state of unbelief. The only way God could eliminate that kind of pride was to eliminate the false idea that man's limited effort was the means by which he lived. If the idea of self-effort is eliminated, then man will never accredit his accomplishments to his own abilities; rather, he will see his livelihood

208

as inextricably connected to the life of God. Furthermore, when he is no longer basing his livelihood upon his limited efforts, the unlimited ability of God becomes his only reality and therefore is manifested in his life.

The apostle Paul so elegantly described this blessed state of unlimited ability in Galatians 2:20: "I am crucified with Christ: nevertheless I live; yet not I, but Christ liveth in me: and the life which I now live in the flesh I live by the faith of the Son of God, who loved me, and gave himself for me." It was in Christ's crucifixion that man's unbelieving, false self was crucified, thereby reinstating God's limitless life into the consciousness of mankind. By faith, Christ's life and effort becomes man's life and effort. In Paul's discourse with the unbelieving intelligentsia of Athens, he states, "...in him *we* live, and move, and have *our* being; as certain also of your own poets have said, For *we* are also his offspring" (Acts 17:28, emphasis mine). Notice here that Paul is including unbelievers into this revelation. Paul is affirming to them that they are alive, able to work, and are living beings, all due to the divine life God has given them. Paul's words were designed to inspire faith in these unbelievers so that they could see themselves as no longer independent, but completely dependent upon the eternal life of God.

When we go back to the very beginning of man's creation, we gain this insight in Genesis 2:7: "And the LORD God formed man of the dust of the ground, and breathed into his nostrils the breath of life; and man became a living soul." By this we know that man was created, vitally connected to the life-breath of God. And then we read in

Genesis 2:8 that "...the LORD God planted a garden eastward in Eden; and there he put the man whom he had formed." Not only did God breathe His life into Adam, but the very environment which God placed him in was created by God as well. It is apparent from these scriptures that Adam's very life, his ability to work, and the environment in which the work took place were all sourced and supplied in God. When the Last Adam came – Jesus Christ – we find Him continually making the claim that He and His Father are inseparable. In John 5:30 Jesus declares "I can of mine own self do nothing." He then turns around and tells his disciples, "...for without me ye can do nothing" (John 15:5). The Lord goes on to say in John 3:27 that "... a man can receive nothing, except it be given him from heaven." Jesus was the manifestation of the creation as well as of the Creator, and demonstrated the vital union between the two. The result was that He reconciled the creation back to the Creator through His perfect obedience to the Father. When we compare the vital unity between the first Adam and his Creator along with the Last Adam and His Father, we see that mankind has always been vitally connected with God. *Unbelief is therefore the greatest sin that man has ever known* – to disbelieve the truth that we are not only made in God's image and likeness, but have our very existence in Him. Any belief that says we are not in perfect union with our Creator gives birth to the lie of an independent self-existence. We must see that *faith in God's life working through us* is the means by which we live the God-kind of life and not through our own limited attempts at doing this or that. By faith, mountains are moved, sickness is healed, the dead are raised, the life of God is experienced, and our lives become pleasing to the Lord.

210

At Deborah's word, Barak left immediately with her and called ten thousand warriors from two tribes in the city of Kedesh. The Hebrew translation of "Kadesh" is "holy place."[5] Walking with the word of God in the person of Deborah, Barak summoned an army that would be known for its holiness. The word "holy" implies being *separate* or *different*. Their difference was not only found in their natural skill on the battle field, but in the place they lived which indicated God's distinct grace on them for warfare. These two tribes were called upon by a commander who would lead them with wisdom far greater than his own – he was being supernaturally supplied and guided by the word of God. Since these warriors were following Barak, who was in turn following the word of the Lord, they would see themselves as an integral part of Israel's destiny, being the instruments divinely used to bring about the prophesied victory. It is significant that the faith which Barak was given to become Israel's military leader, created an opportunity for ten thousand men to fulfill their destiny in becoming heroes in Israel's military history. In other words, Barak's calling made room for thousands of other men's destinies to be fulfilled. It is true that our own calling and destiny will have an impact on countless others as we go forth and journey toward our prophetic promises.

*"And Deborah said unto Barak, Up; for this is the day in which the LORD hath delivered Sisera into thine hand: is not the LORD gone out before thee? So Barak went down from mount Tabor, and ten thousand men after him." - Judges 4:14*

The above verse reveals that Barak was on a specific time table for the events of his destiny to transpire. The time for him to fulfill his destiny would be revealed at the precise time indicated by the prophetess Deborah. This is significant, as we see that the set time for Barak's destiny to unfold was not based upon how many warriors he possessed, how many resources he had, nor how brilliant in warfare that he might have been. The only factor that determined the time of his destiny was the word of God. Not only did Deborah initially call Barak for the mission, but she was there to signify the exact time that the mission was to transpire. That Deborah was there at the beginning as well as at the end of his preparation reveals to us how significant God's word is in revealing the time of our destiny. When we consider what God has said about our purpose in life, we will be tempted to look at our experiences as well as our resources in order to determine when we will be ready to fulfill that purpose. This is a mistake that can lead to premature work which usually ends up aborted. It is only through the word of God that we can know the timing of our destiny. The prophet Habakkuk declares that "...the vision is yet for an appointed time, but at the end it shall *speak*" (2:3, emphasis mine). This verse does not tell us *how* the vision will speak, but simply that it *will* speak. In Barak's case, the vision of God contained in the initial word he received *spoke to him* through the mouth of the prophetess. Her words were "Up; for this is the day..."

It was the Lord who spoke the word which called Barak to champion his people. It was the Lord who spoke the word which defined Barak's mission. It was the Lord who spoke the word signifying the specific time to go forth and fulfill that word. And now,

212

the Lord would sovereignly "discomfort" Sisera, the enemy captain, at the sight of his own men being hewn apart before his eyes by the Israelites. Like Barak, we may trust God to choreograph every detail of our lives, as He is the master of time and movement within our journey.

*"And the LORD discomfited Sisera, and all his chariots, and all his host, with the edge of the sword before Barak; so that Sisera lighted down off his chariot, and fled away on his feet. But Barak pursued after the chariots, and after the host, unto Harosheth of the Gentiles: and all the host of Sisera fell upon the edge of the sword; and there was not a man left." – Judges 4:15*

For the Israelite nation, this victory would have been exhilarating. They witnessed the might of men wielding steel and metal, the bloodshed and tears spilt from hours of militant combat, and the echoing cries of defeat as well as of victory. Still, they were only seeing the very tip of the iceberg. What they could not see beneath the surface of their liberation was the very catalyst for such a glorious outcome – the faith of God which resounded in the heart of their general. In a lightning-flash of a moment, Barak was commissioned by the word of the prophetess, and in that moment he was supernaturally charged by the power of what that heavenly word revealed. The immediate effect of Barak's faith was a glorious discharge of wisdom on the battle field as he and the Israelite army wrought a great victory over the Canaanites. The lasting impact of just one moment of faith brought an even greater reality for Israel: they would experience forty years of peace. Barak's life teaches us that in a moment of time we

213

may be called upon as vessels through which the lightnings and thunderings of heaven are released into the earth. If the Lord has called us, we need not worry about how long or how short the time of preparation is before we are released into that calling; through the divine endowment of faith, we will step into our destiny at exactly the right time.

# CHAPTER TWELVE

# GIDEON

*"Thus was Midian subdued before the children of Israel, so that they lifted up their heads no more. And the country was in quietness forty years in the days of Gideon." - Judges 8:28*

After General Barak and Prophetess Deborah's victory over the Caananites, Israel enjoyed 40 years of rest from enemies. But alas, rebellion took root once again in the people's hearts. As we read Scripture, it is apparent that the enemies of God are attracted to the sin of rebellion. Like flies to a rotting corpse, the sin of man creates the foul odor of rotting flesh which attracts great evil. In this case, Israel's rebellion invited an open invasion and conquest of their land and people by the Midianites, who were descendants of Midian. The name "Midian" aptly means "strife."[1] This conquest caused immense strife in the hearts of the Israelites, so much so that they hid in dens and caves for the constant fear of their oppressors. Along with the Midianites were the Amalekites who also destroyed the increase of the Israelites' crops. Yet, in the midst of this seven year period of bondage, God would do another miracle, requiring another deliverer.

One of the young men hiding from this invasion was from a poor family of the tribe of Manasseh. The first time we encounter him, he is in Ophrah by the wine press. If there was ever a time to be drinking from the wine vats it was now! However, he was not drunk with wine, but was threshing the wheat in order to hide it from the Midianites. His name was Gideon, which means "hewer" in Hebrew. It was in this time that the Angel of the Lord appeared to him with this salutation:

*"The Lord is with thee, thou mighty man of valour." – Judges 6:12*

The first thing that is spoken to Gideon is a direct affirmation of not only who he was, but an indication of the kind of destiny that was in store for him. From this, we must always remember to take note of what God says concerning our lives. The declarations of the Lord are capable of defining who we are and what we are called to do. Each word is meant to not only inform us of our calling, but also begin the time of equipment and empowerment so that we are not able to be subverted by the enemies of our destiny. Gideon learned his first lesson in faith as he encountered the word of God; when God speaks to a person, He is not merely speaking to who they are in the present moment, but who they are destined to become in the future.

Many have depicted Gideon as a coward who was just hiding from the enemy, too scared to do anything. What the Bible says, however, is a different matter. In fact, before we are introduced to Gideon, we read that all of Israel was oppressed and had made homes for themselves in caves and dens in the mountains. Gideon was

217

actually out on a covert mission, risking his life to hide the increase of wheat which had been a target of the Midianites and Amalakites. This was an act of valour. What Gideon did not realize was that, although in seed form, his valour would be used mightily by the Lord for the deliverance of a nation.

*"And Gideon said unto him, Oh my Lord, if the LORD be with us, why then is all this befallen us? and where be all his miracles which our fathers told us of, saying, Did not the LORD bring us up from Egypt? but now the LORD hath forsaken us, and delivered us into the hands of the Midianites." – Judges 6:13*

Now, we must not miss the connection between verse twelve and verse thirteen. When the Angel of the Lord showed up, He mentioned nothing of Himself, nothing of the nation of Israel, nothing of the enemy, but simply appeared with a bold declaration about Gideon. The young man responded, not with "Why, thank you!" but replied, *"if the LORD be with us,* why then is all this befallen us?" There were two important points that Gideon brought up with his response: first, he recognized that this Visitor was the Lord Himself, as he addressed Him "Oh my Lord," and second, he took this appearance as a sign that the Lord might still be with Israel, even in their backslidden condition. Gideon was right. One of the signs of Jehovah's covenant with Israel was that the Angel of the Lord "encampeth around about them, He delivereth them" (Psalm 34:7). Gideon came to the startling recognition through this heavenly encounter that Jehovah had not abandoned the Israelites – a perception that was probably common during Israel's captivity. The challenge that this young man had was reconciling two opposing ideas, Israel's oppression brought about by their own sin, with the fact that God was still with them. There will undoubtedly be times when we can empathize with Gideon, feeling as though our present situation is the result of something we did wrong, and therefore we must suffer through it without hope of redemption. It is during these times that the Lord often appears to us, to reveal our true identity in the midst of the suffering, and the great plans He has prepared for us.

Although jaded, yet certainly amazed at this visitation, Gideon receives the Word of the Lord:

*"...Go in this thy might, and thou shalt save Israel from the hand of the Midianites: have not I sent thee? And he (Gideon) said unto him, Oh my Lord, wherewith shall I save Israel? behold, my family is poor in Manasseh, and I am the least in my father's house." – Judges 6:14*

Gideon's response to this great commission is not unlike our own when God calls us to do something great. We immediately look at our natural life and try to judge God's word based upon our own abilities – strengths and weaknesses. This kind of thinking would only be legitimate if God did not supernaturally empower us; for God's calling is impossible without the supernatural equipment provided by His Spirit. When looking at Gideon's family, one can see from a human standpoint the legitimacy of his concern about the Lord's choosing. He was the son of Joash the Abiezrite, who were descendants of Joseph's son Manasseh. Gideon describes his family as "poor in Manasseh," and himself as "the least" of his father's house, which most likely meant that he was the youngest. The youngest sibling in Hebrew times was seen as the most insignificant of the family. Furthermore, sibling rivalry has been an age old part of the curse incurred at the Fall of mankind, and especially seen with Adam and Eve's first and second born. The elder has tended to persecute the younger (i.e. Cain and Abel, Eliab and David). Gideon most likely dealt with age-related prejudices as well.

Surrounded by enemies, from a poor family, and the youngest and most insignificant of his siblings, Gideon had every human right to doubt the statement of the Lord that afternoon. The Lord compounds the absurdity of this calling, by telling him to go forth in *his* (Gideon's) might and that *he* (Gideon) shall save Israel! Gideon must have thought, "How can I, a man of low rank, save this great nation that was birthed by signs, wonders, miracles and by a Divine hand?" He would soon learn that there was a greater power at work in God's calling than social status, genetics, and hereditary titles. This answer followed from the Lord:

*"And the Lord said unto him, Surely **I will be with thee**, and thou shalt smite the Midianites as one man." – Judges 6:16 (emphasis mine)*

Finally! Now, there seems to be some clarity in this calling! The Lord tells Gideon the missing ingredient to his success: the Lord will be with him. The Lord had spoken, and thus faith was beginning to stir in Gideon's heart, sharing the space with some lingering timidity. Fear will always compete with the word of God, until we are assured of God's character, especially that he cannot lie but rather will cause His word to manifest. Any lack of faith is rooted in a lack of revelation about the nature of God – who He is and therefore what He is able to do. He is all-powerful, all-knowing, and all-seeing; in a word, He is *almighty*. The more we know of His character the more we will be of quick faith, not wavering nor hesitating when He speaks. We will also be more aware of His voice, and therefore will not need signs to prove whether or not He has spoken. Like Job, Gideon had heard of the Lord by the hearing of his ears, but now, he had seen him. Still, he needed reassurance as long as his faith was weak. His dialogue with the Lord continued.


*"And he said unto him, If now I have found grace in thy sight, then shew me a sign that thou talkest with me." – Judges 6:17*


Gideon needed an outward sign to confirm this word because his faith was in a specific stage of development. The first word he received was concerning himself, the second concerning his mission. Now, he desired to see a sign to confirm the first two words, and to validate the One giving the words. We know that faith comes by hearing the word of God. However, it is possible to doubt what we hear as being from the Lord. We could belittle this man for a lack of faith, yet how many times do we need to hear the same word before we transition from unbelief to belief, from fear to confident expectation?

221

How many times do we question if the word we heard was even from God? How great is God's mercy toward us!

The Lord confirmed his word to Gideon upon an altar which Gideon erected – the flesh and unleavened cakes that Gideon placed upon the altar burst into flames. Upon seeing this, the fear of the Lord took hold of Gideon and he unequivocally believed that God had indeed visited him. The Lord revealed his mercy to Gideon, comforting him with these words: "Peace be unto thee; fear not: thou shalt not die." Whenever a significant happening took place in the lives of the patriarchs, they offered some form of sacrifice to God and named the place or the altar upon which the offering was given. Gideon named the alter which held of his offering "Jehovah Shalom," meaning "LORD is Peace."[2] "Shalom" literally means to be at peace, to be finished, to be completed, and signifies a sense of wholeness. In other words, Gideon learned an aspect of God that had been previously hidden from him – that Jehovah was the restorer of peace and wholeness to a nation that had been ravaged by enemies due to their own sin. Even under the Old Covenant, Jehovah had not ceased to express His desire to redeem His people.

Gideon was being recruited for a Special Forces type of mission; small in number, but swift and tactical. His first mission began as the Lord directed him to throw down the altar of Baal and cut down the groves that grew near it. The second part of the mission was to bring a young bullock and offer it upon an alter using the wood from the grove as kindling. In order for deliverance to take place, it was necessary to not only tear down the idols, but to shed the blood of an animal to atone for the sin of Israel. And so, Gideon obeyed immediately by forming a team of 10 men to accompany him; they would go at night to conceal their act. Once the morning had come, and the mission had been completed, the city was in an uproar over their fallen deity.

Obedience to the Lord will usually incur retaliation of some sort. Our friends may not understand why we are doing what we are doing, and so they might distance themselves from us. Our families may get upset because our actions may not fit into their expectations for our lives; consequently, they may remove their support from us. The world around us will surely be bewildered by the unearthly peace that we possess, even as they are sinking in a mire of crushing cares. We plow forward with a confidence they do not know, defiant to everything that would rob us of joy. As a result, we may be mocked for not being like them. The truth is, the Lord does not typically consult with us concerning the backlash that will occur as a result of our obedience. Like Gideon, when God gives the directive, we must obey without thought of the consequences. This is how a healthy faith operates, producing quickness to move, and a fullness of trust in the Lord's ability to shield us from whatever evil may come in direct proportion to that obedience.

Upon discovery that Gideon was the culprit of this deed, the city desired to kill him. But Gideon's father, moved with wisdom said, "If he (Baal) be a god, let him plead for himself." This seemed right in the minds of those who worshiped the idol, and instead of killing him, they gave Gideon a new name: 'Jerubbaal' – 'Let Baal Contend'.[3] Now, it was the same people that wanted to kill him that gave him this name. We find this occurring in scripture quite often – that God's chosen people were renamed with names that pointed to their prophetic destinies. Moses was given his name by Pharoah's daughter, Joseph was given the name "Zaphnathpaaneah" by Pharoah, Daniel was given the name Belteshazzar by Nebuchadnezzar, and Gideon was given his name by fellow countrymen. The significance of this is that the people around us, whether friend or foe, will often give us names unaware that the inspiration comes from God, and as such, prophesy through the names they give us. The name Gideon means "hewer."[4] Gideon began his journey as a hewer of wheat. His name change revealed that his true destiny was to hew down false Gods. Gideon went from hewing the wheat to hewing down the gods of the enemy.

Now, it is true that the people expected their idol to contend with Gideon, however, Gideon had already contended with Baal and won the battle. The apostle Jude reminds us to "earnestly *contend* for the faith which was once delivered unto the saints." In other words, we are to contend against anything that opposes faith in God. The outworking of our faith may be different from case to case, but real faith is militantly on the side of truth. The life of faith refuses to live in an atmosphere dominated by the lies of the enemy, especially when those lies are destroying the spiritual condition of a nation. Gideon contended against the evil in Israel because he believed that the truth which had been forgotten in the midst of oppression was actually the person of God. The result of Gideon's faith in action was that the Lord became manifestly stronger in the eyes of the people, instead of the false god of Baal. The effect that this one act of faith had for Israel was seen literally overnight. A massive overthrow of power occurred in the spiritual realm which had dominated the nation for years, and now the

224

deliverance of a nation was finally at hand. Just one day prior to the dethroning of the idols, the Israelites were militarily oppressed, Baal and Ashteroth were worshiped, no one had the courage to lead an army against the enemy, and no faith was manifesting in the land. All of this would change in a moment of time. A word was given, faith was released, and a national revival was sparked.

*"But the Spirit of the LORD came upon Gideon, and he blew a trumpet; and Abiezer was gathered after him. And he sent messengers throughout all Manasseh; who also was gathered after him: and he sent messengers unto Asher, and unto Zebulun, and unto Naphtali; and they came up to meet them" – Judges 6:34-5*

The Spirit of the Lord came upon him, and in a matter of seconds his family was gathered around him; in a matter of minutes the message went out unto the surrounding tribes, and in a matter of hours an army was put together. When the Spirit of the Lord moves upon us, less human effort will be necessary, and the resources for the success of God's word will be given. In fact, the time it takes for this equipping will be greatly reduced under God's anointing. All of a sudden, we have greater confidence and do not need confirmations of our own calling.

When the Spirit of the Lord came upon Gideon, he was prompted to blow the trumpet, gather his family, and seek the assistance of three tribes known for battle. The three tribes that surrounded Abiezer were Asher, Zebulun, and Nephtali. Asher means "happy" or "blessed"[4]; Zebulun means "exalted"[5], and Netphali means "wrestling."[6] The prophetic picture here is that when God commissions

225

you to do something, there *will* be a battle to fight. However, we should be encouraged and rejoice, for we are not wrestling on an earthly level, but from the exalted place with Jehovah.

*"And Gideon said unto God, If thou wilt save Israel by mine hand, as thou hast said, Behold, I will put a fleece of wool in the floor..."*
*Judges 6:36-37*

We already know from Judges 6:14 and 16 that the Lord called Gideon to deliver the nation of Israel. Yet, Gideon had come to a specific instance where he desired confirmation that this event was one for him to lead. It is normal for us to ask God something more than once. The apostle Paul asked the Lord three times to deliver him from his "thorn"; each time the Lord gave him the same reply, "My grace is sufficient for you." It is not wrong to ask God questions, as long as the motivation is a desire for clearer direction or purpose in a matter. God's first response to us may purposely be vague, not revealing every aspect of the answer. He does this simply so that we will continue to inquire. This continual inquiry on our part is a result of faith. He often reveals His will progressively, and it is not typical for Him to give every detail all at once. Gideon was not questioning whether or not God was for Israel, nor if God wanted Israel to defeat the enemy; he desired to know if he was the one to lead them into battle in this specific instance. When Gideon was first called, he had received the general word that he would be used to deliver the nation; yet he was on

226

the eve of a decisive military engagement that would require more specific information. In answer to his request for a sign, he received a wet piece of wool the next morning. After this, Gideon asked for another sign, this time that the wool would be dry while the earth around it wet. The total number of similar requests was three. What did the Lord do about these continual requests? He answered each one without rebuking Gideon.

When comparing Gideon with Zechariah, the old covenant priest in the Book of Luke, we see that they both received the word of the Lord, they both questioned the Lord, yet God dealt differently with them. Zechariah doubted the word, as he asked the angel this question, "Whereby shall I know this? For I am an old man, and my wife well stricken in years" (1:18). Immediately he was struck with muteness by the angel. Gideon was not a priest, nor did he come from a priestly ancestry. God's grace is revealed in that Zechariah ultimately received the promise of the Lord, as did Gideon. However the former received it as a mute, because being a priest who ministered in God's presence, his heart should not have been unbelieving. Gideon was young compared to Zechariah, and his faith was still developing. And so, God accommodated the timidity he had concerning this great calling by answering the request for 3 signs. Similarly, God will always accommodate us according to our spiritual maturity; however the more spiritually mature we become, the less we will need signs for confirmations.

It was early in the morning that this firebrand youth found himself at the head of 32,000 Israelites. The Midianites were on the north side of them in the valley by the hill of Moreh. It was on this hill that Abraham encamped when he first entered into Canaan. For Abraham, God revealed the future promise land in this place. For Gideon, there would also come a revelation of something God wanted him to see. The name 'Moreh" means "teacher."[7] Gideon was about to gain an education concerning the type of person that is most useful to the Lord.

*"And the LORD said unto Gideon, The people that are with thee are too many for me to give the Midianites into their hands, lest Israel vaunt themselves against me, saying, Mine own hand hath saved me."*
*– Judges 7:2*

Compared to Midian who possessed 135,000 men, Israel believed that they would have a fighting chance with 32,000 men, one fourth the amount of soldiers. The Lord knew that Israel would take the credit if they conquered the Midianites with their present numbers. God, wanting them to understand that He was the source of their victory, required them to reduce the number of their troops. This heavenly wisdom defied the conventional logic of warfare. We must understand that the logic of God is not found in the statistical odds of our situation, nor is it found based merely on natural laws: *God's logic is His word!* That divine word has the ability to define and redefine the outcome of any circumstance.

People of faith are not bound by conventional wisdom, as God will typically engineer their success based upon heavenly wisdom. This is why the believer should not live his or her life based upon statistics, but rather on the word that God has given them. The chances for a person to succeed in a particular area of life may be considerably lower, if that person comes from an impoverished and oppressed region of the world. If God has destined them to succeed, however, they will inevitably break that natural barrier of poverty and oppression until they have attained the success they were created for. Furthermore, when God gives His word to a person, that word ensures that the outcome will ultimately give Him the glory.

In keeping with Gideon's unconventional calling, including his special forces-like raid of Baal's temple, God took the army of Israelites into a special forces-like selection process that would determine not only who was capable of fighting, but those whose hearts were God-ward and given to praise Him for the outcome of the battle. The first phase of this process took place in Gilead, which required Gideon to weed out those who were fearful. The name "Gilead" means "rocky region." In the rocky terrain of testing, we will need to hold fast our faith in the word that was spoken to us. Scriptures such as Psalm 27:1 should encourage us when faced with the fear of man: "The Lord is my light and my salvation; whom shall I fear? The Lord is the strength of my life; of whom shall I be afraid?" God will often bring us many confirmations of our journey's mission, so that our faith is built up and assurance is available whenever the enemy comes with tactics that induce fear. This is why God confirmed His word three separate times to Gideon, so that there would be no fear to cause Gideon's faith to falter. This first test of Gideon's 32,000 was effective: 22,000 had fear in their hearts, and left straightaway from Gilead. The odds just went from one in four to one in thirteen!

For the second phase of the selection process, Gideon is ordered to take the remaining 10,000 down to the water for a test in soldierly behavior. One group lapped the water with their hands; the other group got down on all fours and put their face in the water. The former were chosen to go to war, the latter were sent home. What was the difference? The Bible isn't clear on this, but if these behaviors are analogies for soldierly behavior, the former would have been more prepared for an enemy coming to kill them, as they drank the water with their head *up* as opposed to *down*. We are reminded by the apostle Peter, that in our life of faith we are to "Be sober, be vigilant; because your adversary the devil, as a roaring lion, walketh about, seeking whom he may devour: whom resist steadfast in the faith" (1 Peter 5:8-9).

This second and final phase weeded out 970 Israelites, bringing the once formidable Israelite army from 32,000 men to 300. The odds went from one in four, to one in thirteen, and finally, to one in four hundred and fifty! The absurdity of the outcome would be the perfect opportunity for God to make possible through their faith in His ability, what would be otherwise a total impossibility in their own strength. Israel would learn through this victory that with God on their side, they were already a majority and an unbeatable force. Now they were ready.

*"So the people took victuals in their hand, and their trumpets: and he sent all the rest of Israel every man unto his tent, and retained those three hundred men: and the host of Midian was **beneath him** in the valley." – Judges 7:8 (emphasis mine)*

230

This is a prophetic picture of the life of faith. Our enemies are *beneath* us in the spiritual realm. The apostle Paul says that we are seated "Far above all principality, and power, and might, and dominion, and every name that is named, not only in this world, but also in that which is to come" (Ephesians 1:21). The reason that we are on the spiritual high ground is because Christ, our true identity, is Lord over everything that He has created. Faith simply recognizes that we are in Christ, and therefore we live vicariously above our enemies. In this way, we are living from a place of victory, rather than striving *toward* that victory. The apostle John writes that our victory is not in the wrestling or the striving against sin or evil, but is found *in* our faith (1 John5:4).

In a real spiritual sense, the life of faith lives in the future, beyond the conflict that faces us today. Since the outcome of faith is always victory, the challenges that await the believer have already been assessed by God, the ability has already been given to them, and the reward has already been secured for them. This is the beauty of faith. We do not need to strive for a victory if God has already said we are victorious. If God has spoken a word concerning our life in a particular area, than we know God will perform that word. If God says it, God will do it. Faith gives us that confidence – the supreme confidence of God – that this or that will work out in our favor, for it is God who does it in us, and for us. The person of faith has already touched the "finish line" in the sense that the substance and evidence of the outcome is already a reality.

*"And it came to pass the same night, that the LORD said unto him, Arise, get thee down unto the host; for I have delivered it into thine hand. But if thou fear to go down, go thou with Phurah thy servant down to the host." – Judges 7:9-10*

Phurah was Gideon's armor bearer and was called a support to Gideon in the event that he still had fear in his heart. The grace of God is such that, in light of all He has done to reveal Himself to us, He is still merciful toward us when we grow fearful and even unbelieving. When God looks at a man, He looks at the whole of man's life to determine success, not incidental moments of unbelief within man's heart. If the opposite were so, and God held us accountable every time we doubted His word, we would not only be disqualified from our calling, but God's plans would be circumvented by this inherent weakness in every man. However, the good news is that His word will not return to Him without accomplishing its purpose. Gideon received the word of the Lord, and that word would continue exuding faith so that he could fulfill his mission. To ensure this fulfillment, Phurah was called upon as a helper. The name 'Phurah' means "bough" and gives us a little insight into his ministry.[8] A bough is considered any of the larger branches which come out of a tree; in essence, the bough plays a supporting role for the main part which is the trunk. Praise God for those He sends our way to support the mission He's given us, and help encourage our faith when we are weak!

In addition to ensuring a helper for Gideon's assignment, the Lord created an opportunity to further encourage this young captain. As Gideon was making ready for battle, he overheard a man recounting

232

a dream to a fellow soldier. The man with the dream said that his dream was about Gideon. The man who listened, interpreted it, and said that the Lord of Hosts had delivered Midian into Gideon's hands. Gideon just happened to overhear the right conversation at the right time! The Lord divinely orchestrated this encounter to strengthen Gideon's faith. As we have seen, the Lord appeared in bodily form, supernaturally ignited an altar with fire, miraculously dampened a fleece, miraculously dried the same fleece, and orchestrated a conversation about a dream confirming an upcoming victory; surely, God does not tire nor run out of creativity in confirming the destiny of his chosen vessels!

With the zeal of a warrior burning inside the chest of this young captain, Gideon gathered the 300, divided them into 3 ranks, and equipped each of them with a trumpet, as well as an empty pitcher with a burning lamp inside, giving them these instructions:

*"When I blow with a trumpet, I and all that are with me, then blow ye the trumpets also on every side of all the camp, and say, The sword of the LORD, and of Gideon." - Judges 7:18*

We have already established that victories in our personal lives are dependent upon faith, and faith is dependent upon the word of God. Once the word is spoken, faith will begin to produce some kind of work that will facilitate that victory. After all, faith without works is no faith at all. That work will be uniquely designed for the situation that we are in. We must rely upon the Spirit's direction in each instance, as did Gideon in his creative approach to this battle. Nowhere in the Old Testament are we given a formula to blow a trumpet and chant in order

233

to win a victory over the enemy; the fact that Gideon was inspired to do this reveals the spontaneous and creative nature of God as manifested through faith.

The trumpet represented the proclamation of the Lord against the enemies of Israel. Trumpets are used throughout Scripture, symbolizing the word of the Lord for a person, a spiritual entity, or a nation. When we speak what God is saying in the midst of our circumstances, we are releasing a spiritual sound that invades the natural and spiritual realm, bringing devastation to the enemy that stands between us and our destiny. The empty pitcher was a symbol of the Midianites' physical presence in Israel, which would be broken by the power of God's word. The lamp within the pitchers contained a flame, which represented the spirits of the Midianites made bare, as their physical protection was destroyed. Proverbs 20:27 declares that "The spirit of man is the candle of the Lord." As the Israelites broke the pitchers, they shouted "The sword of the LORD and of Gideon!" The "sword" that is mentioned here is a reference to the word of God, as it is also mentioned as a piece of the believer's armor in Ephesians 6. But it was not just the word of God being declared, it was the Word of Gideon too. God's word became Gideon's word. And as Gideon faithfully obeyed God, his faith connected the Lord's original word to him with his destiny as Israel's deliverer. Gideon and his army of 300 were prophesying victory over their own future as a nation.

The enemy armies were not prepared for what would take place next. They were awoken suddenly out of sleep as they heard the triumphant sound of 300 trumpets surrounding them. Next they heard the breaking of the clay pitchers, and through the dim light of dawn, they saw the fiery lights emerge on the hilltop around them. With all the gusto of the most saintly soldiers, Israel shouted as "one man," thus fulfilling the prophecy in chapter six and verse sixteen.

*"And the three hundred blew the trumpets, and the LORD set every man's sword against his fellow, even throughout all the host: and the host fled..." – Judges 7:22*

Faith is like a dance in which one moves, and the other follows. Gideon moved in step with God's movement. With the help of Jehovah, Gideon and his men slew 120,000 men in a day. The Bible says that Gideon and his army of 300 were "faint, yet pursuing." When the mission has turned bloody, bodies are tired, minds are weary, faith becomes faint, we should glean from the example of Gideon's army who grew faint yet continued to pursue. Faintness is not a sign of failure, but that the manifested victory is near at hand. For there is no one faint in the beginning of a battle, only near the end.

One of the last great acts recorded about this iron clad captain named Gideon, is found in Judges 8:22-23 after Israel's victory over Midian was secured:

*"Then the men of Israel said unto Gideon, Rule thou over us, both thou, and thy son, and thy son's son also: for thou hast delivered us from the hand of Midian." – Judges 8:22*

Remember back to the special-forces selection process in Judges 7, where God weeded out those who would not give Him the glory for the victory. When the war has been won, and faith has brought us through the test, we will have the opportunity to attribute our success to the Lord for the outcome. Furthermore, in this time of success we may be approached by others who view our success as an opportunity to fulfill their own desires. Gideon faced this test at the head of the hosts of Israel who desired that he rule over them as a king. But Gideon understood the purpose of his mission, which was to deliver Israel from the enemy, not to rule over them – that was God's position to fill. With great poise and wisdom, young Gideon said to the multitude:

*"I will not rule over you, neither shall my son rule over you: the LORD shall rule over you." – Judges 8:23*

Gideon was most certainly a hero of faith, who defied all the odds. He defied the familial, social, political, and religious norms, being the youngest in his family, under the oppression of poverty, without any political voice, and believing in a forbidden Lord. And yet, despite the fear that emanated from his countrymen, he obeyed the call of God and delivered a nation from the grip of an overwhelming enemy. His faith brought deliverance to those in bondage, and also reinstated the truth that Jehovah was still God of Israel. In addition to these things, Gideon's faith brought 40 years of peace to his people. Truly, the writer of Hebrews had well written that Gideon, the son of Joash, hewer of the wheat, contender with Baal, and deliverer of Israel, led a life worth remembering in the chronicles of faith.

# CHAPTER THIRTEEN

---

# JEPHTHAH

*"Now Jephthah the Gileadite was a mighty man of valour, and he was the son of an harlot." - Judges 11:1*

Jephthah was a mighty man of war, considered to be a national hero, and known for delivering his countrymen from the threat of invasion. His destiny could be likened to his predecessors, Barak and Gideon, whose unique journeys were inspired by the dynamic power of God's word. Although the outcome of Jephthah's mission would be similar to these two national heroes, his journey would be quite different. Just as several mountain climbers might climb the same mountain to reach the top, and yet climb from completely different vantage points, there are many believers who are called to the same end, and yet will arrive at their destination having completely different experiences along the way. The truth is, no two callings are identical, because no two lives can experience that calling in the exact same way. It is by divine design that this difference exists, for the Lord desires to reveal a unique facet of Himself to each individual, which can only be discovered in the landscape of their own unique experiences. He does

238

this primarily so that all of humanity may see different sides of His manifold wisdom, intending for every person to express a creative glimmer of that wisdom within their respective callings. No matter how many similar endeavors have been undertaken throughout the centuries, every believer has had the opportunity to express God's eternal character in different ways, revealing aspects of that divine glory which were previously hidden. The revealing of God's wisdom occurs through our personal experience within each season of life, some of which are filled with great triumphs and others with fiery persecutions. Those experiences not only reveal to us highly unique aspects of the Lord, but act to supernaturally impress His divine characteristics upon us. This divine impress serves as God's signature upon those He has called to carry out His purposes throughout the earth. We see this demonstrated very clearly in the life of Jacob. Once he encountered the Angel of the Lord, his struggle with Him culminated in a dislocated hip; what followed was a physical limp, serving as the impress of the Lord's omnipotence upon his life, giving him his new identity while incapacitating the old. Jephthah's arrival at his destiny would also reveal the impress of God, testifying not only to the difficulty of rejection in the midst of his journey, but also the redemptive power of God to reveal his true identity – the deliverer of a troubled nation.

*"And Gilead's wife bare him sons; and his wife's sons grew up, and they thrust out Jephthah, and said unto him, Thou shalt not inherit in our father's house; for thou art the son of a strange woman." - Judges 11:2*

In Judges 11:1 we are told that Jephthah was a "mighty man of valour." In verse two, we are told that he was rejected by his brothers because he was the son of a prostitute. Jephthah's beginnings are reminiscent of Joseph's, who received the blow of rejection from his brothers as well. What is interesting is that Jephthah was a descendent of Manasseh, who was the son of Joseph; Jephthah was therefore dealing with the same prejudice from his brothers that his ancestor Joseph dealt with from his siblings. Now, we can infer from verse one that Jephthah proved his valor growing up, and likely had leadership capabilities as well as the reputation of a valiant fighter. Therefore it is possible that his brothers masked their real motive for forcing him out by pointing to his mother's illicit profession – they were jealous of him. Just like Joseph, who was pushed out of his family because of jealousy, Jephthah may have also been kicked out because of jealousy over his destiny. Through these events we see that the *value* of his identity had come under fire, not only in the estimation of his brothers, but his own. Verse one declares that he was a "mighty man of valor." However he was also a man greatly rejected. On the one hand, Jephthah had to know what he was capable of – he was skilled in the art of war and most likely felt fulfilled operating in a military capacity. On the other hand, he was keenly aware of the scandalous history of his mother. It may be said that *there was a battle over the identity of his life.* He was a heroic man, and yet his very existence was tarnished with the immoral reputation of his mother.

At this point, it is important that we understand the thought of God concerning Jephthah. The Lord *always* sees the true identity of an individual – the highest that they have been called to. Since all have

240

been made in the image and likeness of God, all have their true identity as His sons and daughters. It is the primary lie of the enemy to deceive redeemed humanity into thinking that they are less than perfect, less than the divine replicas of God they were created to be. Those who embrace this lie end up living as children of the devil because they do not realize that they are actually children of God. The Lord reveals the stunning truth to Jeremiah that "Before I formed thee in the belly I knew thee; and before thou camest forth out of the womb I sanctified thee, and I ordained thee a prophet unto the nations" (Jeremiah 1:5). This verse reveals two dynamic things to us, the first relating to the *person* of Jeremiah, the second to the *purpose* of Jeremiah. God knew Jeremiah before he was a physical entity. Furthermore, God's eternal knowing is not merely a knowledge that encompasses future events, but involves an intimate awareness of the people through whom these events will occur. That the Lord knew Jeremiah before he was born reveals that the Lord's personal knowledge of His creation is just as tangible before that creation is manifested in the earth. Next, the Lord reveals that the purpose for which Jeremiah was created – to be a prophet to Israel – was determined before he was born. In the same way, the Lord has predetermined our specific function in the earth before we were born. Therefore He may confidently prophesy concerning each person knowing that His word has the ability to define who they are and what they are called to do.

God saw Jephthah as he was created to be – a mighty man of valor and a deliverer of Israel. The problem with his brothers' perspective was that, like so many people today, they were only accessing what was apparent in the natural, physical world. They saw

241

only the facts of Jephthah's life as it related to his natural origins, not the eternal purpose to which he was called. God saw him in light of eternity, whereas his brothers saw him in light of temporal existence. Since it is God who both determines the person and their purpose, we know that only by accessing God's view of a person can we ascertain that individual's true identity. The controversies surrounding Jephthah's early life were actually trying to compete with the image that God had determined him to be. In the midst of whatever controversies that surround us, we can see an even greater reality emerge as we are made aware of God's eternal purpose for our lives. If not enlightened to who we are in Him, we will inevitably believe a lie about ourselves – the same lie that Adam and Eve believed, that they were *not* already like their Creator. We must see the eternal word of God as having the ability to *define* who we really are, therefore rendering all human perceptions about our identity void of power. We may be confident that regardless of the past, we will see the eternal value of our heavenly identity emerge out of the word God has spoken concerning us. It does not matter if the recipient of God's word is a prostitute, drug addict, or a person involved with one of the many religions in the world. All of those endeavors are *fig leaves* designed by man to cover the nakedness of his sinful humanity. Just like Adam and Eve tried to cover themselves with fig leaves after the Fall, humanity has been trying to hide beneath one of a million guises to take away the shame of their sinfulness. However, only God's word can release His faith so that those who are trying to cover themselves may see their true identity in Him. His word is our only reality. All other "realities" are false, mere fig leaves sown together to hide the image and likeness of God.

*"Then Jephthah fled from his brethren, and dwelt in the land of Tob:*
*and there were gathered vain men to Jephthah, and went out with*
*him." - Judges 11:3*

Rejected by his family, Jephthah fled to the land of Tob. The word "vain" in this verse is the Hebrew word "reyq" which means "empty, impoverished, or wicked."[1] The destitute of this land were looking for a leader, and they found one in Jephthah. Even though he was removed from his family, rejected because of his mother, and living in a foreign land, Jephthah could not stop doing what he was created to do – he was not able to hide his true identity. He may have been bitter, he may have also wanted revenge, but no amount of rejection could cover up the leader that he was called to be. In a strange land, we see the assembling of destitute souls around him. Similarly, when David was rejected by Saul and the kingdom of Israel, he joined sides with the Philistine army, the very people that were an enemy to the kingdom in which David was destined to rule! Compounding the irony of this season in David's life, he was able to acquire the sword used by Goliath while on the run. David's newly acquired weapon was the same one he used earlier to cut off Goliath's head! These unique situations may not fit neatly in our preconceived idea of what the man or woman of God should face on their journey; however, we must not adopt the idea that our lives are supposed to fit within the parameters of our cultural norms. Furthermore, we as the Church must be wary of scripting the journey of others based upon our perception of a successful Christian life, instead of God's preordained path for the individual believer. We must get used to the truth that there is no precedent for our individual journey. The reality is that our lives will be scripted based upon one of two plans – the Lord's or the world's. The world's plan does not require faith for the journey; it merely requires that we observe worldly ideas, whether they be from the culture or religious institutions. The Lord's plan, however, has a map that can only be followed by faith, transcending human ingenuity. Neither David nor Jephthah could have imagined while growing up in Israel, that a day would come when their own families would reject them, and they would be forced to inhabit a strange land where destitute people would gather to them. And yet, this *was* their journey. We may find ourselves in ironic situations, dealing with people we otherwise would not; nevertheless they may be an integral part of our pathway. In such cases, we must continue to hear what God is saying, that we may follow his lead and accomplish His purpose.

It is in this stage of Jephthah's life, surrounded by destitute people in the land of Tob, that we can see a vital revelation about God's nature. The Lord does not merely possess faith, He *is* faith. Speaking to his spiritual son, the apostle Paul says, "If we believe not, yet he abideth faithful: *he cannot deny himself"* (2 Timothy 2:13, emphasis mine). Paul is equating the very Person of God with the concept of being faithful, or *full of faith*. In other words, if we could give the tangible substance that constitutes God's spiritual makeup a name, it would include *faithfulness*. We see this truth also expressed in 1 Corinthians 1:30, where Jesus Christ was "made unto us wisdom, and righteousness, and sanctification, and redemption." Christ didn't just come to give us righteousness; He *was* the incarnation of righteousness. It is not as though God possesses things, rather, He is the embodiment of everything He has, and therefore everything He

244

gives. The writer of Hebrews describes faith as "the substance of things hoped for, the evidence of things unseen." Since faith is substance, and God's nature is faithfulness, then we may confidently say that the "substance of things hoped for" is God Himself. We may be expecting a child, a ministry, or a position of work; and yet, these things are made possible because they proceed out of the very Person of God. This mystical reality was understood and communicated by the apostle Paul in his letter to the Colossians; he says, "For by him were all things created, that are in heaven, and that are in earth, visible and invisible, whether they be thrones, or dominions, or principalities, or powers: all things were created by him, and for him: And he is before all things, and by him all things consist." When we read scriptures like these, we are tempted to modify the apostle's strong assertion that "all things" were created by God and for God, in light of the overwhelming evil that has existed throughout the ages. However, Paul is by no means attributing the evil actions of unenlightened, unbelieving creatures to the Lord. He is merely saying that all of those creatures came from the Person of God despite whatever evil actions they may have done.

Since we know that all of creation is a result of God's word, we also know that *God puts Himself into every word that He speaks.* God's word is literally upholding everything that is created, even that which denies His existence! When the apostle says that God "cannot deny Himself," he is really saying *God cannot deny faithfulness.* Therefore we know that faith itself is sourced in the very person of God. Apart from the Lord, man cannot have faith. It must also be said that, although a man may have no faith, God is not dependent upon man to accomplish His will. God has always relied upon His own faith, for He knows that He is the only source of faith. Jephthah may have come to the point of disbelieving his role as a valiant warrior for Israel, but God still believed in the destiny He had scripted for this man. Regardless of how adverse Jephthah's life had become, his God-ordained destiny contained the guarantee of fulfillment, because the Lord who scripted that destiny was faithful to bring it into manifestation.

*"And it was so, that when the children of Ammon made war against Israel, the elders of Gilead went to fetch Jephthah out of the land of Tob: And they said unto Jephthah, Come, and be our captain, that we may fight with the children of Ammon. And Jephthah said unto the elders of Gilead, Did not ye hate me, and expel me out of my father's house? and why are ye come unto me now when ye are in distress?"* - *Judges 11:5-7*

What must have seemed like a million miles away from Jephthah's new home in Tob, Gilead was being invaded by a mighty group of warriors from the nation of Ammon. In a strange turn of events, we find the elders of Gilead traveling to the land of Tob in order to find Jephthah and acquire his military expertise. Not only did the elders desire Jephthah to fight for them, but being aware of his ability on the battlefield, they implored him to be their captain. In verse seven, we find Jephthah's discourse with these men revealing an ironic twist of events, as the elders of Gilead were in fact his brothers! Despite the prejudice which they showed toward him years earlier, they recognized their powerlessness without him. In their present crisis if they were to allow their prejudice to continue any further, they would be faced with an even greater problem than the army of Ammon – a refusal to recognize Jephthah as their captain would actually be to deny God's solution to their problem. Jephthah *was* God's appointed man to bring the military solution as well as righteous order back into the Israelite nation. Even though his brothers had the title of "elders" – signifying their role as the dominant decision makers in Gilead – they did not have the capacity within themselves to lead Israel to a victory. The fact is that Jephthah's brothers were never going to be the most effective leadership for the people of Gilead: they were standing in someone else's place of destiny.

God's destiny for each person is like a geographic location. No two people can stand in the same exact place at the same time. Even so, there are those around us who have assumed positions that they have not been divinely ordained to fulfill. Through self-effort, they try to assume certain duties that have not been given them by God. Therefore, their functioning becomes illegitimate, and their role eventually becomes invalidated as some crisis arises requiring the genuine anointing of God for a successful outcome. If a position of authority is gained through human initiative, the same must be maintained by that human effort. The only way to maintain such an illegitimate position is through controlling who and what is allowed near that position. As a result, those who have not been appointed by God to operate as they are will disallow those whom God has purposed to fulfill that role. The reason given for prohibiting these appointed ones may be related to age, gender, or natural inexperience. However, these all become smoke screens to hide the real reason – the illegitimate leadership was built upon the false idea that man can assume a position apart from a divine ordination. Therefore, insecurity pervades every aspect of their illegitimate leadership. This is why we see the Lord oftentimes sending a great crisis to Israel, to reveal how ill-equipped these leaders were to handle the situation successfully. It is true that we should never assume any position apart from the Lord's initiative. We may ask, "But how will I know if it's my time to lead?" God has personally tailored all of our promotions in such a way that we will *not* be able to mistake their entry into our lives.

It is interesting to note that throughout the history of Israel, we find virtually no cases where God used a man or woman whose human ability was sufficient for the task of providing proper leadership for the nation. In fact, throughout biblical history we find that the common practice of God is to use the *least likely* of each generation to demonstrate that human strength will not be able to accomplish the will of God. We see this pattern of God using the misfits to achieve His ends through the lives of Rahab and Jeremiah, as well as in the life of David, John the Baptist, and all of the first apostles of Christ. Jephthah was no different, as he was literally cast out by the very people he was called to lead. Ironically, the entry-point into his destiny would come at the behest of his brothers – the current leaders of Israel whose illegitimate rule just cracked at the seams due to an Ammonite invasion.

*And Jephthah said unto the elders of Gilead, If ye bring me home again to fight against the children of Ammon, and the LORD deliver them before me, shall I be your head? - Judges 11:9*

248

From the above verse, it is apparent that Jephthah had greater insight into his own destiny than did his brothers. At a glance, it would seem like his request to be made head of his entire tribe was selfish. After all, his brothers had already come to find him, undoubtedly swallowing a great deal of pride, knowing that they had previously ostracized him from the family inheritance. Not only did they face the humiliation of having to approach him, but they desperately needed him to accept their endorsement as military commander over Gilead. Surely his brother's arrival accompanied by their request for his assistance was enough for him to agree to their terms. And yet, Jephthah replied with a telling demand, insisting that if he were to return home with his brothers, fight against the Ammonites and defeat them, he should become their "head." It was as though a thirst had filled his heart which could not be quenched merely by being reinstated into the family, nor by being granted military command over Gilead – his heart was fixed on the greater end of Gilead's problem. He knew that the issue for the Gileadites was not that they needed a military leader, but that they needed a righteous judge to bring godly order back into the nation. And so, whereas the people of Gilead saw a victory over Ammon as the ultimate success, Jephthah saw their hearts returning to the Lord as the ultimate of success. Jephthah shared God's heart which was demonstrated through his prophetic demand to be appointed as the head of his tribe. We must see that opportunities will present themselves to us through human instrumentality. However, just because we are recognized as possessing certain giftings, it does not mean that the people recognizing us understand the scope of our destiny. We must know the destiny God has called us to, so that we do not settle for a lesser outcome, but rather boldly pursue exactly what God has shown us.

*"Then Jephthah went with the elders of Gilead, and the people made him head and captain over them: and Jephthah uttered all his words before the LORD in Mizpeh." - Judges 11:11*

The name "Mizpeh" means "watchtower" or "high place" in Hebrew. We know that this newly elected captain not only lived in the geographically high region of Gilead (see Judges 11:34), but that he spoke words before the Lord in the same place. The phrase "before the LORD" literally translates as "before the face of the LORD." Jephthah was preparing himself at the highest elevation in Gilead through an intimate prayer session with the Lord. The natural location of these preparatory prayers was just an outward picture of the spiritual heights he was accessing for the battle ahead. Similar to Jacob, who had wrestled with the angel of the Lord right before meeting his brother Esau, Jephthah was in direct contact with the Person of God right before his engagement with the enemy. And like Jacob, he would need to see the imprint of God's face upon the army which was coming to threaten the livelihood of his people. When we begin to do as David did, who said that he "foresaw the Lord always before (his) face" (Acts 2:25), we will no longer see an enemy that needs to be overcome; instead, our eyes will see almighty God Who has *already* given us victory over our enemy.

Just before Jephthah was approached by his brothers for leadership he seemed to be living a life of rebellion – he was living in the land of Tob while leading about a group of destitute people. And yet, at the moment he was approached by his brothers, he unashamedly gave the terms of his service, exhibiting a surprising awareness of what his destiny entailed as a leader and judge over the people of Israel. Furthermore, after a season of living amidst these baser individuals, he did not seem to lack any understanding of God's primary role in both his ability to lead as well as in the successful outcome of the upcoming battle. It needs to be said here that to many people, our time of preparation may actually be misinterpreted as rebellion. They mistake our noninvolvement with contemporary methods of ministry or work, for apathy or carelessness, and therefore write us off as rebellious. And yet, we are neither apathetic nor careless, but rather are being trained unconventionally in a setting that is not compatible with a hardened, religious mindset. In this training period, we are being infused with inner strength through the abundance of revelation we are receiving, knowing that the timing of the Lord will cause us to enter into our destiny in the most spontaneous and unexpected way. It would be easy to typecast Jephthah as a "broken man" as a result of sustaining a horrific rejection in his early life, and therefore needing many years to be "fixed up" before he could assume any position of service in his home nation, let alone lead them as a judge. Had Jephthah's brothers entertained this misconception, they would have ultimately been deprived of the natural, territorial freedom which God desired them to have, and more importantly, they would have forfeited the glory of a righteous government established by a righteous judge. We must learn the lesson which Jephthah's brothers undoubtedly learned – that the outward appearance of an individual should never determine their natural or spiritual usefulness; only through the lens of faith will we see the will of God for our lives, which may often be disguised by a set

251

of circumstances which we would reject if left up to our natural vision.

Another critical aspect in this account is the importance that Israelite history would have had in Jephthah's mind. Being an Israelite, he was from the same DNA of men like Joseph, Jacob and Abraham. The first delivered a nation from famine, the second wrestled with God and prevailed, and the third saw the supernatural hand of God open up his wife's barren womb. He must have known about those judges who came before him; how Deborah and Barak wrought a great victory against the Canaanites, along with Gideon and his special-forces army of three hundred who routed one hundred and twenty thousand Midianites, as well as the victory given to Ehud when he slew a host of Moabites, bringing eighty years of rest to Israel. In light of those individual's whom God used mightily in our past, it is essential to see that none of them were able to do what they did apart from the faith which God gave them. This cannot be overstated, for it is only by faith that we can do the works of God in the earth. Knowledge of what men and women have done in the power of God cannot of itself give us the same power; however by recalling what has been done, we may understand that it is the supernatural force of faith which energizes our natural abilities to perform supernatural exploits.

Nearing the day of battle, we see Jephthah's faith demonstrated in a letter he wrote to Sihon, the king of Ammon. Sihon was an idol worshiper whose god was Chemosh, the national deity of the Moabites and the god of the Ammonites. The name "Chemosh" is the Hebrew word meaning "subduer."[2] Like many prophets of the Old

Testament, Jephthah gave an Elijah-like taunt aimed at the king of Ammon saying, "Wilt not thou possess that which Chemosh thy god giveth thee to possess? (Judges 11:24)" In other words, "If your god really has the ability to subdue us, than let him do it!" Jephthah had come to the point where he believed beyond any doubt that only one God existed, and he could not be beaten by any other entity. By faith, Jephthah was living vicariously through the word of God, and therefore was manifesting his bold distain for the false religion of the Ammonites. If God could bring him this far, winning the battle against Ammon would prove relatively easy. Now, we as believers will encounter many forces that seek to "subdue" us. These may include the demonic power behind poverty, greed, and all kinds of evil addictions, or may come as simply as an evil thought which attempts to put fear in our minds. We know that God's original intention for Adam was to keep all of creation "subdued" under his delegated authority (see Genesis 1:28). In the face of any evil opposition, we must be as Jephthah was, unafraid and fully confident in God's ability to work His supernatural power through us. The Bible declares that "Ammon was subdued before the children of Israel" (11:33). The language here wonderfully illustrates the natural fight which the Israelites were engaged in, as well as the spiritual fight of faith that every believer enters into. By the very nature of its demonic origin, Chemosh existed to "subdue" God's people and their possessions. However, when fighting against a man like Jephthah, it was no match for the even greater, subduing power of his faith. In fact, by the end of the battle, the slaughter of the Ammonties was so great that it extended throughout twenty cities! This is a lucid description of the incomparable nature of the life of faith with every other so-called life.

253

It is a spiritual fact that when we operate by faith, we will never bow to any demonic force in the universe; the divine energy operating within faith is as transformative to its surroundings as is the rising sun to a darkened sky. The faith of God which a man or woman exhibits will also create a shield of invincibility around them, making it impossible for any enemy to destroy the purpose to which they have been called.

It is interesting that the name "Jephthah" means "he opens" or could be translated as "whom, or what God sets free."[3] God made an opening for this man to reach his destiny – it was a roadway paved with redemption. He needed this road to take him from rejection to exaltation, from outcast to acceptance. This God-carved pathway was *faith*. Faith became his road connecting what was in his heart – the hope of becoming Gilead's leader – and the substance of that hope, which came through the repentance of his family. This is why scripture declares that "faith is the substance of things hoped for..." We could say that faith *reveals* the substance of our hope, even while that substance is yet in the distance. We may confidently expect to find that God's road for each of us is carved right into life's unpredictable happenings. Faith in God does not keep us from journeying through dark places, but is the very guarantee that we will never be lost in the darkness. Psalm 16:11 says, "Thou wilt shew me the path of life: in thy presence is fullness of joy; at thy right hand there are pleasures for evermore." The path of life is a spiritual roadway, for it is here that the realities of joy and divine pleasures are found. Therefore, it is by faith that we may traverse across the hostilities of natural existence, and yet experience all of God's pleasures.

Just as there is no generic "map" for our spiritual journey, there is equally no set mold into which the man or woman of God must fit. It is an ungodly idea that we are to build a particular ministerial, social or relational framework in which many individuals can attempt to fit. The Lord is not interested in building exterior structures for people to conform to; He is molding each one of us into the image and likeness of Christ, expressed through our own unique destiny. Consequently, everyone's journey is highly unique, and everyone that journeys on the pathway of faith will experience the most concentrated blend of unique situations that will serve as God's molding agents. Jephthah was unique in his background as a warrior, but even more as the son of a prostitute and a reject of his family tribe. From a human standpoint, being the son of a prostitute and an outcast would make his choosing to be captain and judge over Israel an impossible one, if God had not specially called him. It was in spite of the controversies surrounding his life that he emerged as Israel's deliverer.

It is true that the controversies surrounding our own lives will actually serve to rule out all human ingenuity as the means by which we arrive at our destiny; we become aware that only God can move us into our ordained position. It took the threat of an Ammonite invasion to move Jephthah's brothers to find him and install him as their leader. In the same way, it will take nothing less than an act of God to bring us into our expected future. The account of Jephthah's life teaches us that only by faith in the supernatural orchestration of God can we see the pathway to our destiny opened up, in spite of the barricades of human injustice.

# CHAPTER FOURTEEN

# SAMSON

*"...For the child shall be a Nazarite unto God from the womb: and he shall begin to deliver Israel out of the hand of the Philistines." -*

*Judges 13:5*

The nation of Israel was created to be a representative gem of God's kingdom. They were the embodiment of divine favor, having the protection and provision of God continually within reach. At the mention of their name, Israel's enemies would tremble. Their fame was a result of the supernatural triumphs which they experienced at the most impossible of circumstances. Although often outnumbered, they defeated their enemies with the help of angelic forces who would accompany them into battle. To the rest of the world, they were a revelation of God's unfailing faithfulness – no matter what He promised them, His word would be fulfilled in the most spectacular fashion. Like a child to its mother, Israel was nourished by its Creator in the most maternal way. And like a child to its father, they were blessed with the inheritance of being sons of God, the resources of heaven ever at their grasp. The Lord's desire for Israel was that they be utterly captivated by their Creator. And yet, Israel was unfaithful in their devotion toward God, at times likened to a harlot whose affections would repeatedly waver toward false gods. The Israelites devotion toward the Lord too often drifted into a bewitched gaze at the temporal pleasures of the world. Such evil captivations attracted the attack of ambitious nations seeking to fight with them and bring them into captivity. It is through our study of Israel's wavering gaze between the Lord and the world that we find a stunning parallel with the central figure of this chapter – a man who would embody the destructive duality found within Israel. This man was known for his spectacular strength, whose mythical feats were part of Israel's history of deliverance. He demonstrated the warriorship of the Lord which made him a formidable foe in the face of hundreds of enemy combatants. He was called to a life of strict consecration, and in turn was promised a continual torrent of supernatural abilities. In the midst of heroic accolades and a Spartan code of conduct, a paradox emerged: he embodied Israel's damaging duality of both faith and unbelief. His greatest heroics on behalf of Israel were paralleled by his greatest failures to keep himself from indulging in forbidden pleasures. The result of this duality would be his undoing as Israel's deliverer, leading to his capture and confinement in the bowels of a Philistine prison. And yet, it would be the resurgence of faith that would give sight to this man, whose eyes had become darkened through unbelief.    His name was Samson, and through the power of faith, he would deliver the nation of Israel from their oppressors. It is ironic that Samson would be raised up as Israel's deliverer, for he himself would need a deliverance from his enemy. The means through which he would deliver his countrymen, as well as himself, would be the same – the faith of God.

*"And there was a certain man of Zorah, of the family of the Danites, whose name was Manoah; and his wife was barren, and bare not. And the angel of the LORD appeared unto the woman, and said unto her, Behold now, thou art barren, and bearest not: but thou shalt conceive, and bear a son." – Judges 13:2-3*

At the outset of Samson's account, we are introduced to Manoah and his wife, a couple who lived in Zoreh – a town of Dan – in the time of the Philistine's forty year occupation of Israel. As the wife tended to her work in the field, she was suddenly visited by the Angel of the Lord who spoke a startling word regarding her barren condition. He assured her that despite her infertility she would conceive a son. Next, he began detailing the manner in which this child was to be raised – under the auspices of the *Nazarite Vow*. To the Hebrew people, the Nazarite Vow was known as a vow of consecration to the Lord, where an individual would abstain from various foods and activities, such as eating anything from a vine or from cutting his or her hair. In the Hebrew language, the name "Nazarite" literally means "separated."[1] We understand this word "separated" as being synonymous with the word "holy." In other words, those taking this vow would be marked amongst their community as serving a holy purpose unto God. According to the first mention of this vow in scripture, it was a voluntary oath to the Lord made by the individual (see Number 6:1-8). That it was *voluntary* is clearly stated in verse two which says, "When either man or woman *shall separate themselves* to vow a vow of a Nazarite, to *separate them* unto the LORD..." (emphasis mine). The onus was on the individual to make such a

258

commitment. And yet, here we find the Lord explicitly commanding Manoah's wife to raise her son in the Nazarite fashion. It is clear that the Lord had already defined the journey that her son would take, leaving no room for debate. Now, we know that this lifestyle would have required the strictest of discipline. We also know that this unborn child was destined to champion Israel's freedom through the super-human strength which he would receive. This supernatural empowerment would be conditional upon his obedience to the binding oath. Furthermore, we know from his future ministry that he would be tempted continually to break this vow, and that many times he did in fact do so. Therefore, it is likely that the Lord commanded his mother to raise him in such a way to reveal the stark contrast between God's perfect ability displayed through an obedient life, and the failure of man to display divine ability when disobedient to the Lord's commands. God would make it clear to the world through Samson's life that the manifestation of divine strength would be connected to the faithfulness he showed toward his vow.

*"And the woman bare a son, and called his name Samson: and the child grew, and the LORD blessed him. And the Spirit of the LORD began to move him at times in the camp of Dan between Zorah and Eshtaol." - Judges 13:24-25*

The Spirit of the Lord began to "move" Samson between the mountains of Zoreah and Eshtoal as he grew. The word "move" here in the Hebrew language means "to urge, to impel."[2] Merriam Webster defines the word "impel" as "to urge or drive forward, or as if by the exertion of strong moral pressure." At this point we may gather that Samson was still relatively young and had not yet been released into his delivering ministry. What is interesting in this account is that he was being supernaturally "urged" and "driven forward" by the Lord in this time. He was in fact experiencing the "pressure" of his own preparation for supernatural ministry. And this is a significant point to consider, as we are all in varying stages of our own journeys; before God's purposes can be birthed through us, we will experience a degree of pressure just prior to the birthing. The idea of *pressure* can be seen from two very different perspectives: coming from the enemy or brought by the Lord. If we see the pressure mounting around us as having been initiated by the devil, we may despise it in whatever form it takes – physical or spiritual. However, if we trust that God is in control of our lives, we will learn to see the pressure as God's tool to mold us according to the vision He has given us for our lives. It is often true that the greatest form of pressure does not come from the persecution we may face, but from the knowledge of what God has shown us about our future. We are often waiting for things that have not manifested, and the waiting itself can build an enormous amount of pressure which we experience in our minds. At first, our focus may be on how strong our adversity is; however, over time we realize that God is teaching us how much greater He is in us than the external pressures that are testing us. Before Samson could manifest supernatural strength he had to experience the urging of the Lord in the time of his preparation.

*"And Samson went down to Timnath, and saw a woman in Timnath of the daughters of the Philistines. And he came up, and told his father and his mother, and said, I have seen a woman in Timnath of the daughters of the Philistines: now therefore get her for me to wife." –*
*Judges 14:1-2*

There will always be a strategy attached to our calling, some strategic means by which we accomplish our heavenly objective. This strategy is not something we come to merely by intellectual means, rather is revealed over time, throughout the various stages of our journey. We must realize that God is the one who has orchestrated a strategy which, when implemented, becomes the agent of our success. In His divine strategy for us, he includes tangible realities that we come to find indispensable for the fulfillment of our mission. For Adam, part of God's strategy was to give him a wife to aid him in his stewardship over the earth. For Barak, God used the mighty prophetess Deborah as a symbol of His word which brought a military victory for Israel. For David, there was the woman named Abigail who was instrumental in keeping him from needlessly shedding blood. The pattern here is that *relationships* are often the key in the divine strategy. From the above verse we can see that Samson desired a wife from the Philistines, however his motive was something other than matrimony – he was looking for a covert way to get into the Philistine camp. Verse 4 says, "But his father and his mother knew not that it was of the LORD, that he sought an occasion against the Philistines: for at that time the Philistines had dominion over Israel." Notice how this scripture says that Samson's desire for a wife was "of the Lord." God had implanted a strategy into this man's heart that would require the assistance of another individual. Through this act of marriage, Samson would be in a prime position to preemptively strike at the enemy's camp.

*"Then went Samson down, and his father and his mother, to Timnath, and came to the vineyards of Timnath: and, behold, a young lion roared against him. And the Spirit of the LORD came mightily upon him, and he rent him as he would have rent a kid, and he had nothing in his hand. but he told not his father or his mother what he had done."*
*– Judges 14:5-6"*

Before Samson arranged his marriage to the Philistine woman, he passed through the vineyards of Timnath. In this vineyard, Samson would have been surrounded by grapes used for making wine. We already know that he had taken the Nazarite vow which included abstaining from eating anything that came from a grape. Yet, we find him here in the vineyards of Timnath surrounded by grapes! This is a symbolic picture of his propensity to walk in places that encouraged the fall of his mission. This would be the first of many compromising situations that he would find himself in. It was in this vineyard that a roaring lion came out to meet Samson. The apostle Peter declares, "Be sober, be vigilant, because your advesary the devil, *as a roaring lion*, walketh about, seeking whom he may devour" (1 Peter 5:8, emphasis mine). This verse is illustrated perhaps clearer in Samson's case than any other as he walked in the vineyard of Timnath. Although he walked in a potentially compromising situation, the lion could not overcome Samson, for he was appointed by God for the overthrow of the Philistine occupation of Israel. In fact, it was here that we see the first of many spectacular feats of strength. As the lion approached, the Spirit of the Lord came upon Samson giving him the supernatural power to literally rip the lion in half! Although we may be tempted to focus on Samson's tendency toward disobedience, we must realize that God's faithfulness is greater than man's faithlessness. In fact, even in a place of potential compromise, the sovereignty of God may still cause mighty manifestations of supernatural power. Furthermore, we know that the gifts and callings of the Lord upon a person's life are irrevocable, which means they will not be retracted at any time by the Lord (see Romans 11:29). If God has called a person to do a work, then He has also invested Himself into their success.

*"And after a time he returned to take her, and he turned aside to see the carcase of the lion: and, behold, there was a swarm of bees and honey in the carcase of the lion. And he took thereof in his hands, and went on eating, and came to his father and mother, and he gave them, and they did eat: but he told not them that he had taken the honey out of the carcase of the lion." – Judges 14:8-9*

After his initial meeting with his future bride, Samson returned by way of the vineyards to find the carcass of the lion he killed, full of honey and swarming with bees. According to Numbers 6:6, a man taking the vow of a Nazarite was not allowed to touch a corpse. However, Samson not only took honey out of the carcass to eat it, but he brought some home to his parents! Samson purposely did not tell his parents that he had killed the lion, or that he grabbed the honey out of it as they would have known the error in what he had done. Similarly, it would have been a sin for the common man to enter the temple of God and eat the showbread from off of the table. And yet, we find David doing this very thing and being commended by the Lord for doing it! (See Matthew 12). On the one hand, we find David with a group of men, in the presence of a priest, and in a place he knew to be holy. He did not display any crisis of conscience for what he did. And we know that Jesus did not rebuke David's actions when the Lord Himself was being questioned by the Pharisees for having eaten grain on the Sabbath day. On the other hand, we find Samson taking honey out of the lion while alone in a vineyard. Furthermore, we see that he brought some back to his parents, not telling them where the honey came from. It appears that Samson *did* have a crisis of conscience in what he did. And it is in the conscience of an individual that motives of good and evil are formed. If that motive is inspired by faith, then the action will be pure in the sight of God. If not, then the action becomes defiled. This is why the apostle Paul said, "I know, and am persuaded by the Lord Jesus, that there is nothing unclean of itself: but to him that esteemeth any thing to be unclean, to him it is unclean." (Romans 14:14), and goes on to say "whatever is not of faith is sin" (23). David displayed faith in what he did, believing that God cared about him and his men more than the ceremonial law stating "thou shalt not eat the showbread." Therefore his action was acceptable to God. Samson however revealed a lack of faith in that he was ashamed to tell his

264

parents where he got the honey. We know that this act on the part of Samson was recorded for a purpose, specifically to reveal the emerging duality that was forming within this man's conscience. What compromises he was willing to make now, in the beginning of his journey, he would be willing to make later in greater proportions.

*"So his father went down unto the woman: and Samson made there a feast; for so used the young men to do. And it came to pass, when they saw him, that they brought thirty companions to be with him. And Samson said unto them, I will now put forth a riddle unto you: if ye can certainly declare it me within the seven days of the feast, and find it out, then I will give you thirty sheets and thirty change of garments: But if ye cannot declare it me, then shall ye give me thirty sheets and thirty change of garments. And they said unto him, Put forth thy riddle, that we may hear it." – Judges 14:10-13*

Samson went down to the feast which was being prepared for his marriage. He gathered thirty Philistine men on the eve of the traditional seven-day wedding banquet. He was actually operating undercover as he ate, talked with, and conspired against his enemies on their soil. Once they all gathered together, he put forth a riddle and gave the men seven days to find the answer; if they could not unravel the mystery, they would each forfeit one of their garments. Attached to this game was a sadistic taunt which Samson aimed at these men, intending ultimately to humiliate them. This humiliation was a preemptive strike at them emotionally and intellectually before his physical campaign of war would begin. Samson was employing something known today as "psychological warfare." This type of warfare uses psychological manipulation in order to deceive, confuse, and demoralize an enemy so that their resistance is greatly weakened, making them susceptible to surrender.[3] "Psychological warfare aims at the insecurities and desires of its targets and uses these as a means of achieving objectives."[4] This psychological manipulation would become a theme of Samson's military strategy.

Although there are both good and evil connotations connected to the idea of psychological warfare, we must see the redemptive aspect of this military methodology. It was never God's intention that men manipulate other men in order to do them harm. However, God has allowed warfare to continue throughout the ages with the ultimate intent of bringing all human warfare to an end. Since the Fall of creation, evil has been allowed to coexist with good, inevitably leading to confrontations between the two. The instrumentality of war has been used by God as a tool to stop otherwise unstoppable military forces from literally wiping out the human race. Whereas the militaries of mankind have had a place in God's sovereign plan for the world, He has always placed the natural order of human military beneath the greater, spiritual realities of forgiveness, repentance, and redemption. Nevertheless, within the realm of the natural order, God has given leaders throughout the ages various strategies to deal with unrepentant individuals who would otherwise be unrelenting in their quest for human domination. Samson would eventually succeed in confounding the Philistine men, infuriating them because of their inability to meet the challenge set forth by the Israelite. On the seventh day, their nerves were ready to explode. The men pressed Samson's wife for the answer to the riddle, threatening to burn her and her father, along with her house if she failed to give them what they desired. In turn, she began to press Samson for the answer to this riddle.

*"And Samson's wife wept before him, and said, Thou dost but hate me, and lovest me not: thou hast put forth a riddle unto the children of my people, and hast not told it me. And he said unto her, Behold, I have not told it my father nor my mother, and shall I tell it thee? And she wept before him the seven days, while their feast lasted: and it came to pass on the seventh day, that he told her, because she lay sore upon him: and she told the riddle to the children of her people." – Judges 14:16-17*

The book of Proverbs reveals two important scriptures concerning secrecy: "A talebearer revealeth secrets: but he that is of a faithful spirit concealeth the matter" (11:13) and "A fool uttereth all his mind: but a wise man keepeth it in till afterwards" (29:11). Notice how the *talebearer* and the *fool* share the commonality of revealing something that is supposed to remain hidden, whether about someone else or about themselves. Also, notice that it is a *faithful spirit* and a *wise man* that conceal important matters, revealing those matter later on only if it necessary to do so. Here we see faithfulness and wisdom vitally connected to the secrecy that one is able to maintain. Along our journey, there will be certain matters that we are to keep secret. In his second letter to the Corinthians, the apostle Paul said that he "was caught up into paradise, and heard unspeakable words, which it is not lawful for a man to utter" (12:4). And he never did reveal what those things were. Although the primary objective of any believer's ministry is to express the Gospel of Christ through any means necessary, there will still be times that certain truths are to remain secret. These are personal words that the Lord does not want us to share with others, as outside involvement might bring unnecessary opinions from well-meaning or else ill-meaning people. Today, we live in an age where social media is controlling the airwaves of the world, and people are encouraged to reveal the most personal details of their lives for all to see. Online forums are designed to allow individuals a way to interact with others, often at the expense of their privacy. For people of faith, there is a danger in being transparent about what God has spoken to them personally. By divulging such information, we become susceptible to the criticisms of those who are unenlightened as to our destiny. Furthermore, we should never seek to solicit from others affirmation regarding the prophetic words we have received; it only takes one negative comment to strike a blow at our faith in those words. We are taught that faith is like a shield which covers us in spiritual battle. That faith is intimately connected to what God is speaking to us personally, and therefore it serves two purposes: to cause us to believe that word, and to protect that word from outside influences that can damage our trust in what we have heard.

Through the continual manipulative pleas from his new bride, Samson finally gave in and revealed the secret of the riddle. She was able to wear him down to the point that he lowered his defensive shield, losing his edge in the psychological campaign.

*"And the men of the city said unto him on the seventh day before the sun went down, What is sweeter than honey? and what is stronger than a lion? And he said unto them, If ye had not plowed with my heifer, ye had not found out my riddle. And the Spirit of the LORD came upon him, and he went down to Ashkelon, and slew thirty men of them, and*

*took their spoil, and gave change of garments unto them which*
*expounded the riddle. And his anger was kindled, and he went up to his*
*father's house." – Judges 14:18-19*

Anytime we see the phrase "and the Spirit of the Lord came upon him" in scripture, we know that whatever follows is sanctioned by the Lord. After Samson's manipulative wife gave his secret to the thirty men, the Spirit of the Lord moved mightily upon Samson who was able to defeat these thirty men in this, his second mighty act. Ashkelon was a maritime city of the Philistines, the name literally meaning "the fire of infamy: I shall be weighed." It was in the geographic location known for being a place of vindication from dishonor, that Samson slew these men. As we study this particular military victory, it would seem that there were two different motivations manifesting at the same time. The first was related to the divine purpose for such a mighty display of power; God wanted to see His people liberated from the tyranny of the Philistines, and therefore employed Samson to be the catalyst for that deliverance. The second was Samson's human motivation behind all of his military engagements – personal vengeance. Instead of fighting for Israel's deliverance, his own need for vindication became the controlling force. In spite of this, The Lord's plan to deliver Israel would ultimately be successful, for God would not have chosen Samson if Samson's own personal vendetta would have become a hindrance to the divine plan. Similarly, we must realize that God's purposes for our lives may at times conflict with our own reasoning for why we are doing what we are doing. We may feel a personal vendetta against some evil going on

269

around us; however, God may still choose to move through us to accomplish something. And we must likewise withdraw from casting judgment upon those who may appear to be acting out of a wrong motive. Even those whom Paul knew to be preaching the message of Christ from "strife and envy," out of "contention, not seriously" (see Philippians 1:15-16), he excuses by saying, "In every way, whether in pretense, or in truth, Christ is preached" (18). God is not limited by a person's misguided attempts at doing the right thing; on the contrary, the Lord is masterful at using even ill-motived individuals to accomplish His ultimate purpose.

To add fuel to an already burning fire, Samson's Philistine wife was treacherously given to one of his friends by her father. In what must have been a wild frenzy, Samson took three hundred foxes, tied their tails together, lit them on fire, and caused them to run through the Philistine's field. The strategy here was to burn their entire crop to the ground. This violent strike against his enemies revealed great military wisdom, as he was not only effectively destroying part of their food source, but also striking another psychological blow against them. The employment of foxes created an image that revealed Samson's dominance over his enemy. The creativity behind such a strategy was God-given, in the same way that God has given wisdom to military leaders throughout the centuries. Since it was God's desire to see Israel delivered from oppression, He would endow their many deliverers with creative strategies to work strategic deliverances. We know that Joshua's strategy involved marching around Jericho seven times with nothing more than clay pots, fire, and horns. Jehu slew Jezebel by imploring some eunuchs to throw her out of a window.

270

Ehud slew the king of Moab single-handedly just after saying "I have a message from God unto thee." Although the methodology was different in every case, the wisdom behind each method was God-inspired.

In the same way, we know that the Lord does not merely orchestrate the general idea of our destiny, but implements the very strategy that makes walking in our destiny possible. Although we may not be called to deliver a nation through military force, we may be called to wage a campaign against abortion, human slavery, or some other injustice which society has used to oppress its people. What's interesting is that Exodus 15:3 describes the Lord as "a man of war." This attribute reveals God's innate tendency to make war upon everything that is a cancer in the body of society. Samson would make the warfare of God known to the Philistines by employing three hundred foxes to achieve his military objective.

With a double-crossing father-in-law, an unfaithful wife, and an outraged enemy, Samson's next conflict would cost him his new family. The Philistines were livid at Samson's exploit in the field, and so they got revenge upon him by burning his Philistine wife and her father to death. The result was that Samson made war against these Philistines and smote them with what the Bible calls a "great slaughter." This was his fourth mighty act, which was also done in the power of the Spirit. Afterward, Samson went and dwelt on the top of the rock "Etam." This rock was aptly named "The Lair of Wild Beasts."[5] This was a prophetic picture of the nation of Israel which was inhabited by the Philistines. To the Israelites, the Philistines were like "wild beasts." It could also be thought of as a picture of Israel's deliverer. He had been blessed with a tremendous amount of strength and wisdom, and yet his appetite for revenge was beginning to overshadow his God-given assignment. He was becoming more and more unbridled.

*"Then the Philistines went up, and pitched in Judah, and spread themselves in Lehi. And the men of Judah said, Why are ye come up against us? And they answered, To bind Samson are we come up, to do to him as he hath done to us. Then three thousand men of Judah went to the top of the rock Etam, and said to Samson, Knowest thou not that the Philistines are rulers over us? what is this that thou hast done unto us? And they said unto him, We are come down to bind thee, that we may deliver thee into the hand of the Philistines." – Judges 15:9-12*

Now the people of Israel hiked to the top of the rock Etam where Samson was in order to confront him about his mission. We might naturally think that the men of Judah would have thanked Samson, rallied around him in support, and perhaps even lent him their own shields and swords to help in the fight against their enemies. Not only did they *not* support him, but they wanted to bind him up! What is clear here is that the Israelites' fear of the enemy was greater than their faith of the God of Samson. The physical captivity that bound Israel produced a stronghold in their minds, which made them choose to stay beneath the iron fist of their oppressors rather than embrace the deliverance God had specially tailored through their herculean deliverer. Today, we call this phenomenon the "Stockholm Syndrome," where a captive will begin to empathize, sympathize and even defend his or her captors. After forty years in captivity, Israel related more with Her enemy than with Her ally. We see the same

272

tendency when the Israelites were coming out of Egypt, many of whom desired to go back into bondage, longing for the "nourishment" which they received in the form of leeks and onions. It is true that many of us battle this same demon of perversion due in part to the many years of wrong teaching, abusive leadership, and a skewed sense of identity which we have received at the hand of ministers, friends, and even family. We'd rather stay behind the bars of fear because the greatness of our promised future triggers anxiety in our minds. It is here we see that fear has perverted our courage, passion, and faith for the adventure that lies ahead.

This fear-based mindset can also be transmitted to us by our Western culture. Unlike in centuries past, where societies were marked by a pioneer spirit, boldly going into the unknown to discover new worlds, we have allowed ourselves to be reduced to narrow schedules and tiny cubicles. Our lives have become so restrictive that we've choked out the possibility for the unexpected and for the potential of God to be fully revealed through us. Our culture has taught us the path of least resistance, and the Church has adopted that view as well. We have not risen to the challenge of meeting our Philistines head on, and conquering the giants in the land like David did. And those that God raises up as spiritual frontiersman, like Samson, are chided rather than supported, bound up instead of let loose. The Lord's remedy for this condition is *vision* which is transmitted by His word, and accomplished by His faith. Israel had lost Her own sense of vision, for she was under the vision of an abusive leadership.

The name "Philistine" literally means "immigrant." This was a fitting name as they were occupying a land that was not their own. The truth is, they were *illegal immigrants* in the physical land which the Lord gave to the Israelites as their inheritance. Samson was not only interested in destroying the enemy, but in restoring the territory back to God's people. Similarly, the Lord is not only interested in our victory over a particular vice, but in restoring our vision to see the whole of our existence – spirit, soul and body – as it was originally intended. The apostle Paul declares that God accomplished this very thing, revealing that through Christ's death and resurrection, our entire being was reborn into the likeness of Christ. Through Jesus' perfect blood, we have been given entrance into a spiritual kingdom that exists parallel with the natural kingdoms on earth. Everything that is not of that spiritual kingdom – sickness, disease, poverty, and death – is "illegal" in our lives. By faith, we walk in the reality of Christ's victory, and we do not allow the enemy to come and intimidate us or bind us with fear. Since Israel is a type of the Church, we may see God's intent for the physical nation of Israel as a parallel reality to the intent He has for the spiritual nation of the Church (see 1 Peter 2:9). All of our rights as citizens of the heavenly kingdom are found in the New Covenant. The more we know of this Covenant, the more we will detect what is truly "illegal" in our lives.

*"...And Samson said unto them, Swear unto me, that ye will not fall upon me yourselves." – Judges 15:12*

Three thousand Israelites were now set on binding Samson with cords to deliver him unto the Philistines, who wanted him dead. Amazingly, Samson did not resist his own people however made an interesting request. He said, *"Swear unto me, that ye will not fall upon me yourselves."* Now Samson knew what he was capable of when the

Spirit of the Lord came upon him. He had ripped apart a lion, employed three hundred foxes to ignite the Philistine crops, slew thirty men in Ashkelon, and made a great slaughter of the Philistines after they killed his wife and father-in-law. This Israelite was not concerned about what the enemy could do to him, not even after hearing that the Philistines approached his countrymen, wanting him dead. What he was concerned about was that his own people would try to kill him. Although at times the objective of his warfare seemed to be a personal gratification rather than the liberation of his countrymen, Samson had an underlying respect for Israel. He knew that if Israel attacked him, he would be fighting not only against them, but against their Creator. And Samson must have known despite his own moral failings that the incredible strength which he possessed came from this awesome Creator. The Lord honored Samson's respect for Israel by planning yet another mighty spectacle in Lehi.

*"And when he came unto Lehi, the Philistines shouted against him: and the Spirit of the LORD came mightily upon him, and the cords that were upon his arms became as flax that was burnt with fire, and his bands loosed from off his hands. And he found a new jawbone of an ass, and put forth his hand, and took it, and slew a thousand men therewith. And Samson said, With the jawbone of an ass, heaps upon heaps, with the jaw of an ass have I slain a thousand men." - Judges 15:14-16*

The epic journey for this Herculean figure took him to Lehi, bound up by cords which his countrymen had tied. As the Spirit of the Lord came upon him, the cords that bound him became "as flax that was burnt with fire," which indicates that he could break them

275

effortlessly. Just as he broke free of the cords, he found a "new jawbone" from a dead donkey which he used as a weapon against his adversaries. It's fascinating to note that Samson is violating his Nazarite Vow a second time, by using the bone of a dead animal as a weapon to fight the Philistines. Both violations revolved around a dead animal – the first time was for food, the second time was for a weapon. It is remarkable that God continued to anoint him, giving him the victory despite these repeated indiscretions. From this we see a truth, that God's ability to accomplish His purposes in our lives is greater than our own ability to thwart those purposes. Although Samson said "With the jawbone of an ass...have I slain a thousand men," we know in actuality that it was the Spirit of God Who had empowered him to gain his victory. The name "Lehi" literally means "Jaw" in Hebrew,[6] which is a fitting name for the place in which Samson would use the jaw of a donkey in battle.

*"And he was sore athirst, and called on the LORD, and said, Thou hast given this great deliverance into the hand of thy servant: and now shall I die for thirst, and fall into the hand of the uncircumcised? But God clave an hollow place that was in the jaw, and there came water thereout; and when he had drunk, his spirit came again, and he revived: wherefore he called the name thereof Enhakkore, which is in Lehi unto this day." – Judges 15:18-19*

After the battle was over, Samson was thirsty. In response, the Lord caused water to supernaturally flow through the same jawbone that was used to rout the Philistines. By doing this, it would seem that God was violating His own law which He commanded Samson to live by. However, the Lord was demonstrating the fascinating truth that a

276

divine law can actually be superseded by an even greater divine law! We may understand this better by examining the law of gravity. In God's infinite wisdom, He created this natural law as a means to keep physical matter on the earth from floating and colliding into each other. In aviation, for example, we know that the law of gravity is one of the central concerns that engineers have in the construction of an airplane, as well as the aircraft's ability to lift off of a runway and climb to its appropriate altitude. A typical aircraft weighs tens if not hundreds of thousands of pounds. If operating under the law of gravity alone, the plane would not be able to lift itself above gravity's tremendous downward pull. Another law is needed to supersede the law of gravity. Physics teaches us that a principal law for facilitating take-off is called the *law of lift*. In the same way that an airplane pilot must depend upon the law of lift to aid in the plane's ability to break the law of gravity, Samson would experience *the law of God's grace* which superseded the Nazarite law, allowing him to drink from the supernatural water flowing through the jawbone. Similarly, Moses was instructed by God to *command* water to flow out from the rock; instead, he struck the rock with his rod (see Numbers 20). Water came gushing out of the rock even though Moses disobeyed God's command. By the examples of Samson and Moses, it is clear that the law of God's grace for each person supersedes their human ability to fulfill the moral laws of God.

*"Then went Samson to Gaza, and saw there an harlot, and went in unto her. And it was told the Gazites, saying, Samson is come hither. And they compassed him in, and laid wait for him all night in the gate*

*of the city, and were quiet all the night, saying, In the morning, when it is day, we shall kill him." – Judges 16:1-2*

The enemy had heard of Samson's whereabouts in Gaza, and surrounded the harlot's house in which Samson spent the night. He apparently believed that God would continue anointing him with supernatural power, despite living a life of sin. Now in a careless act of fornication, Samson found himself surrounded by the enemy. In the same way that the Philistines knew where to find Samson, surrounding him on all sides, sin gives the enemy access to the "whereabouts" of our spiritual life. The whereabouts refers to the *hidden man of our spirit*. Satan is drawn to the light of our spirit like flies are drawn to natural light. He will attempt to obscure the light which emanates from God's word. Like the Philistines, the enemy of our spirit-man will do whatever he can to put out that light. Satan will tempt us to cave in to a particular lust. And if we do submit to that lust, he knows that we are prone to experience doubt regarding the grace of God, which allows us to receive God's forgiveness. Those twinges of doubt are what the enemy looks for in order to capitalize on our moment of weakness.

Samson would not ultimately be overtaken, as his gifted strength would still be resident in the anointing. He would fight his way through this as he did the other confrontations. However, the sin in his life attracted his enemies. This powerful demonic attraction is for the purpose of making people of faith lose sight of God's faithfulness in the midst of their failings. Satan's greatest weapon becomes *condemnation.* Since Satan cannot ultimately condemn us, sentence us, or finalize the verdict against us, he can only make us *feel* as though God has cast the verdict against us, that we are guilty of trespasses and therefore must face the penalty of our actions. We can take courage in the apostle Paul's words concerning condemnation. He says, "There is therefore now no condemnation for them that are in Christ Jesus." Jesus died to eradicate our sinful consciousness, so that we would only be conscious of His perfection on our behalf. Our knowledge of Christ's finished work on the Cross is our greatest weapon against the devil. Staying aware of our God-given righteousness makes us *invisible* to the enemy. And the invisibility of our condemnation-free existence is only made visible to the degree that we are allowing condemnation to rule in our hearts.

From Gaza, Samson made his way to Sorek. The name "Sorek" in Hebrew literally means "choice vines."[7] This is the second location he went to that was known for its vineyards. When he passed through the first vineyard in Timnath, he encountered a lion. Upon passing through the vineyard of Sorek, he would encounter a far more dangerous enemy – a Philistine woman named Delilah. Her influence would prove to be far more subtle and disarming to Israel's champion. Previously, he dealt with the more obvious means of warfare, including the weaponry of swords, spears, and enemy taunts; this time, the attack wore the subtle face of seduction. The meaning of Delilah's name implies that she was one "pinning with desire" and "feeble."[8] It is apparent from the Bible's account of her life that she was in fact a morally feeble woman laden down with lusts. Primarily, she lusted after wealth. Her desire for Samson may not have been out of love at all, for she would be easily turned when enticed with money. Now it is

279

clear that Samson had a weakness for foreign women, which we can see through this, his third relationship with a non-Israelite. Similarly, the Bible says of Solomon that he "loved many strange women" (1 Kings 11:1), and was warned that they would "surely…turn away his heart after their gods…(2)" Delilah represents anything "foreign" to our purpose, position, and priorities in the destiny which we are called to. She is the mask which the enemy wears to deceive us and bring us into bondage. Although the enemy of our faith is said to walk around as a roaring lion, he disguises himself in those who will yield to his purposes.

When the Philistines found out that Samson was in the valley of Sorek, they came to Delilah and bribed her with money. Because she was desirous of monetary gain, she began to probe Samson as to the source of his strength. Seeing this manipulation as some sort of game, Samson gave her three different answers, each lie causing her to literally wear him down through her manipulative pleas for the truth. Now Samson rightly believed that his physical strength would remain intact as long as he did not reveal the physical access point to his spiritual power – his uncut hair. Through the constant manipulation, and a tolerance for such manipulative pleas, he had lost his *sobriety* and his *vigilance*, even as the apostle Peter speaks of in his epistle (see 1 Peter 5:8, as well as this reference in Samson's first confrontation with the lion). In his immoral intoxication, Samson was deceived into thinking that he could trust Delilah. Just as his first Philistine wife won over Samson's confidence, Delilah would eventually win the battle for Samson's trust.

*"And when Delilah saw that he had told her all his heart, she sent and called for the lords of the Philistines, saying, Come up this once, for he hath shewed me all his heart. Then the lords of the Philistines came up unto her, and brought money in their hand." – Judges 16:18*

From this account, we see the theme of *separateness* emerge that must be considered. The separate nature of Samson's lifestyle under the Nazarite Vow contained the key to his physical power. He was not to mix his separatist lifestyle with the ways of the world. By him disclosing the secret of his power, he would be mixing the very essence of his sanctified existence with the unsanctified motives and intentions of his enemies. In the same way, the life of faith deals with a state of being that is, in essence, hidden, and as such can be seen as a separate conscious reality. This separate reality remains completely *apart* and *hidden* from the unenlightened person. Furthermore, it is true that this hidden life of faith is the very *source* of our spiritual power. The apostle Peter describes this secret life as the "hidden man of the heart" which remains "incorruptible" (1 Peter 3:4). We see major corporations practicing the principle of separateness concerning the way their products are made. If they were to reveal the blueprints of their inventions with the general public, people would have open access to steal or manipulate whatever they wanted, devaluing the inventors and their inventions. People of faith experience the same devaluing and theft when they allow the world's way of doing things to influence their spiritual walk of faith. We are not implying that we should keep the life of God hidden from the world, but that the life of God is by nature separate from the world. James says that "friendship

281

with the world (the Greek word for "world" here is *kosmos* meaning the "world system"[9]) is enmity with God." Our way of living is holy and therefore should not be mixed with that which is unholy. The secrecy of our holiness will give us the winning edge over every form of adversity that seeks to destroy our spiritual life. In the same way that Samson's power was sustained by his separatist vow, the Christian has sustaining power because he or she is separated from the world system. By "separation" we are not saying that we are isolated from the world, but that we are to the world as light is to the darkness. And just as light is a real substance that has the ability to transform its surroundings, so we are the light of the world, able to transform our surroundings by virtue of our all-together different life of faith.

The first thing the Philistines did to Samson was to pluck his eyes out. Second, they brought him down to Gaza (the name "Gaza" literally means "The Strong"[10]). Third, they bound him with fetters of brass. Fourth and finally, they made him do hard labor in the grinding mill. These four parts to Samson's captivity are significant to people of faith today, as we may similarly experience these four effects when entering into sin. The first effect of sin is that it *causes our vision to become distorted*. In other words, the spiritual eyesight which faith gives us is blurred, causing us to receive a skewed view of God's word. We will be apt to think He is angry with us, that we must serve some rigid form of penance in order to be cleansed, or that our destiny has somehow become marred to the point that it will not occur as God said it would. These are all thoughts that coincide with the deception of sin. The immediate result of Adam and Eve's transgression was "they knew that they were naked." This knowledge produced a distorted vision of the truth. Notice how their sin led to spiritual blindness, which resulted in a distorted view of something God had already called good – their nakedness. Likewise, our faith is affected by sin, the vision of which becomes twisted, and that which is good is seen as something to hide from. It is important to know that deception may only work when we are disobedient to God's word; however, even through disobedience there is an even greater force at work called *grace*. It is by the grace of God that we are delivered from the power of that deception. And it is through faith that we can see this glorious grace and its superior countermeasure to all that seeks our demise. Even a weakened faith can be made strong again as God's word is eternally at work energizing that faith which He has given us. To live a life of faith is not simply to believe that God's grace covers us when we sin, but to walk without the *consciousness* of sin. We are to be completely aware of our perfection in Christ that even a sinful action cannot cause us to think less of what Christ accomplished on our behalf.

The second effect of sin is that it leads us to "Gaza," or the place where *strongholds* are built. We know that strongholds are the result of any force – good or evil – that binds us to the point where we cannot escape its grasp. Now, most people understand strongholds as evil things, such as fear, oppression, and lust. However, strongholds may also be good, even as David prayed, "The Lord is...my stronghold" (Psalm 18:2, NKJV). It is true that the strongest person is no match for the power of sin, when that person has entertained sin. However, the most powerful sin is no match for the one who sees him or herself as having already been made perfect in Christ. The

283

understanding of our perfection in Christ must become a greater stronghold in our minds than that of our former, sinful mindset. Had Samson's vision remained pure through faith in God's word, he would not have been able to be overcome – his conscience would have remained untarnished by the lured temptation of Delilah. When we gaze at that which God has already done through Christ, we will find that his strength is made perfect for us in our time of temptation.

The third effect of sin is our inevitable wrangling with the 'brass fetters' of *condemnation*. One of the hallmarks of the Old Covenant was that the Law of God revealed man's sin. That revelation brought about a sense of condemnation to man's conscience over his inability to measure up to God's standards. In the New Covenant, God has eradicated the very root of condemnation, by eliminating the system of Law in which man attempts to become like God by what he does. Why do many feel condemned by their sin? It all comes down to a lack of revelation. We are likely unaware that God does not condemn us for our sin, or are not yet fully persuaded about this truth. When we disobey the voice of God in any particular area, the spirit of condemnation may appear to be our reality. This is a distortion created by sin, and must be washed away by the reality of our condemnation-free existence in the Person of Jesus Christ.

The fourth effect of sin is that we are *given to the hard labor of unbelief.* When the seed of unbelief is planted into our minds, we will ultimately find ourselves in some form of sin, and if that seed is not rooted out, it will grow into a lifestyle of unbelief. A lifestyle of unbelief is most evident in the person's thoughts and actions continually reflecting the false idea that Jesus did not finish the work

284

of salvation on the Cross. And so, those with this mindset will continually strive for what God has already given them freely through Christ. They will continue labor to get more spirituality, more favor, more anointing, and more blessing. The apostle Paul declares that "whatever is not of faith is sin" (Romans 14:23). This means that whatever we do that is not directed by the faith of God within us, misses the mark of His perfect purpose for us. And sin is essentially anything that misses God's perfect standard (see Strong's G266 for the Greek definition of *sin*). In essence, sin leads to sin, imperfection to imperfection, and unbelief to labor an unnecessary labor in order to curry the favor of the Lord. The life of unbelief is a life of heaviness, with self-imposed burdens placed upon the shoulders of the one who is unbelieving. It is only through faith in what God has already done in the Person of Jesus Christ, that we will experience relief from the torment of unbelief's self-induced labor.

*"Howbeit the hair of his head began to grow again after he was shaven." - Judges 16:22*

In the dark prison of his own making, Samson's anointing could not be ultimately eliminated. Although his hair had been cut, the Philistine's knives were not able to remove the follicles that produced his hair. Similarly, beneath the surface of Samson's captivity was a truth that could not be altered, not by the most oppressive of Israel's enemies: God would fulfill His purpose of delivering Israel by the hands of this mighty deliverer. God had already called Samson to a destiny defined by deliverance, and He would not abandon him even in this self-induced darkness. Though a man may be unfaithful, God will always remain faithful, for that is His nature. It was in this prison, surrounded by a party of mockery, with a false deity presiding over the festivities, and enveloped in blindness, that Samson had been reduced to an invalid, needing the leading of a boy to find his way around. And it was here that Samson called upon the Lord for the last time.

*"O Lord GOD, remember me, I pray thee, and strengthen me, I pray thee, only this once, O God, that I may be at once avenged of the Philistines for my two eyes." - Judges 16:28*

Samson was chained between two pillars, one on his right side and the other on his left. His request to the Lord was that God would avenge his two eyes by giving him one final visitation of supernatural strength. As he pressed upon the two pillars which were instrumental in holding up the roof, the pillars broke apart and the roof came falling down. Within this palace were three thousand men and women, all of whom were crushed by the collapsing structure. This, his eighth and final act, was Samson's final blow against the Philistines, completing his destiny as every one of the Philistines died that day. Samson's greatest failure was transformed into the greatest act of deliverance for Israel and the final blow of defeat to the enemy.

Looking back, Samson's life has undoubtedly been used as an object lesson for many purposes – *proper leadership* would not be one of them. He has no record of leading a single person, as he did everything alone. By very definition a leader has to have followers. Rather than a trail of warriors following after his example, he had a trail of enemies that wanted to overtake and destroy him. The very people he was called to deliver did not even support him, but rather desired their Philistine captivity over his ministry of deliverance. Not only did he not display any leadership ability, he also did not show the *personal lifestyle* of one that should be imitated. He was known by his obstinate personality, stumbling in and out of his Nazarite vow, touching things he shouldn't have touched, and flirting in forbidden territory. Further, he did not possess the right *personal relationships*. There is not one mention of him having a close friend, an Israelite man perhaps with whom he could share his adventures with. Although his parents were supernaturally visited by God, given a divine word about their future son, and a miracle for his mother to conceive, they did not receive the respect due to them; he showed them dishonor by offering forbidden honey out of the carcass of a dead animal. He is only recorded as having three relationships with whom he was close, all non-Israelite women who turned his heart against the way of the Lord. In light of his improper leadership, rebellious personal lifestyle, and unhealthy personal relationships, it is with great astonishment that the writer of Hebrews lists Samson along with the others of the Old Testament. The truth is that Samson's greatness was sourced in the faith of God, which gave this cracked vessel the ability to fulfill his destiny. By faith, he wrought some of the most miraculous and unconventional miracles of deliverance the world has ever witnessed. His name means "Like the Sun,"[11] and we may accurately say that to Samson the universe seemed to revolve around him. However God would use the brightness of his faith to bring freedom to Israel in the darkness of captivity.

287

# CHAPTER FIFTEEN

# SAMUEL

*"And Samuel grew, and the LORD was with him, and did let none of his words fall to the ground." - 1 Samuel 3:19*

There was bitter anguish in Hannah's soul as she went before the Lord. As she spoke her petitions, she vowed a vow. Noticing her mouth – moving without any sound coming forth – Eli spoke harshly to her, "How long wilt thou be drunken? put away thy wine from thee." But it wasn't wine that made her mutter; it was the bitter anguish in her soul. She was barren in a day when barrenness was as bitter as a curse. Irrational and desperate, she replied, "No, my lord, I am a woman of a sorrowful spirit: I have drunk neither wine nor strong drink, but have poured out my soul before the LORD." Without hesitation, the priest declared "Go in peace and the God of Israel grant thee thy petition that thou hast asked of him." As high priest, Eli represented the vessel through which the word came. When he spoke these last words to Hannah, it was as if God was answering her prayer that very moment. What had she prayed?

*"O LORD of hosts, if thou wilt indeed look on the affliction of thine handmaid, and remember me, and not forget thine handmaid, but wilt give unto thine handmaid a man child, then I will give him unto the LORD all the days of his life, and there shall no razor come upon his head."– 1 Samuel 1:11*

Many people think that the intensity of their prayer determines how God will respond. However, God only responds to one kind of prayer: the prayer of a righteous man (see James 5:16). And how do righteous men pray? They pray *in faith* believing that God hears them and will grant them whatever they ask. This does not mean that God will not answer the prayers of the one who is trying to drum up physical intensity to match their words – many do this ignorantly. However, there will be times when our need is so great that we will not be able to help the physical intensity that goes into our prayers. Hannah perfectly demonstrates this. The prayer which she prayed became so physically intense that Eli thought she was intoxicated. The result of this faith-induced prayer was that God *heard* her, and responded by opening her barren womb. She became pregnant soon after, and eventually named her child "Samuel," which means "Heard of God."[1]

Hannah fulfilled her promise to the Lord and gave Samuel into the service of Eli the priest:

*"And the child Samuel ministered unto the LORD before Eli. And the word of the LORD was precious in those days; there was no open vision. And it came to pass at that time, when Eli was laid down in his*

There is a connection in these two verses. First, we are told that God's word was rare in Israel during the days of Eli, and then we are told that Eli's eyes began to "wax dim, that he could not see." It is no coincidence these two verses are juxtaposed. In the same way that Eli's natural eyes began to dim, his spiritual eyes were losing the ability to see as well. The result was that Eli, who was commissioned to receive and speak the word of the Lord to Israel, was unable to communicate what God was saying. Matthew 5:8 tells us, "Blessed are the *pure* in heart for they shall *see* God" (emphasis mine). Here the Lord is comparing purity of heart with the degree of one's spiritual eyesight. Eli's heart had become impure and thus he was not able to be the eyes and mouthpiece of the Lord. This created a major problem in this nation, as their government was a theocracy where God employed priests to lead the people! The Lord would now call upon the young boy in Eli's care, putting him to the test. This test would involve two components – the word and faith – and would be crucial to his success as Eli's replacement.

It was night time when Samuel was awakened to hear the voice of God. Now, we have already established that faith comes by hearing God's word. However, it is possible to hear God's word, but be unfamiliar with the way in which that word is conveyed. Samuel was hearing correctly, but needed understanding from the older, more experienced, Eli. Three times God called him, and three times he ran to

290

Eli saying "you called?" Eli was not aware that the Lord was calling unto Samuel until the third time. Finally, Eli perceived that it was Jehovah who called unto Samuel, and said: "Go, lie down: and it shall be, if he call thee, that thou shalt say, Speak, LORD; for thy servant heareth." It would not be unusual for a young boy to question the audible voice of God calling unto him, thinking it to be the voice of another person. It is not acceptable for a high priest who has been walking with the Lord for many years, to question that voice.

It is worth noting that the content of God's word to Samuel was, in fact, for Eli. Yet Eli was losing his ability to hear that voice because of sin in his life. Upon Eli's instruction, Samuel went back to sleep and answered the Lord who called a fourth time, saying, "Speak, for thy servant listeneth." Samuel finally perceived that the voice he heard was from the Lord, and was able to receive the rest of the message. There are times when our understanding is limited and we are unsure of the word of the Lord to us. But as we perceive the various ways God speaks the message we hear will become clearer. For example, one way God speaks is through repetition. He may initially speak one word to us through our friend. Then, He will speak the same word through a co-worker. Finally, we will see yet another confirmation through a Bible verse we have stumbled upon. We must not see these confirming events as merely coincidence, but as the Lord confirming His word in the mouth of two or three witnesses (see Deuteronomy 19:15).

*"And Samuel grew, and the LORD was with him, and did let none of his words fall to the ground." – 1 Samuel 3:19*

If we understand that Samuel's life and ministry was a result of God's word, then we will see the similarity between Samuel's growth as a prophet and the development of God's word in him as well as in us. Samuel's physical growth was paralleled with the growth of God's presence and word in his spoken ministry. It should also be understood that God's presence stays with God's word. Once a divine word is spoken to a person, we can be assured that God will *personally* tend to that word so that it experiences unhindered growth. The result of this union between God and His word is this: the word comes to pass and the man fulfills his destiny. Any word that man speaks which God has not first uttered will be void of God's fulfilling presence and of His fulfilling power. That God was *with* the young prophet demonstrates that the young man was not only carrying God's word, but was in fact the *result* of God's word.

As we read the second part of this verse, we understand that it is God's personal involvement with His spoken word that causes the success of the one who delivers that word. We read on and find out that Samuel's prophetic marksmanship was so accurate, that "all Israel from Dan even to Beersheba knew that Samuel was established to be a prophet of the LORD" (3:20).

*"And the LORD appeared again in Shiloh: for the LORD revealed himself to Samuel in Shiloh by the word of the LORD." – 1 Samuel 3:21*

The next great appearing of the Lord to Samuel occurs in Shiloh. The name "Shiloh" means "place of rest"[2] and was Samuel's temporary home for a season of his life. We gather that Samuel lived in communion with God, which was forged in a "place of rest." Hebrews 4 speaks of the rest that comes to those who live by faith and not by the works of the law. Every prophet and prophetic voice in the earth today will find their success in the ministry of God's word as they learn to abide in the rest of faith.

*"And the word of Samuel came to all Israel. Now Israel went out against the Philistines to battle, and pitched beside Ebenezer: and the Philistines pitched in Aphek." – 1 Samuel 4:1*

There is a spiritual progression in a life of faith that moves from small beginnings in obscurity to a wider sphere of recognition. Samuel began his journey as a young prophet-in-the-making revealing the word of the Lord to the man Eli. As he grew in his spirituality, he was eventually able to give the word of the Lord to "all Israel." Samuel's faith was always evolving as he had become a significant prophetic voice in Israel; he was considered to be a crucial part in their success as a nation. Overall, Israel's destiny was to take the land which was occupied by the Philistines. In order for this to happen, a prophet was needed at the helm of the Israelite army in order for their victory to be sure. Israel's success militarily was dependent upon the specific

293

word that a prophet spoke to them at the time of each conquest. The word that Samuel delivered hinged upon his faith. It is true that the word of the Lord brought clear instruction, but it was the faith of the prophet that caused the word to be released and performed. He believed God, which is evident in the verse "...and the LORD was with him, and did let none of his words fall to the ground." It sounds like this prophet didn't miss the mark! The fact is, we do not have to miss the mark in the gifts God has given us; the degree to which we yield to the voice of God and believe what He says, will be the degree to which we prophecy without hindrance to the divine word. Because of his personal faith in God, the entire nation of Israel benefited.

*"And Samuel spake unto all the house of Israel, saying, If ye do return unto the LORD with all your hearts, then put away the strange gods and Ashtaroth from among you, and prepare your hearts unto the LORD, and serve him only: and he will deliver you out of the hand of the Philistines. Then the children of Israel did put away Baalim and Ashtaroth, and served the LORD only. And Samuel said, Gather all Israel to Mizpeh, and I will pray for you unto the Lord." – 1 Samuel 7:5*

The name "Mizpeh" means "watchtower." A watchtower in the days of Israel was the highest point in the city where watchman would position themselves to warn the people of any impending danger. Samuel was a spiritual watchman for the nation of Israel. His role was to be a spiritual seer, to see the nation of Israel as God saw it

294

and to reveal the purpose of God which would inform and protect the nation. Israel responded to their watchman by destroying their idols. Like Samuel, people of faith are aware of their heavenly vantage point, and understand the devices of the enemy and the working of the Lord from God's panoramic perspective; and like Samuel, we have been given the divine responsibility to see afar off and pray in light of what is revealed to us. In the same way the watchman stood up high to see afar off, and alarm the people of any danger, we are called to stand in the high place of prayer, seeing what is yet to come, and by faith, interceding on behalf of our families, friends, cities, and nations. Faith allows us to pray effectively, and brings the supernatural signs and wonders of God into the situations that surround us.

*"And as Samuel was offering up the burnt offering, the Philistines drew near to battle against Israel: but the LORD thundered with a great thunder on that day upon the Philistines, and discomfited them; and they were smitten before Israel." – 1 Samuel 7:10*

Samuel's offering released the thunder of God to discomfort the Philistines. This led to an Israelite victory over their enemy and an affirmation of the power of one man's faith in God. Samuel prayed and God answered. We can see this same intervention of God today. If a person has faith, he or she can witness the creative acts of God's power in their sphere of influence; however, in order to see answered prayer, we must believe that God hears us. 1 John 5 says, "And this is the confidence that we have in him, that, if we ask any thing according to his will, he heareth us: And if we know that he hear us, whatsoever we ask, we know that we have the petitions that we desired of him." As his name declares, Samuel was confident that he was "heard of God." We must see that we have this same unspeakable privilege today based upon our relationship of faith to the father.

*"And it came to pass, when Samuel was old, that he made his sons judges over Israel." – 1 Samuel 8:1*

There is no death to the life of faith. Faith is an eternal attribute of God, and therefore cannot expire. When a person possesses God's faith, they live their life with God's ability to perform God's will. When the person dies, and their mission on earth is over, the faith which they possessed is still available for others to walk in. The Bible describes Abraham as the "father of faith," or, the father of all those who possess the faith that he received from the Lord. Faith is therefore a gift that is given throughout each generation. At times, when a person dies another may take his or her place and finish what they started; in the same way, Joshua finished what Moses started, leading the children of Israel into their promised land. The faith Moses operated in to lead Israel out of Egypt was the same faith that Joshua walked in to bring the people from the Wilderness into Canaan. And so we see that faith leaves a legacy for the next generation to fulfill. Samuel became old, and he made his sons judges over Israel.

Unfortunately, Samuel's sons were much like Eli's sons who did evil in the sight of God. This provoked the people to cry out for a king to take the place of the God-ordained priesthood. Knowing God's desire to lead His people through Levitical priests, Samuel also knew that this cry was sin. He could have simply rebuked the people for this demand, but instead he sought after God's wisdom. Despite knowing the highest and best that God intends for a person or people-group, we need wisdom to discern the proper course of action for each dilemma. Wisdom provides us with God's immediate solution to an immediate problem.

God replied to Samuel's prayer by comforting the disheartened prophet with these words:

*"And the LORD said unto Samuel, Hearken unto the voice of the people in all that they say unto thee: for they have not rejected thee, but they have rejected me, that I should not reign over them." – 1 Samuel 8:7*

By rejecting Samuel and the priestly order as the ordained leadership, the Israelites were actually rejecting the Lord's leadership over them. Samuel felt hurt as a result, as many of us are hurt when people we are called to lead reject us or take us for granted. However, we cannot afford to allow any form of rejection to take root in our hearts. Like Samuel, we must take our wounds to the Lord, and seek his wisdom. Had Samuel not been faithful to seek the Lord's counsel and command for the rebellious people, he would have become a hindrance to the plan of God.

*"And he went from year to year in circuit to Bethel, and Gilgal, and Mizpeh, and judged Israel in all those places. And his return was to Ramah; for there was his house; and there he judged Israel; and there he built an altar unto the LORD." – 1 Samuel 7:16-17*

In order to fulfill God's word, God must first equip us with His faith to go where He tells us to go, and speak to whom He directs us to. Every act of obedience moves us into a strategic position for divine connections to take place. In other words, we will be at the right place at the right time. While Samuel was accustomed to travel a circuit in order to fulfill his ministry, he was faithful to stay in his hometown when the Lord required. While in Ramah, Samuel was being divinely positioned to meet a young man who, while in search for a lost family possession, was about to collide with his own destiny. The young man's name was Saul. While looking for some of his father's lost animals, he and his servant were not able to find them. The servant – undoubtedly inspired by the Lord – said to his master,

*"... Behold now, there is in this city a man of God, and he is an honourable man; all that he saith cometh surely to pass: now let us go thither; peradventure he can shew us our way that we should go. (Beforetime in Israel, when a man went to enquire of God, thus he spake, Come, and let us go to the seer: for he that is now called a Prophet was beforetime called a Seer.)" – 1 Samuel 9:6 & 9*

Listen to the testimony of Samuel in the mouth of Saul's servant: "all that he saith cometh surely to pass." Not only was Samuel an accurate prophet, but he was famous as a result of his accuracy. When a person does something by faith, whether it is to prophesy to a government official, build a school for underprivileged children, or successfully raise 5 children as a single parent, their faith will produce successful results that will draw the attention of others. Furthermore, a faithful person will be marked by two attributes – success and fame. Contrary to some religious thinking, fame is not evil; it is simply a tool that amplifies the message of one's life. If a person's life exudes the works of God, then God will get the glory. Whereas we are not to seek after fame, a life lived in faith will undoubtedly get the attention of the world around us. It is while the world's attention is on us, that we will have an opportunity to reveal the true nature of our success which is found in Christ.

*"Now the LORD had told Samuel in his ear a day before Saul came, saying Tomorrow about this time I will send thee a man out of the land of Benjamin, and thou shalt anoint him to be captain over my people Israel, that he may save my people out of the hand of the Philistines: for I have looked upon my people, because their cry is come unto me."*
*– 1 Samuel 9:15-16*

An event was going to take place that had no precedent in Israel's history; however, because the prophet lived a life of faith, he became a central figure in the divine plan for this nation's future leadership. Not only was he given the knowledge of God's will, but was the vessel the Lord used to carry out the plan to make Saul a king. Likewise, our faithfulness to the Lord will produce revelation after revelation of God's will, not only for our lives, but for the lives of those around us, and provide direction for the course of nations. Verse 15 present us with the understanding that Samuel's ear belonged to the Lord. In the same way, we need revelation to see that our faith will only function to the degree that we are hearing his word. The more we hear of His word, the more that faith will be generated. We may "practice" hearing God's voice by doing as Samuel did when he was a boy in the temple. We should say "Lord, please speak, for your servant is listening." After we pray this prayer, we must not forget to listen!

Once we hear God's voice in some particular area, we are then energized to obey what we hear. It is not as though God's part is merely to speak a word to us, leaving us with the arduous responsibility of obeying that word; not only does He speak a word to us, but He releases His faith with that word. The faith of God then produces the willingness and ability on our part to perform that word. In actuality, to the person who lives by faith, obedience is as effortless as breathing. It is not normal for a person to think about breathing, nor does thinking aid the body in its respiratory function. Likewise, it is not normal for a person living by faith to wrestle with the idea of obedience before they obey; obedience is simply the natural response of a man or woman who has received a supernatural word. The less we analyze obedience the more natural it will become when God speaks a word of direction to us.

*"And when Samuel saw Saul, the LORD said unto him, Behold the man whom I spake to thee of! this same shall reign over my people." –*
*1 Samuel 9:17*

The conversation that began with a whisper in the ear, continued the next day as the Lord confirmed his word to the prophet, pointing out Saul, the man He had just spoken about. When God speaks to us, He may be indicating something that will happen in the future, but may not reveal all of the events and people that will come into play in the unfolding of that word. Sometimes He will give us only part of a word, so that we stay in a mode of listening – we never know for sure when the second part will come, and so we are filled with a kind of eager expectation.

Samuel encounters the young man Saul, and says confidently, "I am the seer: go up before me unto the high place; for ye shall eat with me today, and tomorrow I will let thee go, and will tell thee all that is in thine heart." To be effective as a man or woman in God's service, we will need more than just education and good morals. We will need the supernatural equipment provided for us by the Holy Spirit. When we reveal the "secrets of men's hearts" by the Spirit's enabling, they will be made open and willing to receive the mind of God for their lives. Jesus was given continual insight into the thoughts as well as the motives of people's hearts because His faith never wavered. We will be given the same insight in proportion to our faith.

*"Behold, here I am: witness against me before the LORD, and before his anointed: whose ox have I taken? or whose ass have I taken? or whom have I defrauded? whom have I oppressed? or of whose hand have I received any bribe to blind mine eyes therewith?" – 1 Samuel 12:3*

In the twelfth chapter of 1 Samuel, the prophet asks a series of rhetorical questions in front of the Israelites about his character during the many decades he served as their chief leader. He received an astounding response from the people: they could not accuse him of one single act of sin. Samuel heard the voice of God, was heard by God, prophesied God's word, and anointed Israel's first king; however, the most amazing thing about his life was that he possessed character that could not be blamed. This is a testimony to the life of faith, which is demonstrated loudly through blameless character. It needs to be said that, although there is distinction made in Scripture between the outworking of the Spirit in the form of gifts and character, we are wrong to emphasize one over the other. There are some who emphasize the need for supernatural giftings to manifest, such as miracles and prophecy. There are others who emphasize the need for greater character, such as love and patience. However, both godly giftings and godly character emanate from the same source: the Holy Spirit. Instead, we are to see that the same faith which activates the gifts of the Spirit as the faith that activates the character of the Spirit – also known as the fruits of the Spirit. The person who lives by faith will have both areas of spirituality manifesting through their lives. Any deficit in supernatural gifting or supernatural character must be traced back to a deficit in faith. When we believe we have been given the very Source of the gifts and of the character, we will begin seeing, as Samuel did, a manifestation of both which will be evident to those around us.

*"Then said Samuel, Bring ye hither to me Agag the king of the Amalekites. And Agag came unto him delicately. And Agag said, Surely the bitterness of death is past. And Samuel said, As thy sword hath made women childless, so shall thy mother be childless among women. And Samuel hewed Agag in pieces before the LORD in Gilgal." – 1 Samuel 11:32-33*

Samuel was a man of prayer, a man of character, and a man of passion. When it came to the morality of the leadership of Israel, Samuel took it very personally. He was the last of the judges commissioned to lead the people before the appointing of their first king. He knew the heart of God. It was not a democratic, aristocratic, or communistic rule that God desired, but a theocracy – a government presided over by God Himself. Samuel was simply the middle-man between the Lord and the nation of Israel for many decades. So, when God gave the people the king that they pined for, Samuel was distressed. Not only did he know this wasn't God's perfect will, he understood the sinful nature of man, and the inevitability of corrupt human rule. The result of this sin would bring the entire nation into moral chaos. Saul had been disobedient to God's plan in destroying all of the Agagites, by saving their king. When we read the above passage, we see the passion of the prophet as he slew the enemy king.

*"And Samuel came no more to see Saul until the day of his death: nevertheless Samuel mourned for Saul: and the LORD repented that he had made Saul king over Israel." – 1 Samuel 15:35*

Samuel's passion is seen in his mourning over Saul's failed leadership. The above verse juxtaposes two things - Samuel's tears and the repenting of the Lord. Both God and man were expressing passion over the same thing. This is because the life of faith *feels* the passion of God, and responds as though God were responding. When God is angered, the person becomes angered; when God is satisfied, the person of faith is satisfied. Speaking of this relationship, Jesus said that He came to give us abundant life. The word that is used for *life* here is the Greek word *zoe,* which means "the God kind of life" or "the life that God lives."[3] Furthermore, the apostle Paul said that we live by the faith of Christ (Gal. 2:20). Therefore, the life of faith is the God-kind of life inspired by the God-kind of faith. It is faith that causes us to experience the powerful emotions of God, even as Samuel experienced these emotions over the nation's backslidden leader.

*"And the LORD said unto Samuel, How long wilt thou mourn for Saul, seeing I have rejected him from reigning over Israel? fill thine horn with oil, and go, I will send thee to Jesse the Bethlehemite: for I have provided me a king among his sons. And Samuel said, How can I go? if Saul hear it, he will kill me. And the LORD said, Take an heifer with thee, and say, I am come to sacrifice to the LORD." – 1 Samuel 16:1-2*

In spite of the dangers that are embedded in our journey, when the Lord says "Go here" and "Say this" we have to trust in his protection over us. Faith sees the potential, the possibilities, and the final outcome of our obedience to the Lord. For example, God has shown us a vision of us preaching to a group of people on a street corner down town. We know that it is a particularly dangerous neighborhood, and so we may get a twinge of fear. But we are emboldened by our faith in the vision He gave us in prayer. We remember Jesus' words to His disciples saying, "I give you power to tread on serpents and scorpions and over all the power of the enemy; and nothing shall by any means hurt you." So, we go to that street corner, and we preach boldly without any fear, leaving all the consequences of our obedience to the Lord. We see this very clearly with Samuel, who feared being killed by Saul, but obeyed the divine instructions and went to Bethlehem to find the next king.

*"And Samuel did that which the LORD spake, and came to Bethlehem. And the elders of the town trembled at his coming, and said, Comest thou peaceably?" – 1 Samuel 16:4*

The ministry which God has given us will do something profound in the presence of those to whom we are sent. People will perceive the gift in us which will create an expectancy of that gift operating at any given time. If we are especially gifted in exhortation, then our presence will signify to those around us that the exhorter's ministry may operate at any time. This will prepare them for the word of encouragement. If our ministry is that of a teacher, then those around us will perceive that the teaching ministry of the word may operate spontaneously. Samuel was known for his prophetic ministry,

305

and was revered by all who heard of him as having the word of the Lord. In the above verse we read that the town *trembled* at his coming, indicating their great respect for Samuel's authority – a direct result of his accuracy when it came to hearing the voice of God, and delivering God's word to the nation. The more accurate we become in perceiving and operating in our gifting, the more spiritual authority we will have in the spiritual (i.e. the demonic spirits in Acts 19:15 who *knew* the apostle Paul) and in the natural realm. The purpose for this authority is to create the atmosphere of receptivity for our gift to operate. When people are receptive to God's gift in us, then will the plans and purposes of God be revealed to them.

Being a person of faith does not mean that our human judgment will never interfere. Samuel knew the heart of God, and spoke as His representative. However, his humanity was still operating, evident in the sixth verse of chapter 16. Looking for the next king of Israel in the sons of Jesse, Samuel sees Eliab and said to himself, "Surely the LORD'S anointed is before him." Judging by his natural eyesight was not something he was supposed to do as a prophet and a man of faith. Likewise, we have all made the same mistake of trying to see God's will for our lives or for the lives of others through our natural vision. The problem with natural sight is that it's limited to a three dimensional perspective, seeing only natural facts and figures which are always subject to change. God's realm is more like a 4-dimentional reality, as it encompasses the natural realm, but includes a hidden dimension that can only be seen with spiritual eyesight. The power of faith is that it sees what God sees beyond the dimensions of time and space. Faith is the substance of things not seen with the human eye.

The invisible realm where God's will is located is unveiled by faith, and we are able to prophesy into existence what is in that dimension. What God tells Samuel next is a major key to operating in this faith which unveils the will of God.

*"But the LORD said unto Samuel, Look not on his countenance, or on the height of his stature; because I have refused him: for the LORD seeth not as man seeth; for man looketh on the outward appearance, but the LORD looketh on the heart." 1 Samuel 16:7*

Two things are apparent with this verse. The first is man's inclination to look on the external, visible part of a situation to determine something. The second is that God looks on the internal, invisible aspects of a situation to determine something. In order for us to perform God's will, we must be able to see as He does and then speak or act accordingly. This is only made possible by faith. The decision Samuel needed to make would be based upon his ability to see the spiritual reality behind the outward appearance of the young men standing before him. As the account goes, seven men passed before him, all of whom were denied by the Lord. Now, when David arrived, the Bible says that he was "of a beautiful countenance, and goodly to look at." By this we know that David had an attractive outward look, however he most likely did not possess a mature physique like his brothers, or the more seasoned experience in physical combat. The good news is that God does not take into account our physical stature or our experience when he calls us; rather, He calls us according to what He has planned for us in the future! This is why it is essential that we see people through the eyes of faith, which unveils the spiritual dimension, revealing God's will for their future.

One of the last great events that revealed the power of Samuel's faith was the account of Saul's men going out to kill David, who was hiding in Samuel's house. Each time a band of soldiers came in the vicinity of the house, the Spirit of the Lord fell upon them and they started to prophesy. When Saul himself came, after sending three unsuccessful bands, he fell down, stripped naked, and began to prophesy all day and all night. What Saul and his men failed to realize was that Samuel walked in greater authority then the very king of Israel, because he lived the life of faith. Being in the presence of Samuel was the same as being in the presence of the Lord. Entering Samuel's sphere of life, Saul *had* to strip naked, because he was in the presence of a man whose ministry exposed the sinfulness of the nation, especially that of its king. Samuel could not be defeated nor his gifts stamped out because his life was a life of faith, yielded to Almighty God. Samuel's sphere of authority had grown to the point that prophecy, miracles, signs and wonders manifested continually. Not only that, but those who were attempting to do him harm came under the very power that emanated out of him, prophesying under the same spirit! A life of faith will likewise transform our lives in such a way that we not only manifest signs and wonders, but allow the world to become participants in the divine life, as they experience God's divine power through their contact with us.

Samuel's entire life could be summarized as an unending conversation with the Lord. From the time of his childhood, to the last days of his life, Samuel possessed the unique characteristic of faith in God which opened his ears more and more to hear the full counsel of God for a nation, and to speak on behalf of that nation's creator. His very existence was a result of the heartfelt prayer his mother prayed before he was even born. Without her faith, this national prophet would not have existed. It was as if faith was written into his DNA. From his first encounter with the voice of God as a child, to the great exploits performed in front of the nation of Israel, Samuel's life inspires us to see our lives as a continual exchange with Christ, not merely from major event to major event, but in the simplicity of a "voice in the ear" spoken throughout each day.

# CHAPTER SIXTEEN

# DAVID

*"And when he had removed him, he raised up unto them David to be their king; to whom also he gave testimony, and said, I have found David the son of Jesse, a man after mine own heart, which shall fulfil all my will." – Acts 13:22*

Few figures throughout human history have had a more prolific life than David the Bethlehemite. As one of the most well recognized figures in the Old Testament, he is known for shepherding, slaying giants, and ruling over Israel as king. His life has been the study of people groups around the world for his wisdom as a national leader, his military achievements, and the iconic psalms which he wrote throughout the various stages of his journey. Behind his spiritual and physical prowess was the faith of God, which so empowered him that the writer of Hebrews put him in the same class as the other paramount figures of faith. All of the attributes ascribed to him – warrior, leader, and lover of God's heart – resulted from the power of God's word to him, which set him on the journey of faith toward his destiny as king.

The prophet of the Old Testament was the voice of God in the earth. He or she represented God's word, and God's will. They were loved by many, hated by some, and feared by all. They were God's instruments to reveal His divine plans and purposes for each generation. It was the prophet Samuel who installed the first king over Israel – king Saul – and it was the same prophetic ministry that God used to tear Saul's kingdom from his hands. When the first king sinned against God, he was not fit to lead the nation anymore. And so, God sent Samuel to find the next king.

*"And the LORD said unto Samuel, How long wilt thou mourn for Saul, seeing I have rejected him from reigning over Israel? fill thine horn with oil, and go, I will send thee to Jesse the Bethlehemite: for I have* **provided** *me a king among his sons." – 1 Samuel 16:1 (emphasis mine)*

The Hebrew word for "provided" is *ra'ah,* which has the specific meaning in this verse as "to see about anything, to provide or care for it."[1] The word *ra'ah* is used when Abraham says "God will *provide* for Himself a lamb for a burnt offering" (Genesis 22:8). In essence, God was telling Samuel that He had observed who the next king would be, and carefully chosen him according to His predetermined plan. It was as though God were saying, "I have already seen the next king, I already know him, and I have made provisions for him to become who I've called him to be." The Lord already knew who the next king would be, for He had already seen him through the divine lens of faith. In fact, God does everything through faith, whether it is to "frame the worlds" or to choose a king. Now, unlike Saul, who was chosen based upon the Israelite's preferences, the new king would be chosen solely on God's preferences. Since the next king would be chosen based on God's qualifications and not Israel's, the chosen vessel would reveal much about God's character, God's nature. The Lord was looking for someone in particular, someone who possessed a God-like heart. Below, we read of the Lord's desire, even in the midst of Saul's reign, to find a man whose heart was literally cut from the mold of divinity.

*"But now thy kingdom shall not continue: the LORD hath sought him a man **after** his own heart, and the LORD hath commanded him to be captain over his people, because thou hast not kept that which the LORD commanded thee." – 1 Samuel 13:14 (emphasis mine)*

A key word in this verse is "after" which denotes a specific class or mold from which that man originated. The next king of Israel would possess a heart that was like God's, having desires that reflected the nature of God. As such, God's choice would not be based upon man's idea of what a king should look like, but on His own. When the Lord sent the prophet Samuel to anoint the next king, He already knew that the majority of Jesse's sons would seem like good choices to Samuel, and so He gave him this word of admonishment, *"Look not on his countenance..."* (1 Samuel 16:7). The Lord was not looking for a man who possessed a specific outward appearance, rather someone who had an inward tendency to yield to God's leadership. The same is true today. The Lord is only impressed with what He sees of Himself in a man or woman, and not with what that man or woman can do or how impressive they are in appearance. Furthermore, since it takes faith for that man or woman to emanate the divine nature, it is necessary that a divine word be spoken to them first. Within that divine word is the revelation of the purpose God has for them, something that

312

will inspire faith and even promote the desire to see that thing come to pass.

As the prophet Samuel inspected seven of Jesse's sons, he was not aware that there was an eighth son missing from the lineup. He simply did his duty by observing the seven, and by revelation came to the conclusion that God had not chosen any of them for Israel's kingship. The chosen king was not present, as he was in the field looking over the family sheep – he was Jesse's eighth and youngest son. The Lord would not allow Samuel to rest until the eighth son passed before the prophet. And so, David was called away from the sheep so that he could stand before Samuel.

*"Then Samuel took the horn of oil, and anointed him in the midst of his brethren: and the Spirit of the LORD came upon David from that day forward. So Samuel rose up, and went to Ramah. But the Spirit of the LORD departed from Saul, and an evil spirit from the LORD troubled him." – 1 Samuel 16:13-14*

Now, David was young when he was anointed by the prophet. The anointing was for the kingly position that awaited him sometime in the future. David was not given any details of his calling, except that he was to be the next king of Israel. He was not told what would happen to Saul, the existing king. He was not given the particulars on how to prepare for his calling. He was not given any insight into the type of king he was to become. He was not told about the things he would have to suffer in order to reach his destiny. All he knew was that he was anointed by the prophet Samuel, and that a kingship awaited him. Similarly, we may receive God's word that reveals some grand

313

plan about our future. Yet, we are given no details as to the exact course we are to take in order to arrive at God's intended destination. All we are made to know is God's word. Immediately we receive that word, faith begins to energize our imaginations and we are infused with a new spiritual fortitude to press onward into the unknown, with nothing more than a glimpse of that destiny in the horizon.

According to the above scripture verse, as soon as David was confirmed as the next king, three things happened. First, he was anointed by the prophet. Second, the Spirit of the Lord came upon him. And third, the Spirit of the Lord departed from Saul, leaving him open to an evil spirit. By these three occurrences, we see a prophetic picture of the life lived by faith. When God reveals His word to us, we are anointed to fulfill that word. In other words, we received the divine enablement – the anointing – to walk a supernatural path that will require supernatural abilities in order to arrive successfully at our destination. Next, we begin to see the Spirit of the Lord as our shepherd, leading us toward that goal, teaching and guiding us so that we do not miss anything needful along way. And lastly, a problem will typically arise that can only be solved by the anointing which we have received, and the wisdom which has been revealed to us on the journey. The same Spirit Who came upon David for his kingly destiny permitted an evil spirit to come upon Saul, the existing king of Israel. As a result, Saul needed someone who was anointed to deal with that evil spirit. Thus, David was called into the palace to play his harp for the troubled king.

Through the anointing he carried, David was able to launch a spiritual assault upon the evil spirit, so much so that each time he

314

played, the spirit left Saul. Although Saul was not aware that David had been anointed as his successor, he was benefiting from the kingly anointing that rested upon this youth, emanating from his music. From this account, we may glean understanding about our own destiny. What God has spoken to us about our future will indicate the kind of spiritual equipment He is installed within us, and will make room for divine opportunities leading to the fulfillment of that destiny. We may receive a prophetic word that our talent will one day be broadcast to the world; in the meantime, doors of opportunity may open where that emerging talent will be able to impact people on a smaller scale. It is not that our abilities are anything in themselves, but that our abilities provide opportunity for God to demonstrate His power.

*"And David rose up early in the morning, and left the sheep with a keeper, and took, and went, as Jesse had commanded him; and he came to the trench, as the host was going forth to the fight, and shouted for the battle." – 1 Samuel 17:20*

Now, along with being called upon to minister in the palace, David was also released back to his home when needed, to tend to his responsibilities there. One morning, he was instructed by his father to take food to his brothers on the battlefield. As he approached the field, the Bible says that David "shouted for the battle" which was brewing between the Israelites and the Philistines. It is remarkable that David, who was not a trained soldier, displayed no fear at his first sight of the Philistine army and their giant captain. Meanwhile, the entire Israelite army, including their king, was in dread fear because of the enemy across the field! By this, we see a truth that, although we have never stepped out onto some "battlefield" of life, we may do so with the courage of the most seasoned warrior. This is because our natural experience in a particular area of life is not a prerequisite to our success in that area in the future; this kind of experience is *not* central to the life of faith. Rather it is the level of confidence in God's ability through us that will determine success in that area of our life. Although David had seen God's power demonstrated in other areas of his life, he had no experience fighting a giant; therefore his confidence was not based upon a history of giant-slaying but in the power God which inspires the faith needed in the exact time of need.

*"And Saul said to David,Thou art not able to go against this Philistine to fight with him: for thou art but a youth, and he a man of war from his youth. And David said unto Saul, Thy servant kept his father's sheep, and there came a lion, and a bear, and took a lamb out of the flock: And I went out after him, and smote him, and delivered it out of his mouth: and when he arose against me, I caught him by his beard, and smote him, and slew him. Thy servant slew both the lion and the bear: and this uncircumcised Philistine shall be as one of them, seeing he hath defied the armies of the living God. David said moreover, The LORD that delivered me out of the paw of the lion, and out of the paw of the bear, he will deliver me out of the hand of this Philistine. And Saul said unto David, Go, and the LORD be with thee." – 1 Samuel 17:34-37*

316

The above verses reveal that Saul compared the youth standing before him with the warrior standing before the armies of Israel; however, David saw the confrontation not between Goliath and himself, but between a man and Almighty God. One can see the clear line of distinction between unbelief and faith when looking at the perspectives of Saul and David. Although Saul had seen military success in his past, he was not able to reconcile this present situation with the fact that God could actually give him the victory. By this we may safely conclude that he did not give God the glory for all of his past victories, as did David. Notice that David accredits his past victories to the Lord. In David's eyes, it mattered little whether the enemy was a lion, a bear, or a giant man. The specific situation of deliverance was not David's focus, rather it was the Lord. Ultimately, our enemy will attempt to turn our attention away from the Lord, and toward our own ability to win or lose the battle. It is when we see the victory as already belonging to the Lord that we will exude the confidence of David, knowing that the outcome will always be in our favor.

After giving David permission to pursue Goliath, Saul gave David his armor to wear into battle. Unlike those who were trained for war with conventional armor, David refused the armor saying that it had not been "proved." The word "proved" here means "to test, to try, to put to the proof."[2] In other words, David had had no experience in conventional armor in his past battles in the sheep fields. Rather, he was used to the unconventional means of protection that he had proven, especially against the lion and the bear. It was because of this mindset that David would become one of the most unconventional

317

leaders of the Old Covenant (we will look at the concept of unconventional leadership later on). David would meet the giant with nothing more than a slingshot and 5 smooth stones.

*"Then said David to the Philistine, Thou comest to me with a sword, and with a spear, and with a shield: but I come to thee in the name of the LORD of hosts, the God of the armies of Israel, whom thou hast defied. This day will the LORD deliver thee into mine hand; and I will smite thee, and take thine head from thee; and I will give the carcases of the host of the Philistines this day unto the fowls of the air, and to the wild beasts of the earth; that all the earth may know that there is a God in Israel. And all this assembly shall know that the LORD saveth not with sword and spear: for the battle is the LORD'S, and he will give you into our hands." – 1 Samuel 17:45-47*

Upon studying the above three verses, we find four definitive statements made by David. Notice that all of them are spoken in *future* tense.

1. "This uncircumcised Philistine *shall* be as one of them";
2. "The LORD...he *will* deliver me out of the hand of this Philistine";
3. "This day *will* the LORD deliver thee into mine hand; and I *will* smite thee...and I *will* give the carcasses of the host of the Philistines this day unto the fowls of the air...";
4. "For the battle is the LORD'S, and he *will* give you into our hands."

318

David was declaring what would happen in the future, prophesying the victory that he and the Israelite people were about to gain over the Philistines. This was not just some young boy's fantastical imagination running wild, as his elder brothers thought (see 1 Samuel 17:28). David was given God's faith which enabled him to see success as the *predictable* outcome. In fact, when we see our situation the way God does, we will always have hope of a successful outcome because faith can completely alter our circumstance. It is when we speak out of the confidence of our faith, tangible results will follow. David's boldness was a precursor to the kingship he was destined for, and was manifested in the face of an intimidating foe.

*"And all this assembly shall know that the LORD saveth not with sword and spear: for the battle is the LORD'S, and he will give you into our hands'...And David put his hand in his bag, and took thence a stone, and slang it, and smote the Philistine in his forehead..." – 1 Samuel 17:47 & 49*

These two verses depict the brilliant simplicity of faith operating with corresponding works. The first demonstrates David's belief in what was about to take place. The second reveals the work which David performed, bringing the manifestation to what he had just declared. When Peter spoke with the man at the gate called Beautiful, he said by inspiration of the Holy Spirit, *"Silver and gold have I none; but such as I have give I thee."* (see Acts 3:6) Peter spoke this to the crippled man out of the faith of Christ abiding in him. The same faith that gave him bold words prompted him to do what we find in the next verse: "And he took him by the right hand, and lifted him up: and immediately his feet and ankle bones received strength." We must

319

remember that faith does not plan events or actions. Faith sees into the future and responds according to what is seen. The response of faith is not formulated in the intellect but manifests out of the spontaneity of the Spirit. Peter was on his way to pray and David was on his way to slay. But it was faith that prompted the response to pick the crippled man up and the use of a sling and stone to kill the giant.

The life of faith is a constant, as is the life of God Himself. Faith is always a present reality. To have "little faith" or "no faith" does not mean faith is not present, any more than the one who does not believe in gravity negates the gravitational force all around them. If faith is not activated in someone's heart, it is simply a matter of that person's blindness to the truth of God – their ignorance to God's life all around them. The *conscious* life of faith is a life of constant trust in God. The more constant the reality of faith is to the believer, the more constant the life of God will manifest through the believer. Even if, like David, we see a great victory preceding a great obstacle, we still can see the life of God manifest in our situation.

Amazingly, after David slew Goliath with a single stone, the entire Israelite army "...arose, and shouted, and pursued the Philistines." The Israelites did exactly what David did when he first saw the enemy armies led by their giant captain. What caused this sudden reversal in the tone of the once fearful Israelites? They saw the manifestation of David's faith, slaying the giant and cutting his head off, and suddenly they believed in the power of God to defeat their enemy. In essence, the Israelites demonstrate to us that, when our faith is manifested in some declarative act, that faith may be seen by others, and may cause those who see to believe and do what they formerly did

320

not have the courage to do. David's faith was seen and therefore it was emulated.

*"And the women answered one another as they played, and said, Saul hath slain his thousands, and David his ten thousands. And Saul was very wroth, and the saying displeased him; and he said, They have ascribed unto David ten thousands, and to me they have ascribed but thousands: and what can he have more but the kingdom? And Saul eyed David from that day and forward." – 1 Samuel 18:7-9*

Now, David was anointed by the prophet as the future king, yet he was not set in his kingly office yet. He was living in the tension between the anointing he had received and the kingly office he would inherit as a result of that anointing. The tension was, and is, the place where faith in God's word is put into the fire of affliction. The faith of God stirring within David's heart was not quenched by Saul's new-found animosity; it was simply ignited by the circumstances of Saul's hatred. The calling was great, and the testing would be equally as great. David's faith did not change, but David himself changed in the fire of Saul's anger. In fact, a close study of the interactions between David and Saul reveal that Saul attempted to kill David eleven times throughout the course of Saul's reign!

It is at this point in David's life that he experienced a divine disconnect in his relationship with Saul and the kingdom of Israel. This "divine disconnect" is typical in the life of faith. There comes a point

321

when we aren't able to stay connected to those people we have previously worked with. This disconnect often happens just prior to the Lord revealing what we formerly did not know. The reasons for the disconnection can be varied; some may be due to a geographical move we are to undertake, others because of a change in the specific type of work we are called to, and still others because of an unresolvable conflict with those we have worked with. Nonetheless, we reach a point where we are speaking different languages, and the peace we once knew has turned into confusion. Abraham could not see his destiny come to fruition until he parted with his nephew Lot. Paul could not continue ministering with Barnabas because of a heated contention over John Mark. David could not continue where he was any longer, for the celebration of his great exploits on the battlefields turned into a nightmarish season of continual hatred, coming in the form of violent assaults from the king. When we find there to be no more peace in a particular relationship, it may be that the assignment has ended and the Lord is moving us in a different direction. And so, David fled from Saul's kingdom and became an outcast in the wilderness.

This next season of David's life would be comprised of the unconventional preparation that is typical to those biblical figures we have been studying. It is a season of perplexity that seems to follow some great revelation, some valiant deed, or some conquered enemy. Abraham left the familiarity of his family in Haran, as the Lord called him to a foreign land. Joseph was taken captive away from his family after two monumental prophetic dreams. Moses left the glory of his position in Egypt, after delivering a fellow Hebrew from an oppressive captor: he spent the next 40 years living in the wilderness. John the Baptist, who was in line to succeed his father Zechariah – the high priest in Israel – left his rightful place in the temple to prepare for the coming Messiah. It appears that the Lord has appointed a time for us to leave our surroundings, and venture out into a more solitary place for greater preparation. It is in this place that we become prepared in an unconventional way. God's ways are *unconventional* in that they typically defy cultural norms – that which is accepted by our society, albeit Christian society – as the way we are to prepare for our calling. Although Bible colleges may present us with an education on biblical issues, they will never be an adequate substitute for the experiential preparation which has been tailor-made for creating the kind of man or woman God desires us to become.

David was on the run. The royal life he tasted in the palace had turned bitter in the face of new found persecution, resulting in rejection and great perplexity. At one point, we find him in the city of Nob asking the priest Ahimelech for some food. Before leaving, Ahimelech gave him the sword of Goliath, the same sword David used to cut off his head after he had killed him with the slingshot. Upon eating the holy bread laid in the temple and acquiring the sword, David made his way to the Philistine king of Gath. Because he was known by the Philistines as the Israelite war hero, David "changed his behavior" before them, acting insane as he scribbled on the gate doors and let his spit fall onto his beard. Not only did the Philistines allow him access into their kingdom, but would later form an even closer alliance with him.

*"David therefore departed thence, and escaped to the cave Adullam: and when his brethren and all his father's house heard it, they went down thither to him. And every one that was in distress, and every one that was in debt, and every one that was discontented, gathered themselves unto him; and he became a captain over them: and there were with him about four hundred men." – 1 Samuel 22:1-2*

After some time on the run, David made his way into the cave of Adullam. It was in this place that his family, as well as the mighty warriors loyal to David, found him and stayed with him. Although he had been deemed an enemy of Saul's kingdom, he was still seen by some as a beacon of hope, though only to a remnant. In fact, he was able to instill courage into their hearts, as they were "in distress…in debt, and…discontented." The fact that he was able to become their captain reveals the kind of spiritual fortitude he had. It would have been easy for him to have succumbed to the depression of being rejected, yet he was driven by something deeper than mere emotion; he had the oil of a kingly anointing still smeared upon his heart and could not deny his true identity: he was destined to become the king of Israel. Thus, he acted kingly, turning the troubled multitude in front of him into a stalwart army.

*"Then David arose, and cut off the skirt of Saul's robe privily. And it came to pass afterward, that David's heart smote him, because he had cut off Saul's skirt. And he said unto his men, The LORD forbid that I should do this thing unto my master, the LORD'S anointed, to stretch*

*forth mine hand against him, seeing he is the anointed of the LORD."*

*– 1 Samuel 24:4-6*

Having being warned by the prophet Gad, David and his men left the cave of Adullam because Saul and his men were on their way. There were a few specific instances after they departed when David could easily have killed Saul. Now, it is important to remember that although David knew he was anointed to be king, he believed that his destiny was something that could not be arrived at through human wisdom or human strength. From a human standpoint, David had every right to attack and kill Saul, the man whose mission it was to hunt and destroy him. He could have reasoned that, since he was already anointed by the prophet Samuel, he was therefore ready to be a king. He could have looked at his success on the battlefield and saw himself as a greater warrior than Saul. He could have been influenced by the fact that a host of mighty men were at his command, and could invade the kingdom of Israel with probable success. David could have taken his kingship by force, but his reign would have been illegitimate in the eyes of God, in the same way that Saul's reign became illegitimate through the sin of a self-imposed sacrifice (see 1 Samuel 13). Likewise, there will inevitably be times that we are tempted to fulfill God's word through humanly devised planning. However, we must see that God's word is not fulfilled by human will-power, but by the Lord Himself, who has a set time and set means through which to accomplish that word. Any humanly devised plan will inevitably cause us to compromise our integrity in the same way that David's character would have been compromised had he killed Saul.

325

*"And David said in his heart, I shall now perish one day by the hand of Saul: there is nothing better for me than that I should speedily escape into the land of the Philistines; and Saul shall despair of me, to seek me any more in any coast of Israel: so shall I escape out of his hand." – 1 Samuel 27:1*

In a monumental decision, David chose to be part of the Philistine nation, at the risk of being killed by a people he had previously fought to destroy. This radical choice reveals a stunning quality in David's life; he would rather fight for the enemy of Israel than to assume the kingly position over Israel – a position he knew only God could ordain. Here we see the evidence of faith working in the life of David. His belief in God's sovereignty over the affairs of Israel far outweighed his desire for personal gain. It took faith to not only relinquish opportunities for self-promotion, but also to choose citizenship with Israel's enemy, rather than to usurp God's order and oppose God Himself. As long as Saul was king over Israel, David knew that he would be Israel's enemy. And so he lived with the Philistine people for a year and four months.

When considering the choice to live with the Philistines, it becomes apparent that David was not allowing any romantic notions about his future destiny to dictate what he did in his present moment. In other words, he lived in each season making the decisions that were needed, not basing them on human logic. If he was intellectualizing his destiny, making decisions based upon what he thought should happen, it would have been doubtful that he'd choose to reside with the Philistines. If he were of that mindset, the sheer humiliation of submitting to the nation he once championed, all because his home land had rejected him would have been a death blow to his pride. But David demonstrates true faith here as it is not bound by intellectual reasoning. In fact, the wisdom of faith always bypasses natural reasoning because its nature is of heavenly origination. Heavenly wisdom must transcend our natural way of thinking if we are to rightly discern what we are to do in any given circumstance. Typically, the decision that is based in heavenly wisdom will defy common sense; however it will have imprinted upon it the signature of God's peace. Whether we are in a prison like Joseph, who was positioned there to reveal the king's dreams, or an outcast like David who became an instrument of God's power in the Philistine nation, we may expect to see God's purposes revealed in unconventional situations.

*"So Saul died, and his three sons, and his armor bearer, and all his men, that same day together." – 1 Samuel 31:6*

Upon hearing of the king's death, David did not rejoice but rather mourned. In a poetic benediction, David included these words, "Saul and Jonathan were lovely and pleasant in their lives, and in their death they were not divided: they were swifter than eagles, they were stronger than lions" (2 Samuel 1:23). These words were released in a moment of overwhelming grief. It is a fact that many of the iconic psalms which David wrote were inspired by the sufferings he endured on the road to his kingship. It was the crushing blow of rejection, violence, and misunderstanding that produced such a depth of words and songs from out of his heart. By this we see a truth, that spiritual creativity can be produced through the pain of our suffering. In

David's case, it resulted in the writing of many of his psalms. Just as the crushing of the olive is necessary to produce oil, God will allow us to experience painful emotions in order to release a greater expression of creativity in our calling. That creative expression is the anointing oil flowing through us for the benefit of others.

*"And the time that David was king in Hebron over the house of Judah was seven years and six months." – 2 Samuel 2:11*

Many years after his first anointing by the prophet Samuel, David received his second anointing as king over Hebron, the chief city of Judah. He was thirty years old when he began to reign there. Although the fulfillment of the first prophetic word had not yet occurred, as he was not yet reigning over all of Israel, he had finally stepped into an official position as king. By this time, David was not the same young man that he was when he left the sheep fields at home. He had experienced many wars. He had defeated many adversaries. He had tasted the delights of a kingdom, as well as the power of rejection. He had married wives but knew the feeling of having to separate from them because the dangers of his journey did not always permit their accompanying him.

He had gained the loyalty of a distinct warrior class of men, all of whom did mighty exploits recorded in scripture. These were men who understood unconventional warfare. It is recorded that one of them slew eight hundred men at once, and another slew three hundred with a spear. At one point, David longed for a drink of the water in the well of Bethlehem; however, it was guarded by a garrison of the Philistines. In order to satisfy their leader, three of his mighty men were able to break through the Philistine garrison, fill a cup with the sacred water, and return it to him. These were just some of the many exploits these men were capable of. The fact that they followed David reveals the kind of leadership he provided for them, and the kind of leader he was. David had slayed a lion and a bear. He singlehandedly killed the giant goliath when no one else could muster the courage to do so. He rallied an entire nation around the purpose of God for them, which was to claim the land that was rightfully theirs. He did all these things most likely before the age of twenty. He not only had skill on the battlefield but he knew how to ignite the fires of destiny within others. Not only do we see him doing this upon slaying the giant, but also upon gathering to himself thousands of Israelites in the cave of Adullam, and leading them out with greater confidence.

He led many more military victories in the seven and a half years he spent reigning in Judah, until the time when his destiny would ultimately be fulfilled.

*"Then came all the tribes of Israel to David unto Hebron, and spake, saying, Behold, we are thy bone and thy flesh. Also in time past, when Saul was king over us, thou wast he that leddest out and broughtest in Israel: and the LORD said to thee, Thou shalt feed my people Israel, and thou shalt be a captain over Israel. So all the elders of Israel came to the king to Hebron; and king David made a league with them in Hebron before the LORD: and they anointed David king over Israel."*
*– 2 Samuel 5:1-3*

This was the third and final anointing David received. At last, he had become king over all of Israel. What is significant here is that

David knew from the time he was still a boy, that he was called to rule over all of Israel. Yet, throughout his life we find him consistently denying opportunities to exalt himself into his kingship. David did not seek to realize his destiny through politicizing himself in front of the people. David realized his kingship apart from his own devices. The fact that Israel who was formerly David's enemy publicly recognized him as their king, confirmed that it was God's appointed time for David to reign. By this we know that an individual should never seek public recognition as a means to promote who they are and what they are called to do. Those whom God has called for a specific purpose will find that human recognition is merely a byproduct of God's appointed time. We see this in the lives of many biblical figures. It wasn't time for Joseph's destiny to be fulfilled, and so, despite all the good he did in the prison, he wasn't publically recognized until the time that was appointed for him. Similarly, the scriptures say that John the Baptist was in the wilderness "till the day of his shewing unto Israel" (see Luke 1:80), signifying that there was a set time when his ministry would "appear" to Israel. Furthermore, when the apostle Paul was first commissioned to fulfill his apostolic calling, the company of prophets and teachers around him recognized that it was the set time for him to go forth. In the same way, if we wait for the Holy Spirit to release us into our calling, we will simultaneously find that He will promote that very calling, and subsequently, there will be an element of recognition by the people around us.

Scripture reveals a fascinating truth about David's life – he was known as a man whose heart was *perfect*. David's son Solomon, who succeeded him as king over Israel, is described as having an *imperfect*

330

heart. We see this in 1 Kings 11:4 which declares, "For it came to pass, when Solomon was old, that his wives turned away his heart after other gods: and his heart was not perfect with the LORD his God, as was the heart of David his father." Now, Solomon was a man of unparalleled wisdom, by which he saw decades of peace in Israel after he began to reign. However, he sinned by allowing many of his foreign wives to "turn away his heart after other gods." How is it then, that Solomon is described as having an "imperfect heart" before the Lord, whereas David, who committed murder and adultery during his kingship, had a perfect heart before the Lord? The answer is found when we consider the life of faith. David continued in faith toward God whereas Solomon did not. The fact is, the *heart* is the focus of both David's and Solomon's life because it is in the heart of a man that faith is either present or absent. In David's case, faith remained; in Solomon's case, faith had departed.

Now, we know from scripture that a person is not made righteous by their works, but by faith. It is therefore right to say that a person's righteousness is not based upon the sins which they commit in their life, nor is it based upon the good works they perform. If it were based upon their sin, then David's testimony would have been as his sons – that his heart had become imperfect before the Lord. We know that David committed adultery with Bathsheba and had her husband murdered to cover up his affair. If it were based upon good works, then both David and Solomon would have been given the same testimony, that they had perfect hearts as a result of the godly deeds they performed. We must conclude therefore that it wasn't the specific cases of sin or the wonderful deeds done, but rather *the continuance of faith* which determined the perfection of their hearts. It must be seen that David lived his life in faith, for even when he sinned, he did not allow that sin to keep him from the grace of God, through which he was forgiven and restored. Thus we have the apostle Paul speaking on the righteousness of faith, and quoting the psalm of David saying, "But to him that worketh not, but believeth on him that justifieth the ungodly, his faith is counted for righteousness. Even as David also describeth the blessedness of the man, unto whom God imputeth righteousness without works, saying, blessed is he whose transgressions is forgiven, whose sin is covered" (Romans 4:5-7). It was this revelation of David's that would describe the blessed state of man under the New Covenant, as Jesus Christ saved us not based upon our works but upon His finished work on the Cross. David is an example to us of the fact that perfection is made possible only through faith in God.

This man David embodied the extraordinary life which is given to all those who will believe in the word of God and the power of God to fulfill that word. David was a slayer of evil, a prophet declaring the way of God, and a priest ministering before God's presence. David had the heart of a warrior and a worshipper. He believed in the power of God's presence to guide the military might of his sword. Whether in the fields tending sheep, in the wilderness as an outcast, or on the battlefield as a king, he saw victory as the inevitable outcome of the one whose faith is in the Lord.

# TOUCHING THE

# FINISH LINE

One of the greatest examples of a life modeled after Christ is the apostle Paul. He not only modeled the work of the ministry, but the everyday life of the believer. It was in his ministry to the Church that we see the main thrust of his teachings, pointing heavily toward the supernatural kingdom awaiting each individual. Substantiating his message were the supernatural encounters that continually flowed throughout his life. Paul's personal revelation of heavenly realities enabled him to contact the heavenly destiny that awaited him. In other words, Paul experienced the end of his race while he was still running, and therefore *touched the finish line* of his faith. He describes an experience in which he was "caught up to the third heaven" in an out-of-body experience (see 2 Corinthians 12). This supernatural occurrence was for the purpose of seeing "visions and revelations of the Lord." Not only that, but he "heard unspeakable words, which it is not lawful for a man to utter." We are not made aware of any other "third heaven" experiences he may have had, suffice it to say that he was a man well acquainted with the supernatural dimensions of God's kingdom. We know that he was divinely converted on the road to Damascus, having lost his sight for three days after encountering the blinding, white light of Jesus Christ. From 1 Corinthians 9:1, we know that Paul also had an occasion of "seeing" the Lord Jesus Christ. Since the encounter he had at his conversion took place while he was physically blinded, we know that this "seeing" of the Lord was a separate occasion. When studying the Book of Acts, a biblical account that focuses primarily upon Paul's apostolic journey, we see that he was well acquainted with the supernatural operations of the Spirit, performing many signs, wonders, and miracles. It is clear that he possessed in depth personal revelation from the Lord, as he wrote one half of the New Testament, most of which was revelation that had not previously been communicated about the Church. Furthermore, according to Galatians 1, the Gospel which Paul preached was not received from man, neither was he taught it by men – he received it "by the revelation of Jesus Christ." Paul goes on to say in chapter 2 that none of the apostles of his day "added anything" to his ministry or message. By all of this, we understand that Paul was a man specially called, taught, and commissioned by Jesus Christ.

Now, consider the wealth of Paul's supernatural experiences in light of our insight into the life of faith. By his continual contact with the supernatural realm of the Lord Jesus Christ, Paul had in essence *touched the finish line* of his destiny. He had not only received the Lord Jesus – the living Word – but witnessed one manifestation after another of that living Word. It wasn't merely that he heard a word about his future, but that the Word of God spoke to Paul, imparted divine life within him, and set him on a journey that would eventually

335

culminate in his uniting with the Lord in heaven. Upon his death, Paul was confident that he would forever be united with that living Word. Listen to the words of the apostle to the Philippian church below:

*"According to my earnest expectation and my hope, that in nothing I shall be ashamed, but that with all boldness, as always, so now also Christ shall be magnified in my body, whether it be by life, or by death. For to me to live is Christ, and to die is gain. But if I live in the flesh, this is the fruit of my labour: yet what I shall choose I wot not. For I am in a strait betwixt two, having a desire to depart, and to be with Christ; which is far better: Nevertheless to abide in the flesh is more needful for you." – Philippians 1:20-24*

Paul had come to a point in his life where he desired to depart the earthly "tent" of his body so that he could be with the Lord in Heaven. Yet he knew that his earthly ministry was profiting the Church. And so, he reasoned that it was more needful for him to stay with the people for their continued edification. What is significant about Paul's desire to depart is that his desire was based upon having already experienced his future in heaven. Through all of his encounters with the Lord, being converted by Jesus Christ, taught the Gospel by Jesus Christ, and commissioned by Jesus Christ, he had *touched* the One with whom he was destined to be with for eternity. Paul's ministry illustrates to us that the word we encounter is the word wherein we are destined to arrive. Paul touched the finish line when he was caught up into heaven. He experienced his heavenly citizenship. He witnessed the ultimate destination of being united in body with the Lord Jesus Christ. He saw unspeakable things in that eternal realm.

Faith sees similarly into timeless eternity as we receive God's word. When we experience that supernatural word, we *touch* the finish line of our faith. Our faith merely connects the word we receive to the future fulfillment of that word in our lives. In Paul's case, he had a tangible reality of what was in store, not only for him, but for every believer. In essence, we find him saying to the Philippians, "I would rather die, so that I can be with Jesus uninterrupted by this temporary life. However it is necessary for you that I stay here, even though I am in the constant tension of being here and being there at the same time."

Now, we know that we *are* with the Lord, however in a hidden, spiritual way. We have not yet shed our earthly, mortal bodies and been given our heavenly, eternal bodies. We have not yet seen the Lord face-to-face in the same way that we will, once we arrive in heaven. But we have experienced touch after touch of God's divine presence, energizing our faith for that future reality. In essence, we have *touched the finish line* of our faith. Philippians 1:6 says "Being confident of this very thing, that he which hath begun a good work in you will perform it until the day of Jesus Christ." Notice that it is the Lord beginning the good work in us, it is the Lord who performs that good work, and it is the Lord Who becomes our destination after that work has been accomplished. Once again, Paul is outlining the very life of faith, begun by the word of God, carried out by the faith with which He supplies, finding its culmination in the very Person of the Lord Jesus Christ.

When we look back at all of these heroes and heroines of the faith, it is important that we see their lives as having the same essential thread that is woven into our own. When speaking of Elijah, the apostle James makes a remarkable statement. He says, "Elias was a man subject to *like passions* as we are, and he prayed earnestly that it might not rain: and it rained not on the earth by the space of three years and six months. And he prayed again, and the heaven gave rain, and the earth brought forth her fruit" (5:17-18 emphasis mine). The words "like passions" here, literally mean "suffering with another, of like feelings or affections." James is revealing that Elijah, a prophet under the Old Covenant, was a man who experienced the *same* emotions that we do today. Furthermore, he is paralleling Elijah's ministry of prayer to ours under the New Testament. The parallel is such because both Elijah and the New Testament believer have the same power source for their ministry: *faith*. Because of many misconceptions about Old Testament individuals and New Testament believers, many view those under the Old as people to study for nothing more than historical information. And yet, since the dawn of time, it is God who has desired to work in and through every generation of man. Elijah's ministry proves to us that, whereas we may not be under the Mosaic Law as was he, we may still pray as he did and see God's awesome response simply because of the faith with which we pray. James is making the parallel between Elijah and the New Testament believer to reveal that we are *all* given the same ability, to not only do the works of God, but to please God. We must see the faith of God as the common thread that is sown throughout all the ages of mankind. This way we will begin to personally relate with those in Scripture, rather than see them as an isolated group of people who were out of touch with the life and ministry of today.

Instead of isolating the "Old" from the "New," we ought to read passages about individuals like Moses, Rahab, and David, with the anticipation of finding the mystical life of God in each of their historical accounts. Instantly we are able relate with their struggles, their victories, their hopes, their failures, and God's word in their lives. We can empathize with the wanderings of Abraham, as he moved from one foreign place to another with only the word of God to inspire his hope for a promised land. We can see ourselves under the duress of Rahab, as she faced the onslaught of the invading army, as well as her heroism which brought salvation for her entire family. We may relate to the plight of Jephthah, a man who was born in scandal, treated as an outcast by his own family, and yet possessed the ability to deliver his own people from tyranny. Finally, we may draw inspiration from the life of David, as he faced the huntsmen of Saul for many long years, all the while his soul being replenished with the anointing for kingship that still burned within him.

The writer of Hebrews ends the iconic eleventh chapter with the words, "And these all, having obtained a good report through faith received not the promise: God having provided some better thing for us, that they without us should not be made perfect" (39-40). What scripture is pointing out to us here is that, while each of the sixteen men and women mentioned in this book obtained their individual promises, there was the *corporate promise* which had not yet been manifested. The individual promises were according to the word God spoke to them concerning their specific role on earth. The corporate promise was the manifestation of the Messiah. This is why the scripture says that God provided "some better *thing* for us," speaking of the Christ who would save the world from its sin. These verses also indicate that those who came before the New Covenant were not yet made "perfect." The word "perfect" here means "to bring to the end goal proposed." Much like a child, those lived before the New Covenant were living in an immature state, in that the maturity of God's eternal promise – to send forth the Messiah to redeem humanity – had not yet been physically revealed. Those people presented in this book, although having never seen the Messiah with their physical eyes, saw him at a distance – by faith – and therefore touched the corporate promise to mankind. Now that Christ has come and fulfilled His Messianic mission, both those who came before Christ and we who come after have been gloriously perfected. We look back toward the finished work of Christ, whereas they looked ahead. Both they and we have been united in Christ's accomplishment, and have touched the finish line of God's word through the awesome power of faith.

# REFERENCES

INTRODUCTION

1 Blue Letter Bible. "Dictionary and Word Search for peripateō (Strong's 4043)". Blue Letter Bible. 1996-2013. 6 Jun 2013. < http://www.blueletterbible.org/lang/lexicon/lexicon.cfm? Strongs=G4043&t=KJV >

2 Blue Letter Bible. "Dictionary and Word Search for hamartia (Strong's 266)". Blue Letter Bible. 1996-2013. 6 Jun 2013. < http://www.blueletterbible.org/lang/lexicon/lexicon.cfm? Strongs=G266&t=KJV >

CHAPTER ONE

1 Blue Letter Bible. "Dictionary and Word Search for Chavvah (Strong's 2332)". Blue Letter Bible. 1996-2013. 6 Jun 2013. < http://www.blueletterbible.org/lang/lexicon/lexicon.cfm? Strongs=H2332&t=KJV >

2 Blue Letter Bible. "Dictionary and Word Search for `abad (Strong's 5647)". Blue Letter Bible. 1996-2013. 6 Jun 2013. < http://www.blueletterbible.org/lang/lexicon/lexicon.cfm? Strongs=H5647&t=KJV >

3 Blue Letter Bible. "Dictionary and Word Search for Qayin (Strong's 7014)". Blue Letter Bible. 1996-2013. 6 Jun 2013. < http://www.blueletterbible.org/lang/lexicon/lexicon.cfm? Strongs=H7014&t=KJV >

4 Blue Letter Bible. "Dictionary and Word Search for sha`ah (Strong's 8159)". Blue Letter Bible. 1996-2013. 6 Jun 2013. < http://www.blueletterbible.org/lang/lexicon/lexicon.cfm? Strongs=H8159&t=KJV >

5 Blue Letter Bible. "Dictionary and Word Search for pleiōn (Strong's 4119)". Blue Letter Bible. 1996-2013. 6 Jun 2013. < http://www.blueletterbible.org/lang/lexicon/lexicon.cfm? Strongs=G4119&t=KJV >

6 Blue Letter Bible. "Dictionary and Word Search for chemah (Strong's 2534)". Blue Letter Bible. 1996-2013. 6 Jun 2013. < http://www.blueletterbible.org/lang/lexicon/lexicon.cfm? Strongs=H2534&t=KJV >

7 Blue Letter Bible. "Dictionary and Word Search for charah (Strong's 2734)". Blue Letter Bible. 1996-2013. 6 Jun 2013. < http://www.blueletterbible.org/lang/lexicon/lexicon.cfm? Strongs=H2734&t=KJV >

CHAPTER TWO

1 Blue Letter Bible. "Dictionary and Word Search for halak (Strong's 1980)". Blue Letter Bible. 1996-2013. 6 Jun 2013. < http://www.blueletterbible.org/lang/lexicon/lexicon.cfm? Strongs=H1980&t=KJV >

2 Blue Letter Bible. "Dictionary and Word Search for Chanowk (Strong's 2585)". Blue Letter Bible. 1996-2013. 6 Jun 2013. < http:// www.blueletterbible.org/lang/lexicon/lexicon.cfm? Strongs=H2585&t=KJV >

3 Blue Letter Bible. "Dictionary and Word Search for naba' (Strong's 5012)". Blue Letter Bible. 1996-2013. 6 Jun 2013. < http:// www.blueletterbible.org/lang/lexicon/lexicon.cfm? Strongs=H5012&t=KJV >

4 "The Methuselah Prophecy." n.p. n.d. Web. 25 June, 2013 <http://www.christconnections.com/Word/Methuselah.pdf>

5 Blue Letter Bible. "Dictionary and Word Search for laqach (Strong's 3947)". Blue Letter Bible. 1996-2013. 6 Jun 2013. < http:// www.blueletterbible.org/lang/lexicon/lexicon.cfm? Strongs=H3947&t=KJV >

6 Blue Letter Bible. "Dictionary and Word Search for metatithēmi (Strong's 3346)". Blue Letter Bible. 1996-2013. 6 Jun 2013. < http:// www.blueletterbible.org/lang/lexicon/lexicon.cfm? Strongs=G3346&t=KJV >

CHAPTER THREE

1 Blue Letter Bible. "Dictionary and Word Search for Noach (Strong's 5146)". Blue Letter Bible. 1996-2013. 6 Jun 2013. < http:// www.blueletterbible.org/lang/lexicon/lexicon.cfm? Strongs=H5146&t=KJV >

2 Blue Letter Bible. "Dictionary and Word Search for Iēsous (Strong's 2424)". Blue Letter Bible. 1996-2013. 6 Jun 2013. < http:// www.blueletterbible.org/lang/lexicon/lexicon.cfm? Strongs=G2424&t=KJV >

3 Blue Letter Bible. "Dictionary and Word Search for charis (Strong's 5485)". Blue Letter Bible. 1996-2013. 6 Jun 2013. < http:// www.blueletterbible.org/lang/lexicon/lexicon.cfm? Strongs=G5485&t=KJV >

4 Blue Letter Bible. "Dictionary and Word Search for matsa' (Strong's 4672)". Blue Letter Bible. 1996-2013. 6 Jun 2013. < http:// www.blueletterbible.org/lang/lexicon/lexicon.cfm? Strongs=H4672&t=KJV >

5 Blue Letter Bible. "Dictionary and Word Search for towlĕdah (Strong's 8435)". Blue Letter Bible. 1996-2013. 6 Jun 2013. < http:// www.blueletterbible.org/lang/lexicon/lexicon.cfm? Strongs=H8435&t=KJV >

6 Blue Letter Bible. "Dictionary and Word Search for katakrinō (Strong's 2632)". Blue Letter Bible. 1996-2013. 6 Jun 2013. < http:// www.blueletterbible.org/lang/lexicon/lexicon.cfm? Strongs=G2632&t=KJV >

CHAPTER FOUR

1 Blue Letter Bible. "Dictionary and Word Search for Shĕkem (Strong's 7927)". Blue Letter Bible. 1996-2013. 7 Jun 2013. < http:// www.blueletterbible.org/lang/lexicon/lexicon.cfm? Strongs=H7927&t=KJV >

2 Blue Letter Bible. "Dictionary and Word Search for Mowreh (Strong's 4176)". Blue Letter Bible. 1996-2013. 7 Jun 2013. < http://www.blueletterbible.org/lang/lexicon/lexicon.cfm? Strongs=H4176&t=KJV >

3 Blue Letter Bible. "Dictionary and Word Search for Beyth-'El (Strong's 1008)". Blue Letter Bible. 1996-2013. 7 Jun 2013. < http://www.blueletterbible.org/lang/lexicon/lexicon.cfm? Strongs=H1008&t=KJV >

4 Blue Letter Bible. "Dictionary and Word Search for `Ay (Strong's 5857)". Blue Letter Bible. 1996-2013. 7 Jun 2013. < http://www.blueletterbible.org/lang/lexicon/lexicon.cfm? Strongs=H5857&t=KJV >

5 Blue Letter Bible. "Dictionary and Word Search for Mamre' (Strong's 4471)". Blue Letter Bible. 1996-2013. 7 Jun 2013. < http://www.blueletterbible.org/lang/lexicon/lexicon.cfm? Strongs=H4471&t=KJV >

6 Blue Letter Bible. "Dictionary and Word Search for Chebrown (Strong's 2275)". Blue Letter Bible. 1996-2013. 7 Jun 2013. < http://www.blueletterbible.org/lang/lexicon/lexicon.cfm? Strongs=H2275&t=KJV >

7 Blue Letter Bible. "Dictionary and Word Search for Malkiy-Tsedeq (Strong's 4442)". Blue Letter Bible. 1996-2013. 7 Jun 2013. < http://www.blueletterbible.org/lang/lexicon/lexicon.cfm? Strongs=H4442&t=KJV >

8 Blue Letter Bible. "Dictionary and Word Search for Shalem (Strong's 8004)". Blue Letter Bible. 1996-2013. 7 Jun 2013. < http://www.blueletterbible.org/lang/lexicon/lexicon.cfm? Strongs=H8004&t=KJV >

9 Blue Letter Bible. "Dictionary and Word Search for homoiotēs (Strong's 3665)". Blue Letter Bible. 1996-2013. 7 Jun 2013. < http://www.blueletterbible.org/lang/lexicon/lexicon.cfm? Strongs=G3665&t=KJV >

10 Blue Letter Bible. "Dictionary and Word Search for dĕmuwth (Strong's 1823)". Blue Letter Bible. 1996-2013. 7 Jun 2013. < http://www.blueletterbible.org/lang/lexicon/lexicon.cfm? Strongs=H1823&t=KJV >

11 "Nearsightedness." *Medline Plus*. US National Library of Medicine, n.p. 3 Sept. 2012. web. 25 June, 2013. <http://www.nlm.nih.gov/medlineplus/ency/article/001023.htm>

12 Ibid

13 Blue Letter Bible. "Dictionary and Word Search for tamiym (Strong's 8549)". Blue Letter Bible. 1996-2013. 7 Jun 2013. < http://www.blueletterbible.org/lang/lexicon/lexicon.cfm? Strongs=H8549&t=KJV >

14 Blue Letter Bible. "Dictionary and Word Search for 'Abram (Strong's 87)". Blue Letter Bible. 1996-2013. 7 Jun 2013. < http://www.blueletterbible.org/lang/lexicon/lexicon.cfm? Strongs=H87&t=KJV >

15 Blue Letter Bible. "Dictionary and Word Search for 'Abraham (Strong's 85)". Blue Letter Bible. 1996-2013. 7 Jun 2013. < http://www.blueletterbible.org/lang/lexicon/lexicon.cfm? Strongs=H85&t=KJV >

16 "The Letter Hey." *Hebrew 4 Christians*. n.p. n.d. web. 25 June, 2013. <http://www.hebrew4christians.com/Grammar/Unit_One/Aleph-Bet/Hey/hey.html>

CHAPTER FIVE

1 Blue Letter Bible. "Dictionary and Word Search for Saray (Strong's 8297)". Blue Letter Bible. 1996-2013. 11 Jun 2013. < http://www.blueletterbible.org/lang/lexicon/lexicon.cfm? Strongs=H8297&t=KJV >

2 Blue Letter Bible. "Dictionary and Word Search for qalal (Strong's 7043)". Blue Letter Bible. 1996-2013. 11 Jun 2013. < http://www.blueletterbible.org/lang/lexicon/lexicon.cfm? Strongs=H7043&t=KJV >

3 Blue Letter Bible. "Dictionary and Word Search for Hagar (Strong's 1904)". Blue Letter Bible. 1996-2013. 11 Jun 2013. < http://www.blueletterbible.org/lang/lexicon/lexicon.cfm? Strongs=H1904&t=KJV >

4 Blue Letter Bible. "Dictionary and Word Search for Sarah (Strong's 8283)". Blue Letter Bible. 1996-2013. 11 Jun 2013. < http://www.blueletterbible.org/lang/lexicon/lexicon.cfm? Strongs=H8283&t=KJV >

5 Blue Letter Bible. "Dictionary and Word Search for dynamis (Strong's 1411)". Blue Letter Bible. 1996-2013. 11 Jun 2013. < http://www.blueletterbible.org/lang/lexicon/lexicon.cfm? Strongs=G1411&t=KJV >

6 Blue Letter Bible. "Dictionary and Word Search for hēgeomai (Strong's 2233)". Blue Letter Bible. 1996-2013. 11 Jun 2013. < http://www.blueletterbible.org/lang/lexicon/lexicon.cfm? Strongs=G2233&t=KJV >

7 Blue Letter Bible. "Dictionary and Word Search for misthapodotēs (Strong's 3406)". Blue Letter Bible. 1996-2013. 11 Jun 2013. < http://www.blueletterbible.org/lang/lexicon/lexicon.cfm? Strongs=G3406&t=KJV >

8 Blue Letter Bible. "Dictionary and Word Search for Yitschaq (Strong's 3327)". Blue Letter Bible. 1996-2013. 11 Jun 2013. < http://www.blueletterbible.org/lang/lexicon/lexicon.cfm? Strongs=H3327&t=KJV >

CHAPTER SIX

1 Blue Letter Bible. "Dictionary and Word Search for tsachaq (Strong's 6711)". Blue Letter Bible. 1996-2013. 11 Jun 2013. < http://www.blueletterbible.org/lang/lexicon/lexicon.cfm? Strongs=H6711&t=KJV >

2 Blue Letter Bible. "Dictionary and Word Search for mystērion (Strong's 3466)". Blue Letter Bible. 1996-2013. 11 Jun 2013. < http://www.blueletterbible.org/lang/lexicon/lexicon.cfm? Strongs=G3466&t=KJV >

3 Blue Letter Bible. "Dictionary and Word Search for `athar (Strong's 6279)". Blue Letter Bible. 1996-2013. 11 Jun 2013. < http:// www.blueletterbible.org/lang/lexicon/lexicon.cfm? Strongs=H6279&t=KJV >

4 Blue Letter Bible. "Dictionary and Word Search for Ribqah (Strong's 7259)". Blue Letter Bible. 1996-2013. 11 Jun 2013. < http:// www.blueletterbible.org/lang/lexicon/lexicon.cfm? Strongs=H7259&t=KJV >

5 Blue Letter Bible. "Dictionary and Word Search for Gĕrar (Strong's 1642)". Blue Letter Bible. 1996-2013. 11 Jun 2013. < http:// www.blueletterbible.org/lang/lexicon/lexicon.cfm? Strongs=H1642&t=KJV >

6 Blue Letter Bible. "Dictionary and Word Search for `Eseq (Strong's 6230)". Blue Letter Bible. 1996-2013. 11 Jun 2013. < http:// www.blueletterbible.org/lang/lexicon/lexicon.cfm? Strongs=H6230&t=KJV >

7 Blue Letter Bible. "Dictionary and Word Search for Sitnah (Strong's 7856)". Blue Letter Bible. 1996-2013. 11 Jun 2013. < http:// www.blueletterbible.org/lang/lexicon/lexicon.cfm? Strongs=H7856&t=KJV >

8 Blue Letter Bible. "Dictionary and Word Search for Rĕchobowth (Strong's 7344)". Blue Letter Bible. 1996-2013. 11 Jun 2013. < http:// www.blueletterbible.org/lang/lexicon/lexicon.cfm? Strongs=H7344&t=KJV >

## CHAPTER SEVEN

1 Blue Letter Bible. "Dictionary and Word Search for `Eber (Strong's 5677)". Blue Letter Bible. 1996-2013. 12 Jun 2013. < http:// www.blueletterbible.org/lang/lexicon/lexicon.cfm? Strongs=H5677&t=KJV >

2 Blue Letter Bible. "Dictionary and Word Search for tam (Strong's 8535)". Blue Letter Bible. 1996-2013. 13 Jun 2013. < http:// www.blueletterbible.org/lang/lexicon/lexicon.cfm? Strongs=H8535&t=KJV >

3 Blue Letter Bible. "Dictionary and Word Search for Ya`aqob (Strong's 3290)". Blue Letter Bible. 1996-2013. 13 Jun 2013. < http:// www.blueletterbible.org/lang/lexicon/lexicon.cfm? Strongs=H3290&t=KJV >

4 Blue Letter Bible. "Dictionary and Word Search for Beyth-'El (Strong's 1008)". Blue Letter Bible. 1996-2013. 13 Jun 2013. < http:// www.blueletterbible.org/lang/lexicon/lexicon.cfm? Strongs=H1008&t=KJV >

5 Blue Letter Bible. "Dictionary and Word Search for Yowceph (Strong's 3130)". Blue Letter Bible. 1996-2013. 13 Jun 2013. < http:// www.blueletterbible.org/lang/lexicon/lexicon.cfm? Strongs=H3130&t=KJV >

6 Blue Letter Bible. "Dictionary and Word Search for kabowd (Strong's 3519)". Blue Letter Bible. 1996-2013. 13 Jun 2013. < http:// www.blueletterbible.org/lang/lexicon/lexicon.cfm? Strongs=H3519&t=KJV >

7 Blue Letter Bible. "Dictionary and Word Search for Gil`ad (Strong's 1568)". Blue Letter Bible. 1996-2013. 13 Jun 2013. < http://www.blueletterbible.org/lang/lexicon/lexicon.cfm? Strongs=H1568&t=KJV >

8 Blue Letter Bible. "Dictionary and Word Search for Mitspah (Strong's 4709)". Blue Letter Bible. 1996-2013. 13 Jun 2013. < http://www.blueletterbible.org/lang/lexicon/lexicon.cfm? Strongs=H4709&t=KJV >

9 Blue Letter Bible. "Dictionary and Word Search for Cukkowth (Strong's 5523)". Blue Letter Bible. 1996-2013. 13 Jun 2013. < http://www.blueletterbible.org/lang/lexicon/lexicon.cfm? Strongs=H5523&t=KJV >

10 Blue Letter Bible. "Dictionary and Word Search for Pĕnuw'el (Strong's 6439)". Blue Letter Bible. 1996-2013. 13 Jun 2013. < http://www.blueletterbible.org/lang/lexicon/lexicon.cfm? Strongs=H6439&t=KJV >

11 Blue Letter Bible. "Dictionary and Word Search for Ben-'Owniy (Strong's 1126)". Blue Letter Bible. 1996-2013. 13 Jun 2013. < http://www.blueletterbible.org/lang/lexicon/lexicon.cfm? Strongs=H1126&t=KJV >

12 Blue Letter Bible. "Dictionary and Word Search for Binyamiyn (Strong's 1144)". Blue Letter Bible. 1996-2013. 13 Jun 2013. < http://www.blueletterbible.org/lang/lexicon/lexicon.cfm? Strongs=H1144&t=KJV >

## CHAPTER EIGHT

1 Blue Letter Bible. "Dictionary and Word Search for to'ar (Strong's 8389)". Blue Letter Bible. 1996-2013. 13 Jun 2013. < http://www.blueletterbible.org/lang/lexicon/lexicon.cfm? Strongs=H8389&t=KJV >

2 Blue Letter Bible. "Dictionary and Word Search for Mĕnashsheh (Strong's 4519)". Blue Letter Bible. 1996-2013. 13 Jun 2013. < http://www.blueletterbible.org/lang/lexicon/lexicon.cfm? Strongs=H4519&t=KJV >

3 Blue Letter Bible. "Dictionary and Word Search for 'Ephrayim (Strong's 669)". Blue Letter Bible. 1996-2013. 13 Jun 2013. < http://www.blueletterbible.org/lang/lexicon/lexicon.cfm? Strongs=H669&t=KJV >

4 Blue Letter Bible. "Dictionary and Word Search for Tsophnath Pa`neach (Strong's 6847)". Blue Letter Bible. 1996-2013. 13 Jun 2013. < http://www.blueletterbible.org/lang/lexicon/lexicon.cfm? Strongs=H6847&t=KJV >

## CHAPTER NINE

1 Blue Letter Bible. "Dictionary and Word Search for Mosheh (Strong's 4872)". Blue Letter Bible. 1996-2013. 1 Aug 2013. < http://www.blueletterbible.org/lang/lexicon/lexicon.cfm? Strongs=H4872&t=KJV>

2 Blue Letter Bible. "Dictionary and Word Search for kosmos (Strong's 2889)". Blue Letter Bible. 1996-2013. 13 Jun 2013. < http://www.blueletterbible.org/lang/lexicon/lexicon.cfm? Strongs=G2889&t=KJV >

3 Blue Letter Bible. "Dictionary and Word Search for natsal (Strong's 5337)". Blue Letter Bible. 1996-2013. 13 Jun 2013. < http://www.blueletterbible.org/lang/lexicon/lexicon.cfm? Strongs=H5337&t=KJV >

4 Blue Letter Bible. "Dictionary and Word Search for yatsa' (Strong's 3318)". Blue Letter Bible. 1996-2013. 13 Jun 2013. < http://www.blueletterbible.org/lang/lexicon/lexicon.cfm? Strongs=H3318&t=KJV >

CHAPTER TEN

1 Blue Letter Bible. "Dictionary and Word Search for Salmown (Strong's 8012)". Blue Letter Bible. 1996-2013. 13 Jun 2013. < http://www.blueletterbible.org/lang/lexicon/lexicon.cfm? Strongs=H8012&t=KJV >

2 Blue Letter Bible. "Dictionary and Word Search for Rachab (Strong's 7343)". Blue Letter Bible. 1996-2013. 13 Jun 2013. < http://www.blueletterbible.org/lang/lexicon/lexicon.cfm? Strongs=H7343&t=KJV >

CHAPTER ELEVEN

1 Blue Letter Bible. "Dictionary and Word Search for para` (Strong's 6544)". Blue Letter Bible. 1996-2013. 13 Jun 2013. < http://www.blueletterbible.org/lang/lexicon/lexicon.cfm? Strongs=H6544&t=KJV >

2 Blue Letter Bible. "Dictionary and Word Search for 'Allown Bakuwth (Strong's 439)". Blue Letter Bible. 1996-2013. 13 Jun 2013. < http://www.blueletterbible.org/lang/lexicon/lexicon.cfm? Strongs=H439&t=KJV >

3 Blue Letter Bible. "Dictionary and Word Search for Baraq (Strong's 1301)". Blue Letter Bible. 1996-2013. 13 Jun 2013. < http://www.blueletterbible.org/lang/lexicon/lexicon.cfm? Strongs=H1301&t=KJV >

4 Blue Letter Bible. "Dictionary and Word Search for Děbowrah (Strong's 1683)". Blue Letter Bible. 1996-2013. 13 Jun 2013. < http://www.blueletterbible.org/lang/lexicon/lexicon.cfm? Strongs=H1683&t=KJV >

5 Blue Letter Bible. "Dictionary and Word Search for Qedesh (Strong's 6943)". Blue Letter Bible. 1996-2013. 13 Jun 2013. < http://www.blueletterbible.org/lang/lexicon/lexicon.cfm? Strongs=H6943&t=KJV >

CHAPTER TWELVE

1 Blue Letter Bible. "Dictionary and Word Search for Midyan (Strong's 4080)". Blue Letter Bible. 1996-2013. 13 Jun 2013. < http://www.blueletterbible.org/lang/lexicon/lexicon.cfm? Strongs=H4080&t=KJV >

2 Blue Letter Bible. "Dictionary and Word Search for Yěhavah shalowm (Strong's 3073)". Blue Letter Bible. 1996-2013. 13 Jun 2013. < http://www.blueletterbible.org/lang/lexicon/lexicon.cfm? Strongs=H3073&t=KJV >

3 Blue Letter Bible. "Dictionary and Word Search for Yĕrubba`al (Strong's 3378)". Blue Letter Bible. 1996-2013. 13 Jun 2013. < http://www.blueletterbible.org/lang/lexicon/lexicon.cfm? Strongs=H3378&t=KJV >

4 Blue Letter Bible. "Dictionary and Word Search for 'Asher (Strong's 836)". Blue Letter Bible. 1996-2013. 13 Jun 2013. < http://www.blueletterbible.org/lang/lexicon/lexicon.cfm? Strongs=H836&t=KJV >

5 Blue Letter Bible. "Dictionary and Word Search for Zĕbuwluwn (Strong's 2074)". Blue Letter Bible. 1996-2013. 13 Jun 2013. < http://www.blueletterbible.org/lang/lexicon/lexicon.cfm? Strongs=H2074&t=KJV >

6 Blue Letter Bible. "Dictionary and Word Search for Naphtaliy (Strong's 5321)". Blue Letter Bible. 1996-2013. 13 Jun 2013. < http://www.blueletterbible.org/lang/lexicon/lexicon.cfm? Strongs=H5321&t=KJV >

7 Blue Letter Bible. "Dictionary and Word Search for Mowreh (Strong's 4176)". Blue Letter Bible. 1996-2013. 13 Jun 2013. < http://www.blueletterbible.org/lang/lexicon/lexicon.cfm? Strongs=H4176&t=KJV >

8 Blue Letter Bible. "Dictionary and Word Search for Purah (Strong's 6513)". Blue Letter Bible. 1996-2013. 13 Jun 2013. < http://www.blueletterbible.org/lang/lexicon/lexicon.cfm? Strongs=H6513&t=KJV >

## CHAPTER THIRTEEN

1 Blue Letter Bible. "Dictionary and Word Search for reyq (Strong's 7386)". Blue Letter Bible. 1996-2013. 14 Jun 2013. < http://www.blueletterbible.org/lang/lexicon/lexicon.cfm? Strongs=H7386&t=KJV >

2 Blue Letter Bible. "Dictionary and Word Search for Kĕmowsh (Strong's 3645)". Blue Letter Bible. 1996-2013. 14 Jun 2013. < http://www.blueletterbible.org/lang/lexicon/lexicon.cfm? Strongs=H3645&t=KJV >

3 Blue Letter Bible. "Dictionary and Word Search for Yiphtach (Strong's 3316)". Blue Letter Bible. 1996-2013. 14 Jun 2013. < http://www.blueletterbible.org/lang/lexicon/lexicon.cfm? Strongs=H3316&t=KJV >

## CHAPTER FOURTEEN

1 Blue Letter Bible. "Dictionary and Word Search for naziyr (Strong's 5139)". Blue Letter Bible. 1996-2013. 17 Jun 2013. < http://www.blueletterbible.org/lang/lexicon/lexicon.cfm? Strongs=H5139&t=KJV >

2 Blue Letter Bible. "Dictionary and Word Search for pa`am (Strong's 6470)". Blue Letter Bible. 1996-2013. 17 Jun 2013. < http://www.blueletterbible.org/lang/lexicon/lexicon.cfm? Strongs=H6470&t=KJV >

3 Corbett, James. The Corbett Report. 24 Oct. 2012. Web. 25 June 2013. <http://www.corbettreport.com/psyops-101-an-introduction-to-psychological-operations/>

4 The Psychology of Warfare. n.p. n.d. Web. 25 June 2013. <http://www-cs-faculty.stanford.edu/~eroberts/courses/ww2/projects/psychological-warfare/index.html.>

5 Blue Letter Bible. "Dictionary and Word Search for `Eytam (Strong's 5862)". Blue Letter Bible. 1996-2013. 17 Jun 2013. < http://www.blueletterbible.org/lang/lexicon/lexicon.cfm? Strongs=H5862&t=KJV >

6 Blue Letter Bible. "Dictionary and Word Search for Lechiy (Strong's 3896)". Blue Letter Bible. 1996-2013. 17 Jun 2013. < http://www.blueletterbible.org/lang/lexicon/lexicon.cfm? Strongs=H3896&t=KJV >

7 Blue Letter Bible. "Dictionary and Word Search for Sowreq (Strong's 7796)". Blue Letter Bible. 1996-2013. 17 Jun 2013. < http://www.blueletterbible.org/lang/lexicon/lexicon.cfm? Strongs=H7796&t=KJV >

8 Blue Letter Bible. "Dictionary and Word Search for Dĕliylah (Strong's 1807)". Blue Letter Bible. 1996-2013. 17 Jun 2013. < http://www.blueletterbible.org/lang/lexicon/lexicon.cfm? Strongs=H1807&t=KJV >

9 Blue Letter Bible. "Dictionary and Word Search for kosmos (Strong's 2889)". Blue Letter Bible. 1996-2013. 17 Jun 2013. < http://www.blueletterbible.org/lang/lexicon/lexicon.cfm? Strongs=G2889&t=KJV >

10 Blue Letter Bible. "Dictionary and Word Search for `Azzah (Strong's 5804)". Blue Letter Bible. 1996-2013. 17 Jun 2013. < http://www.blueletterbible.org/lang/lexicon/lexicon.cfm? Strongs=H5804&t=KJV >

11 Blue Letter Bible. "Dictionary and Word Search for Shimshown (Strong's 8123)". Blue Letter Bible. 1996-2013. 17 Jun 2013. < http://www.blueletterbible.org/lang/lexicon/lexicon.cfm? Strongs=H8123&t=KJV >

## CHAPTER FIFTEEN

1 Blue Letter Bible. "Dictionary and Word Search for Shĕmuw'el (Strong's 8050)". Blue Letter Bible. 1996-2013. 14 Jun 2013. < http://www.blueletterbible.org/lang/lexicon/lexicon.cfm? Strongs=H8050&t=KJV >

2 Blue Letter Bible. "Dictionary and Word Search for Shiyloh (Strong's 7886)". Blue Letter Bible. 1996-2013. 14 Jun 2013. < http://www.blueletterbible.org/lang/lexicon/lexicon.cfm? Strongs=H7886&t=KJV >

3 Blue Letter Bible. "Dictionary and Word Search for zōē (Strong's 2222)". Blue Letter Bible. 1996-2013. 14 Jun 2013. < http://www.blueletterbible.org/lang/lexicon/lexicon.cfm? Strongs=G2222&t=KJV >

## CHAPTER SIXTEEN

1 Blue Letter Bible. "Dictionary and Word Search for ra'ah (Strong's 7200)". Blue Letter Bible. 1996-2013. 14 Jun 2013. < http://www.blueletterbible.org/lang/lexicon/lexicon.cfm? Strongs=H7200&t=KJV >

2 Blue Letter Bible. "Dictionary and Word Search for nacah (Strong's 5254)". Blue Letter Bible. 1996-2013. 14 Jun 2013. < http://www.blueletterbible.org/lang/lexicon/lexicon.cfm? Strongs=H5254&t=KJV >

www.ingramcontent.com/pod-product-compliance
Lightning Source LLC
LaVergne TN
LVHW051450080426
835509LV00017B/1721

* 9 7 8 0 6 1 5 8 8 6 8 4 8 *